Arctic Daughter

Arctic Daughter

A Wilderness Journey

by Jean Aspen

Menasha
Ridge
Press

Menasha Ridge Press
3169 Cahaba Heights Road
Birmingham, AL 35243

ISBN 0-89732-121-9

Cover design: Paul Bacon
Illustrations by Jean Aspen
Map by Elizabeth Barnard

For my mother, Constance Helmericks,
who taught me to dream.

I LOVE THE SUMMERS in this land. But I also love the feel of winter winds against my cheek, when the snow squeals underfoot, and the ptarmigan, the white grouse, come whirling down from the Arrigetch Peaks once more—or any peaks in Alaska!—to talk along the valley by my house. I love the colors of the bleak wastelands where nobody goes. When the circling sun falls low, and the leaves hang and rattle in the wind, and cranberries turn to mahogany brown, and frosted blueberries taste of wine, then my cabin on the river will be snug and tight against the arctic gale. When wild grass has turned to hay and the wild geese wing their way once more over mountain and valley to the southern land below, the canoe is put away and the snowshoe will appear. But when the arctic turns to green again and the geese return with the sun, I shall take my canoe from off the tall cache, and I shall travel on the river to see some new place.

We Live in the Arctic
Constance Helmericks, 1947

Acknowledgments

I wish to acknowledge the following people who, through their love and support, helped to create this book:

Anny Boice, my sister, provided a home for me while I wrote the first drafts.

Phil's parents, Cliff and Marion Beisel, stood behind us with love while knowing not the journey.

Friends that encouraged me in my writing and rewriting: Charlotte Cardon, Sue Clemans, Terrel Miedaner, Celia Weber and Janet Cutler.

Jennie Leach and my long-time friend, John Earl, undertook the taks of amending the creative spelling of the first drafts.

Donald Sayner taught me the techniques of illustration and Dr. Douglas Canfiled guided my early efforts in writing.

My editor and friend, Barb Wieser, guided me in tightening the manuscript into a book.

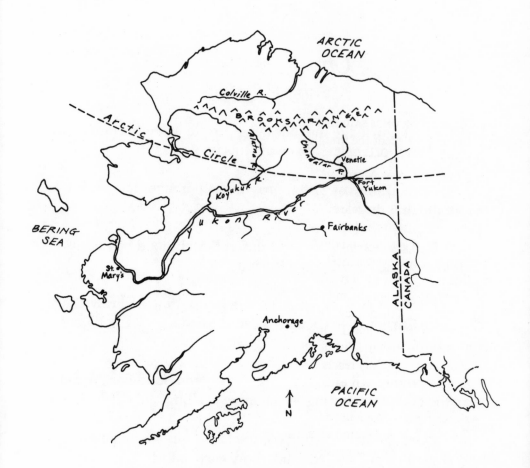

Chapter 1

My mother once said that I must have been imprinted very early on the Arctic for I spent the first three years of my life there. As a child I can remember people asking me, "Are you going to be an author and Arctic explorer like your Mommy?"

"No," I would answer. "I'm going to be a doctor."

In my family the role of Arctic explorer was occupied. Long before I was born my parents had spent years in Alaska's wilderness, living off the land, traveling by canoe and dog sled and on foot. Later they pioneered in tiny planes across the vastness. Writing books and lecturing together had been their way of life until twelve years of companionship ended in an angry divorce about the time my memory begins.

I inherited the legacy. I grew up in Tucson, Arizona, listening to stories and leafing through the heavy family albums where across the pages of *Life* magazine little Jeanie toddles on her snowshoes. But she remained somehow out of my reach; a fairy child. Still I felt that undeniable pull, almost a memory. An eaglet hatched in a hen house never really forgets. Across the dusty years it called, echoing between the sky and water of my restless soul—like a promise.

Yes, I was drawn to the Arctic, but not by the glamour of being an explorer. There was something more. Maybe the smell of autumn leaves. Or the stillness of a winter night. The faint song of running water heard even as I gazed upon the arid playground and waited out my childhood sentence in the public schools of Tucson. Perhaps it was the half-remembered family warmth of my first three years in a little cabin on the Alatna River. Whatever drew me, it pulled me north, unerringly as the geese, as soon as I could fly, to repeat another cycle. At the time I denied any connection with my parents. But somehow I always knew that I would return.

My mother was also serving out her time in Tucson. She once said that she had lived her life by the first commandment, "Thou shalt have no other gods before me," for she saw God everywhere in the natural world and her love of nature came first, even before her children. She was a wild

1

spirit and she fretted being shackled, as she saw it, to the demands of two small children and poverty in the summer city heat, away from her beloved wilderness.

My earliest memories are of wild places, campfires and trails along desert streams. "More walk, less talk," she would say, confined even there by my short legs. As my legs grew she began to dream of returning to the wilderness with her daughters. She managed to get her publisher, Little, Brown and Company, to advance her the money for the three of us to canoe 3000 miles down the Mackenzie River system in northern Canada, a journey spanning two summers and resulting in her seventh book, *Down the Wild River North*. I was fourteen then and my sister, Anny, twelve. My mother was nearing fifty.

Before I turned twenty-two I put together my own expedition. Phil, my long-time friend and companion, was a year older. Looking at our pictures now I can see how very young we were, a couple of kids on an adventure. The year was 1972, a time when other kids our age were dying in the jungles of Vietnam. So perhaps not so young after all. I see myself with more clarity now than I did then, as if who I was to become was already in me. There I stand, a familiar stranger: a lovely blond girl of medium height, a bit chubby, with tanned skin and even white teeth. There is a sense of determination in the set of the jaw, confidence and excitement almost masking the questing in the blue-gray eyes.

We had prepared well for an extended journey into the wilderness: two years spent in gleaning information from my mother, reading books and pouring over maps. We would drift down the Yukon River, which flows westward across Alaska from Canada to empty into the Bering Sea, and then pull our canoe up a tributary north into the Brooks Range. There we planned to build a cabin and live alone for a year or more entirely off the land. The day after final exams of my junior year in college, we started north.

I have been asked why I would undertake such a journey. Why, I might counter, would any young person choose instead a mortgage and forty-hour-a-week job when they could be free to explore a wild and beautiful land?

⊀

At two A.M. the sun was just coming up as Phil's old pickup truck plowed through the last mud hole and into the tiny settlement of Circle, Alaska. End of the line. Three of us had driven north for ten days, Phil and I and a friend who had come along to take the truck back to Tucson. Gradually we had left darkness behind as we neared the Arctic Circle, an imaginary line around the earth where the sun doesn't set for one day each summer and fails to rise one day each winter. Now at last our rutted dirt track simply vanished into the biggest piece of river I had ever seen: the mighty, muddy Yukon. Like a moving lake, it reflected the early morning sun into our tired eyes.

Phil switched off the truck's engine and stretched. Silence rushed into the cab. We sat a moment, numb from the hours of jostling. Then I flipped up the door handle, enveloping us in the waiting mosquitoes. Within minutes we had our tents up beside the truck.

By six A.M. the sweltering heat of an early June day on the Yukon Flats drove us from sleep. We were camped on a sloping grassy bank facing miles of open water and pale blue sky. The land spread flat and lush beneath the endless summer sun. Behind us a few tattered buildings were hidden from view in the dark green spruce trees. Steam rising from the damp earth and foliage made the air feel heavy and hard to breath. Even the mosquitoes were hiding in the shade.

Feeling tired and cranky, I wandered down to the river and splashed muddy water over my face, drying it with the tail of my blue cotton work shirt. Then I brushed out my long hair, twisted it into a knot and clipped it up with a large barrette.

Phil was already unloading our canoe and half a ton of equipment from the truck when I joined him. He looked up at my approach and paused to fold a red bandanna, slipping it over his chestnut hair as a sweatband. He was handsome in his way: heavy bones framing wide green eyes, square jaw beginning to disappear under a dark beard. The mouth was small for his face, over-shadowed by a craggy nose, victim of high school sports. He was of average height, with a body well built and graceful, although his personal inclination was to bull his way through rather than use finesse when confronted with physical challenge. But perhaps his most striking feature was his eyebrows (or rather, eyebrow) for it spanned both eyes in a single dramatic sweep.

It was hard for me to see his features objectively. Through the years of friendship, they had become as familiar as my own. We had been close since high school, hiking, rock climbing, dating. We met in the Southern Arizona Rescue Association when I was sixteen. Our friends had referred to us as "Phil-and-Jeanie" ever since, as if we had somehow joined to form a third organism. And to me, in a way we had. I wanted it to be that way. He had given me an engagement ring just before we started our journey, and the little diamond winked at me as I took a hand at unloading duffel.

We worked quietly together unpacking mounds of gear and piling it on the grass. The canoe and supplies that had crowded the front room of the

3

little house we rented together that last semester in school now seemed to shrink before miles of open water.

My attention was interrupted as a shadow fell across me. I looked up at an older man in a dirty T-shirt and whiskers. Although his remaining hair was gray, the blistered red face and cracked lips were those of a fair-haired person with too many seasons in the weather. From a flat metal can he took a fresh chew of tobacco and tucked it thoughtfully under his lower lip.

"Whar ya goin'?" It came out more like a demand than a question.

I straightened slowly, wiping a sleeve over my forehead.

"Up the Chandalar River into the mountains above Venetie."

"In that?" He spat towards the "Lady Grayling," our nineteen-foot aluminum canoe, lying out of her element among the dandelions.

She did look small beside the Yukon.

"I fly up in that country sometimes in the winter and hunt wolves," he wheezed, watching me. "My neighbor, he gets lots of them buggers from the air, but I don't believe in it," he continued. "Mainly 'cause I ain't got no plane."

I glanced up in surprise, half expecting a grin. His face was impassive but for the slow rumination of the jaws and the shrewd china blue eyes. His self-assurance intimidated me: the solid way he planted his boots on the dandelions.

Go away, I thought. I bent over and went back to packing clothes. Choosing equipment and supplies had been no small task and this last day of organizing it was important. There would be no one to help if we forgot something.

"They say we shouldn't poison these here bugs," he stated, still searching for something we could disagree upon. He shifted his weight, watching me as I worked.

I nodded. "They're a big part of the food chain," I told him, fresh from my biology classes. Absently I scratched a welt-speckled arm.

He spit again, a stream of juice aimed expertly between stained teeth. "Shit." He studied me a moment. "I been pilotin' the River 'fore you was born, huntin' and trappin' this country."

I followed his gaze northward over the glittering water.

"'Course I ain't trapped now in years, not that I couldn't still do it." He seemed to have forgotten me, his eyes lingering on the river. "Jest ain't the game thar was. Wolves is mostly to blame. Wolves and Indians. I could teach you young pups a thing or two about trappin'." His attention came back to me defiantly.

"I imagine you could," I answered in a gentler note. Then I retreated

4

into myself until he was gone.

Soon another man appeared, slowly treading the beach with a cane. He looked to be over seventy, a tiny prune of an Indian, dark and wrinkled. He was dressed in dark cotton clothing of indeterminate color, short rubber overshoes and a purple baseball cap.

"You want whitefish? I give you big whitefish." His voice was soft and difficult to catch. He glanced up at me and then politely away.

He came only to my shoulder as I ambled beside him along the beach, asking questions about the Chandalar River, a tributary of the Yukon that I had chosen from the map. The only maps available were six miles to the inch with eighty-foot contour intervals. But the Chandalar appeared to have no major waterfalls, to be fairly well timbered, and it cut deep into an uninhabited area of the Brooks Range. The Brooks is actually a mass of seven mountain ranges extending east to west across the entire northern third of the state. No one we knew had ever heard of the Chandalar River; few in fact knew of this massive mountain range. The old man beside me had, but he understood very little English and merely bobbed and smiled at most of what I said.

"I catch too many fish. Only me and my wife and no dogs anymore. Every day I come ask white people if they want fish. But they say no," he grinned, showing worn teeth. "That there my wife." He pointed toward a tiny fat prune just disappearing into a small cabin of unpeeled logs. "I build that one her own house. Fifty-two year we married now. Church married! But I can't live with her."

He shook his head stubbornly. We halted beside his leaning cache and he reached into a slimy pail to hand me a fish. Then he stooped and wiped his hands in the grass. I thanked him and returned to the beach to clean the fish.

As I scraped the scales, my eyes were drawn back to the river. I had calculated that we had perhaps a 75% chance of surviving, green as we were. Neither of us had even hunted big game before. I wondered if I had misjudged the odds.

By late afternoon I was dizzy with fatigue. I crawled into the truck cab and curled up on the seat to nap, rolling the windows tight against the bugs. Phil was still loading and reloading the canoe, a job he wished to do alone. He was inexperienced with canoes, but had a natural ability with equipment and a tendency to take charge.

When Phil woke me it was nearly midnight and the sun was setting into the Yukon. He looked very tired. I shivered slightly in the big breath of the river, rubbing the seat print from my cheek. Time to go. We would find our own place to camp away from the curious eyes of the village. I checked around the pickup a last time for overlooked items and sleepily headed down the bank to the canoe.

"It looks awfully full . . ." I protested.

Phil nodded toward the grassy bank where, even at this hour, the total population of ten had come down to watch us sink. "Pretend you know what you're doing," he intoned under his breath.

Together we shoved the grounded craft and I felt the heavy gauge aluminum give under my weight before she slid free into the river. The little ship wallowed deeply but remained afloat. Gingerly I climbed into the bow. My initial alarm increased when I turned to see Phil settling into the stern. We were inches from the river.

"We're crazy, Phil," I declared. "We're dangerously overloaded and we're just going to have to get rid of some of this junk!" I had forgotten the spectators and started to get out.

But we were already underway. Quickly the current snatched our little tub and spun it from shore, sweeping us into the orange and purple sunset. As the truck dwindled into the evening, we waved goodbye. Pursued by a cloud of mosquitoes, we set forth upon the Yukon.

I glanced back at the sound when Phil started our little outboard motor. The canoe gave a sluggish lurch. As he cut back on the power with a gentle curse, we watched a wave ride easily up and over the stern. Lady Grayling settled deeper, and Phil motored quietly with one hand and bailed with the other.

"Got to watch that," he said shakily, staring in fascination at the two inches of freeboard separating us from the river. The glossy orange river betrayed no hint of its depth. Our little engine purred as we wove through the sky-dappled river for the fringe of far-away shore, the finely drawn ribbon of black reality that divided our world from the clouds and gave it order. The mosquitoes were reluctant to give up the chase, but one by one they stowed away or were left behind.

"We're off at last!" I called back cheerfully. I smiled, feeling the thrill of an irrevocable choice.

Phil had finished bailing and was peering toward that phantom shore. Absently he swatted at a lingering bug.

"I just knocked my glasses overboard."

"You're kidding," I said, knowing that he wasn't. "You're new ones?"
"Yes."

I studied the flawless surface that had swallowed Phil's new glasses. "Let's camp at the first spot."

He nodded wearily.

Very soon the sun was gone, sliding into the spruce forest, and a diffused pink glow of boundless sky softened the summer. The shore we finally reached shelved smoothly from a willow bar into a quiet stretch of river. There we beached the canoe, making her fast to a large sunken log. We snapped a fitted nylon tarp over the load and pitched our camp among the supple bushes. Without bothering with dinner, we crawled into our small orange tent and zipped it tight against the bugs. Soon I had drifted into a sound sleep, lulled by the lap of wavelets against the canoe and the shrill cries of arctic terns as they darted for insects in the cool dawn sky.

Early day burned bright and hot when we deserted the stuffy tent for the smell of open water. I knelt in the sand, feeding sticks to a young fire and enjoying the stir of wind on my face. A gossamer mist of mosquitoes swirled in the eddy of my body, attracted by the warm animal smell.

The beach was a story of river moods, gathered from countless other shores. Along it wavered a series of parallel lines marking recent water levels in trails of twigs. Here small plants were forcing their first two leaves upward through the mud. Because the Arctic receives most of its sunlight in an intense burst, plants and animals grow rapidly during the brief summer. But environments with low productivity, such as deserts and the Arctic, are delicate, each niche being filled with a single species.

Further inland hardy young willows formed a living net of fluttering green that locked down the sand with tough red roots. Behind these stood older willows and the fast-growing balsam poplar. And behind the poplar, sheltered from the careless river, two-foot spruce trees pushed through to claim the future.

I leaned back on my ankles and buttoned the throat of my denim shirt against the bugs, feeling contented. I smiled to myself, thinking that we were actually underway. This trip had started in my head, and we had taken one step after another to find ourselves here. Phil dropped an arm-load of firewood and grinned down at me. It was the first smile I'd seen in days.

"I want to repack the canoe after breakfast," he said. "It's poorly balanced. I think less weight in the stern would help."

"I'll make us some breakfast, if you want to get started."

All our bulk staples, like corn meal, flour and sugar, were packed in square five-gallon cans. We had designed a grub box, already dubbed "Wonderbox," with racks of plastic bottles to be refilled at intervals for easy access in camp. Freeze-dried camper foods were just coming onto the market and were far too expensive for our budget. I had also reasoned that we could pack more actual food as bulk staples. We hoped to supplement our supplies with rabbits and fish during the summer, and would of course

7

need big game before winter. My mother had told me an active person consumes his weight in prepared food each month, but a canoe's capacity is small, even ours with it's eleven-hundred-pound limit.

Into a bucket of boiling water I dumped a handful of dried and salted horse meat, an animal we had bought and butchered for the trip. At forty-seven dollars it was protein we could afford and had furnished our first butchering experience. We had oven-dried the meat with a good deal of salt and then broken it into chips which I planned to use in cooking until we found game. I was inexperienced in cooking with staples, and Phil was useless. To the boiling horsemeat I added flour, lard, salt and pepper to make a kind of horse-chip gravy. I stirred the pot and bedded it in the coals to simmer. Then I stripped off my clothes and dashed for the river. Phil was still repacking.

"Come on and have a bath," I called, safely submerged. "You'll feel much better."

"When I'm done," came the voice from the duffel.

I upended with a splash, driving the mosquitoes from my scalp. "Come on, you'll enjoy it." I could imagine the specter of my disembodied head floating on a swirling sea of cocoa amid its own little black cloud.

Reluctantly Phil undressed in the smoke of the fire (mosquitoes hate smoke) and proffered one toe to the river. "It's cold!" he accused me. He wasn't big on water under any circumstances.

"Just rush in and get it over with," I advised him. The cloud of bugs was settling contentedly onto his naked skin. With a grimace he splashed through the water to join me.

Later I stood beside the driftwood fire as Phil brushed out my long hair. Over us a cruising gull dipped sharply, head pivoting in keen interest, white on blue. The sudden, wet hiss of the pot shifting startled me and I shoved a handy branch under the bail, lifting it to rake out more coals.

Thoughtfully my eyes trailed over the muddy beach where the tools and supplies that were to see us through a year alone lay heaped in the sunlight. Every item had been chosen with care, from the folding sheet-metal Yukon stove for the cabin, to down clothing and rifles. We had discussed our possible needs at length, each of us making decisions in the areas we were most familiar with.

Phil had been arranging the load in layers. On the bottom were the water-tight five-gallon cans of food and winter clothes as well as the gas tanks he had built to fit the canoe contours. Items like axes, wire, saw blades, one hundred feet of half-inch polypropylene rope, snowshoes and a few traps were stuffed down beside these. Many kits, such as sewing, photography, medical, maps, journal, and personal items were packed in a middle layer. On top would be everyday items, the tent and sleeping bags tucked into a canvas duffel sack and the large ensolite pad for the tent floor rolled and tied. All the cookware nested in a seven-gallon kettle we called "Mightypot." To insure that equipment would not be washed overboard in case of capsize, everything was lashed in.

This was our future. There were wicks for the tallow candles we hoped to light our winter with and a few special books. We needed fuel for the second-hand outboard motor and rope to pull the canoe with during the later stages of our journey. We had winter clothing, backpacks and canoe patching materials. There were knives and whetstones, files, matches embedded in wax, an auger, tin snips, nails, hinges, bullets, panes of Plexiglas for cabin windows, measuring tape and nylon twine. We had a fish net, binoculars, rivets, a plastic tarp to water-proof the sod roof, window putty, four small bottles of military mosquito repellent (the strongest available), film, and a small gas lantern: in short, everything we could conceive of needing and could manage to fit in.

Like many partners, we tended to specialize. Phil was physically stronger than I and was good at building things. I, with my knowledge of the North and my dream, was the momentum behind the trip. And somewhere, unseen, was my mother with her stories and advice.

When repacking was completed and cargo once more towered over the little craft, we turned to enjoying our breakfast. It was terrible. The jerky had the texture of cardboard and was so salty as to be nearly inedible.

Overhead the arctic terns still hovered and wheeled, dazzling flashes of life engrossed in their great summer task, a job of such importance that they had flown from the Antarctic, a round trip of 36,000 miles, for these few weeks of sun and insects to perform it. In all the world, only terns can make more terns.

It was late in the day before we got underway. As camp was swept behind on a sea of dancing sun diamonds, we discovered that we were not yet across the river. In fact, with the kaleidoscope of wandering channels, big islands, merging backwaters and sloughs, being "on shore" was actually a matter of definition within a width of ten miles or so. From the air, this area of the Yukon Flats resembles a plate of spaghetti. But we were comfortably ignorant of this, for the map that might have helped us had somehow been forgotten in the truck, a mistake that could well have proved fatal. God looks after fools, they say. But not always, I came to find out.

As we slowly motored, we searched for that elusive other shore and our next landmark, the small town of Fort Yukon, some days' travel away. When we stopped the engine far from land and drifted, we found ourselves on a smooth lake of sunlit water melting into flat blue sky where magic islands seemed to float. Only the uneasy boils on the smooth surface and hypnotic hiss of silt against the hull told of our travel.

Night had already settled upon the lands to the south as our tireless sun circled the sky, dipping into the north as evening descended. From shore came the first sigh of cool dampness as the earth awoke from its afternoon doze. We spun past high cutbanks anchored in shadow and guarded by fallen trees, "sweepers" thrashing in the current. It was no place to practice our beaching techniques. Here, close to land, we were suddenly reminded of the speed and power of the water. The dark shore seemed ominous after the innocent dazzle of the river. I squinted and rubbed my salt-crusted eyes, searching the shadows where soon we must land. I ought to have a hat, I thought irritably. Uncertainly I chewed my lower lip where the skin was already peeling. A few more days of this and I'll be fried. I had forgotten the Arctic could be so hot.

A riffle broke the surface ahead and the cutbank suddenly dropped to meet it. A cutbank is where the river is eating into the shore, leaving a raw drop. "There!" I called, pointing.

Phil turned the canoe sharply upstream before nosing in to shore. Our motor conked out in the thick silt and in slow motion we slid to a stop in shallow water. It was the end of the day and we both had dry feet. We glanced at one another and shrugged.

The medium through which our canoe would not pass was far from solid. I climbed stiffly overboard and felt the penetrating stab of boots filling with cold water. Last bubbles of air hiccupped free as together we dragged our load further aground.

"Bugs!" I had forgotten them.

"I can unpack. You start a smudge fire," Phil urged, then choked on a mosquito.

Waving my arms futilely, I snapped off twigs from the lower trunks of spruce trees for a fire. The bank was a snarl of dense trees, matted with the wreckage of spring breakup and still slippery with mud. But already plants were shooting up, pushing aside their dead in the wild summer urge to grow. I cleared a space in the underbrush and soon had a fire billowing smoke from a pile of waterlogged wood. The mosquitoes were thinning when I skidded down the short cutbank to help Phil.

"Empty the cooking things out by the fire and fetch a bucket of water," he called back as he lugged duffel up the bank, churning through dark mud. "I'll get the rest."

I noticed that he had fastened the canoe from three separate places, apprehensive that it might get away during the night.

"Think I'll try to find us a rabbit while you start supper," Phil said. I was staking down the tent floor in a thicket of wild roses. He joined me on his knees, pulling his pliers from their holster to nip off the thorny bushes. I could see that he was anxious to be off.

"Yes, you go ahead. I can finish pitching camp." I felt somehow disappointed to be left with the camp chores while he went off hunting. I didn't plan this trip to be left out, I thought resentfully.

I watched him pick up my old .22 rifle, holding it comfortably in one hand. It was the same gun that my mother, little sister and I had carried to the Arctic Ocean in our canoe.

"Phil, please don't lose sight of the river. A person could really get lost in this jungle. There just aren't any landmarks." The dank forest crowded thickly to the water's edge.

"Doesn't look much like rabbit country either, does it?" He squatted by the fire to dig through the journal box and paused to hold up his compass. Then he repacked the box and levered the lid shut. In a moment he had disappeared.

Soon I had finished pitching camp. I stirred dinner, a horse chip-and-rice dish, before moving it onto coals away from the main fire. Then I got out the tackle box. Wouldn't it be fun, I thought as I rigged my pole, if I caught a fish while he was gone.

Away from the smoke I was again immersed in a sea of mosquitoes. Carefully I traversed the broken bank, seeking a spot to fish. None seemed promising. My first cast sank through shallow muddy water and hooked into a submerged log. I wallowed out to retrieve my lure. After a few tries I retreated to the fire.

Time dragged. I glanced at my watch. Where was that Phil? I wondered, awash with irritation and concern. Positioning another log on the blaze, I wagged to keep my body in the smoke and face free as I sifted the forest noises. Evening cool was definitely upon us now, and a damp breeze from the darkening woods crept out over the gold expanse of moving water. I watched the current, caught in its timeless song. Rivers are somehow important to me. At night I often dream of drifting down rivers, the adventure of each bend unfolding before me. I have since childhood. They are the living blood of the earth. More than just moving water, there is something grand in their presence.

I sniffed the night, listening uneasily for Phil. Surely he had sense enough to stay near the water . . . ?

My mind wandered to my fourteenth summer and canoeing the Slave River in Canada. Or was it the Mackenzie the following year? I know it wasn't the Peace. The country had this same wild look, a summertime rain forest, flooded in breakup, strangled in vegetation. The sky had been rich blue that day, piled with cotton clouds. I had wanted to hunt rabbits (I never got one that year, but I looked) and I recall my mother saying:

"Jean," (she always called me that) "don't lose sight of the river or you may never find it again."

"Okay, sure," I had answered, impatient to be gone.

"I mean it now," she insisted, peering wisely over her reading glasses and laying aside her journal and pen. "You don't know everything yet." She remained sitting cross-legged in the moss by the smudge fire, looking up at me, a plump, middle-aged woman with red hair. It is curious how our relationship reversed that summer, my mother suddenly depending on my strength and youth and judgement.

Shooting her a look of annoyance, I had taken that same .22 (old even then) and started downstream. Over the river I noticed the thunderheads building. The going was rough along the high cutbank and soon I met massive driftwood barricades which forced me inland.

The forest had been gloomy in the hush of oppressively wet air. I followed the debris until I discovered a place to crawl over it. Here I turned back toward the river only to be checked once more. I found myself bashing through ever denser thickets. Finally I decided I would have to turn around.

But I didn't emerge on shore. A gnawing fear whispered inside me, growing with the wind that rocked the spruce tops way above my head. I was suddenly aware of the rapidly changing sky. Lightning flashed and the first big drops splattered between the trees. Could I be mixed up? I glanced about, really frightened for the first time, listening for the river. Now the wind spoke and every tree complained darkly under the burden of it. The mosquitoes had vanished. Nearby something cracked explosively before the singing air. Tears streaked my scratched cheeks as confusion gave way to terror. Slowly I rotated and suddenly each direction looked identical.

I don't recall how long I wandered or if I prayed. Time means very little in moments like that. I only remember that first glint of open sky. Heedless of the grasping branches I scrambled forward and burst into the face of the storm. The river! Despite my backtracking, I felt certain that I was still below camp. I scurried upstream along the bank, pelted by hail and spray. But no camp came into view.

"Mother!" I bawled into the wind, pivoting in frightened indecision. "Moth . . . ther!"

As if in answer, I heard the tiny "Pop!" of a rifle out of the gray ahead. I scrambled over the last few obstacles and found myself in camp.

I hugged my mother, feeling safe and foolish.

"Come on, let's get out of the storm," she said warmly, ignoring my tears and drenched clothes. She put her arm about me and started for the tent. "I fired the 30.06 hoping you could hear it over the thunder."

And I never forgot it.

But now where was that damn Phil?

The fire glowed red in the midnight dusk. Uneasily I rose for another bundle of sticks. I listened: nothing but the faraway call of geese, the hum of insects and the muted crackle of fire sluggishly pushing smoke into the calm, moist air. What if he doesn't come back? At last the thought surfaced in a black wave. What would I do? I could never find this place again if I went for help, and what good would it do anyway? I would wait here all summer if need be, but oh, please God! bring him safely back!

I was digging out the 30.06 when Phil appeared in camp, heralded by clouds of fresh mosquitoes. He took a breath and plunged into the smoke.

"What happened?" I asked as he turned to prop the .22 against a log. His dirty face was scratched and his hair was matted with twigs. Gently I drew my arms about his waist and he stroked my hair. For a long moment we stood there, holding to the security of each other's warmth.

"Come sit down," I said at last, taking his hand.

"I'm sure glad I took the compass," he told me sheepishly. "There was a period of time when I was certain that the compass was wrong, but it seemed unwise to argue with it."

"Dinner is ready." I placed the pot between his feet and pried up the lid. Steam enveloped him, fogging his spare glasses a moment. I seated myself across from him and smiled mischievously. "Let me tell you a story," I said.

⋆

As the days slid by under that constant summer sun, we fell into a rhythm with the river: a watchful harmony, an unequal truce. On a horizon of determined water we floated timelessly towards the sea, past hundreds of sunbaked islands, dense forest, hidden channels, eddies and submerged logs, crumbling cutbanks and sandbars. The earth and sun stood still amid vast plains of water-sky where giant islands rode slowly up to meet us, then dwindled behind into yesterday. And above the silence we could feel a careless song of power.

That song was with us always, even as we slept, one ear tuned for the canoe. We heard it by day as we drifted beneath cutbanks where muddy water sucked at the earth and trees held desperately to one last season, their boughs weighted with cones that the dying offer. A wall of earth would suddenly collapse, rending the thin carpet of roots, sending spray

upward as the earth slid into the river. We felt small, a speck of flotsam adrift in time and space. The river's song was with us, too, far from land in the whisper of silt against the canoe and the gentle swirl of the current.

From shore came the smells of a breathing forest under a midday sun, of balsam poplar and spruce and something akin to fresh, hot caramel candy. A solemn train of dark spruce slid past, interspersed with the bright green flurries of new sandbars covered with willows. A venturesome yellow butterfly lilted toward us, alighting as a splash of living butter on our silver bow.

Drowsiness would steal upon us in the warm, still air; a trust in this big friendly river. Then from nowhere a tremor would slam through the canoe, swinging our stern crazily sideways, shipping water as we collided with an unseen bar. In panic we would fight the current, leaping overboard into the soft, invisible sand, shocked at our speed. I would brace against the straining craft while Phil changed another sheer pin. Our old outboard didn't have a clutch, so the propeller turned as long as the engine was running. The "sheer pin" was designed to break whenever the screw hit something. Once the pin was replaced, we would lead Lady Grayling into deeper water and climb aboard, gushing water from our boots, and be off again, not a visible speck of land for a mile on either side.

One evening we were camped on the head of a sandbar that had recently emerged from spring flood. Bars are new land, a gift of the river. Bedraggled willows in full leaf were knitting over the scars of breakup, healing the ice-furrowed ground in shimmering layers of green. How resilient they seemed. We sat before a driftwood fire enjoying the breeze that kept away the mosquitoes. Before us our island clove the current, brushing aside the Yukon. This combined with the breeze to give an illusion of motion, as if the island itself were traveling upstream through the water.

"But our civilization cuts us off from nature," I was arguing, "and from one another. Compare your relationship with other automobile drivers to your interaction with people walking."

Phil leaned contentedly against a bleached and battered stump, digging his bare toes into the fine, warm sand. His feet, broad and flat, turned decidedly inward.

"You can't just throw it out," he answered. "After all, you've never plowed with a stick . . ."

"Even our play is organized," I broke in. "There is no spontaneity. What price do we pay for our physical comfort? What is 'quality of life'? Primitive people were able to spend more time together. They had a sense of community that we've lost. I'm not certain that all our toys are worth what we pay for them."

Phil was looking his old self as I watched him through the bright hot blaze of our driftwood fire. He was very brown, the light eyes striking in his tanned, bearded face and looking slightly owlish behind spare glasses. His dark hair was already frosted red-gold by the sun. Mine was nearly white on top.

I pulled off my soggy boots, summer "shoepacks" with leather uppers and rubber bottoms, worn with felt insoles. Thoughtfully I wiped the lint from between my toes. Good feet, they have given me faithful service and often been hard used. It felt good to let them dry and air after days of wet boots.

Tasting my tea (saccharin-sweetened to conserve sugar), I settled the white enamel mug beside me in the sand. A few feet away Lady Grayling rested, belly in the mud, while bright ripples of late afternoon sky and water reflected over her silver sides. Already a waterline two inches below the gunwale marked our loaded freeboard. Nearby a distraught sandpiper teetered along the shoal, piping her discomfort at our presence.

"Each generation must examine its world and choose," I said, flashing Phil a glance. I do interrupt too much, I thought. Now he'll give me the silent treatment. "Coyotes may adapt to the L.A. freeways, but we build them."

Phil was studiously pruning his ragged cuticles with a pocket knife. His nails were still grease-stained, and I wondered idly how he managed to maintain this trace of his old life as a mechanic.

"We throw away our power as individuals for a feeling of security," I continued. "We have somehow lost our sense of communion with the planet and with each other."

I stared moodily into the flames, watching the sticks disintegrate under its almost invisible touch. Water had leached the driftwood, leaving it porous and brittle.

At length he snapped his knife shut. "Finished?"

"Yes." I kept my eyes on the fire. A frantic colony of ants boiled from one end of a log, driven out by heat and smoke. Taking a twig, I helped the survivors to safety, knowing even as I did that an ant without its colony is dead. They are not individuals in the same way we are.

"You cannot separate yourself from your culture," he told me. "It's sophomoric to propose simple solutions. What you're talking about isn't just a matter of technology."

"Maybe," I conceded. "But I've had it with the artificial culture we have built. I've had it with forms to fill out in triplicate. I've had it with rules. I would rather risk being killed than have a government restrict me for my own good."

"It's more complicated than that," he insisted once more. "Regulations are meant to protect others from you as well."

I snorted in exasperation. "I know there are good reasons behind most laws, but the end result is a bleak world devoid of creativity and personal responsibility. Kids might fall out of trees and parents might sue – so down come the trees. School yards look like prison camps."

"Parents do sue . . ."

"Bleak." I interrupted again. "Who wants to grow up, no matter how safely, in a bleak and joyless world?"

I took a deep breath and let my eyes rest on the beach. It was so quietly itself, undisturbed by my arguments. "Phil, I need to know what being an animal means before I can understand what it is to be human. I want to be like these willows, sinking my roots into the earth and knowing the direction of the sun. I can't do it in the city." I studied him, this stranger that I wanted to spend a lifetime with, wondering if we can ever know anyone.

Whatever Phil was thinking, he only said, "I'd like to try to photograph the geese before dinner. I didn't hear them leave."

He pulled on his wet socks and boots and set off across the twenty-acre bar, camera and lenses slung around his neck, leaving large, pigeon-toed tracks in the sand. I smiled at his retreating back, thinking of the wise old honkers I have chased.

There were sociable congregations of Canada geese on the Yukon, and nearly every sandspit boasted a wary clan. My mother called them "bachelor birds," for they are not nesting. The breeding pairs were already established on ponds inland. The geese see everything, and soon I heard the excited bark of many voices followed by the flip-flap of weighty bodies becoming airborne. With every beat the jaws flew open, warning all other geese up and down the river. The cry was taken up on neighboring islands where black stalks of agitated necks bristled alertly. Then they too burst into flight.

Theirs is a world of sky and water. I marveled at the V of poetry staining the late afternoon where parting notes still lingered. I focused on them, drawing my mind to a point. Perhaps it is a question of vision, I decided. Some people find more inspiration in their back yards than others do in the Himalayas. Still, wouldn't it be easier here? The wild geese of my school years were silver V's of bombers flying out of Davis Monthan Airbase.

Smoke curled with the steam from our unmistakable horse-chip dinner as I sat in the stillness beneath a hemisphere of sunset and birds. When you live under it, the sky makes up half your life. Down the beach I could see the silhouette of Phil returning, looking small yet somehow complete, at home here as much as I. He greeted me with a soft smile and a handful of wildflowers then joined me beside the fire to recount the things he had seen.

I finished eating and handed the pot and spoon to Phil where he sat tracing circles in the cooling sand with a polished stick. Across the channel an elevated cutbank stood sharply defined by the sinking sun. I could see that it had been the site of a burn in recent years. It was clothed in vigorous new bushes and wild flowers and the carcasses of trees that had once lived there. A time for everything, I thought. Some life thrives only on old burns.

"I wonder if sea gulls are good to eat or legal to shoot," I said, breaking the stillness.

"Probably not much there but feathers," Phil replied, roused from his own contemplations.

"I bet they taste fishy. But at least it would be fresh meat." I had been raised believing that milk, eggs, and meat were the only proteins and hadn't known to pack more whole grains. We had fallen into the habit of two meals of horse chips a day. It seemed a bother to stop for lunch, and we were also conscious of conserving food.

"We do need some fresh food soon," he agreed, "to improve our outlook as well as our diet." We had yet to catch a single rabbit or fish, not a promising omen for people who intended to live off the land.

"Why don't we try to camp in a slough tomorrow and set out the fish net," I suggested. "There'll be LOTS of bugs, but we won't catch anything here. At least not without fresh bait. The current would carry our net away or shred it. And it's too muddy for fish to see a lure."

"Okay," Phil nodded in agreement. I rose from the chilly ground and dusted off my trousers. My clothes were sooty and stained from life on the ground, but it didn't seem important. A lone duck flapped overhead, going somewhere. He veered sharply off to the north when he spotted us, members of a species universally shunned. I watched him, thinking that ducks were never meant to fly. But they do.

Chapter 2

BEFORE I WAS BORN, my parents had wintered in a small cabin in the Brooks Range, much as Phil and I intended. The following year they crossed the Continental Divide and floated down to the Arctic Ocean. There they met a truly wild people, Eskimos living much as their ancestors had for hundreds of years. Life on the tundra is very different from the forest. The people were nomadic, following the seasonal migrations of game. They took my parents in, and without their help, my parents would never have survived the winter.

My mother told me stories of these people. There was an old man who had never owned a rifle. He caught seals in a hand-made net under the ice. He was eaten by a polar bear. Another old man had only an ancient single-shot .22 rifle to hunt grizzly with. He would lie on his stomach on the tundra in the path of the browsing bear and move his hands to imitate ground squirrels. He once told my mother that he had seen "many babies left in the snow." These were good people who loved their children, but they were realists too. They knew that in a bad year the entire family would starve if there were too many of them.

Alaskan Indians were different from the Eskimos in many ways, but they shared a common heritage of recent primitive existence in this wild northern land. Life close to nature can be a tough teacher.

⭑

When we arrived in Fort Yukon, we nosed our canoe among a group of flat-bottomed boats. I jumped ashore with a line and stood ankle deep in thick mud, holding the bow.

"Is it okay to leave our outfit here?" Phil called to the small solitary figure leaning against the general store and watching a fish wheel revolve in the current.

The man was an older Indian, dressed in dark and dusty street clothes and beaded moose-hide moccasins. The visor of his blue baseball cap was flipped back to reveal a stubble of salt-and-pepper hair and obliquely observant eyes creased between wrinkles.

His mouth moved in what may have been a smile as he shook his head. "They steal everything here."

The summer sun stood hot and high in the early morning, reflecting off a string of big boats that rocked in a backwater of floating debris. The smell of the river mingled with a fishy odor. Not a hint of breeze stirred the muggy air. Behind us the featureless blue sky was separated from its reflection by a ragged thread of green islands.

I tied the bow painter fast to the covey of boats and lumbered up the bank, pulling each foot free with an audible "sssssluck." Running a self-conscious hand over my wispy braids, I grinned at the quiet little man.

"Is this your fish wheel?" I asked him. "Are you catching any? Could we buy some?" A fish wheel is a wonder of simple technology. Turned by the current, it scoops the migrating salmon into a basket.

He smiled down at his feet saying in a low voice, "No good for fish here."

Why put a fish wheel where there were no fish? I wondered. From atop the bank I could see a rambling clutter of wooden buildings and log cabins, some leaning at unusual angles.

"I think you'd better stay with the canoe while I try to buy a few things," Phil said, coming up behind me.

I settled myself on the grassy bank a few feet above the canoe just as a river boat loaded with shouting Indians zoomed past a hundred feet from shore. Momentarily caught up in their speed, I watched them skim over a shallow bar, noting how they could raise their motor vertically to avoid hitting ground. The engine seemed to be mounted on a lift. The lift and the shallow draft of the big flat-bottomed boat formed a practical combination for rapid river travel. I felt a twinge of envy, followed by alarm as their bow waves struck our canoe, causing it to wallow deeply in the heaving muddy water.

"Where you going?" came the soft voice behind me. I turned in surprise and saw the old man watching the bucking canoe, his face carefully neutral. I hadn't expected him to speak.

I explained our plans to him, feeling foolish. It was obvious, even to me, that we didn't really know what we were doing. At length the old gentleman ventured tactfully, "Chandalar very fast river. Many rocks."

"How will we find it?" I asked, eager to meet someone who had actually been there. Somehow we had imagined ourselves drifting downstream until we spotted the tributary entering from the north. Now we were beginning to realize the complexity of the Yukon.

"That side," he motioned with the flat of his hand. "You stay always that side."

The boat shot by again and I stared at the rocking canoe in hypnotic fascination, afraid it would sink before the town.

"Isaiah Daniel," he answered when I asked his name. Isaiah Daniel from Venetie. He was visiting friends here in Fort Yukon. Could we buy gas in Venetie? Yes.

"How far is it to Venetie from here?"

He shrugged. "One drum of gas."

Fifty-five gallons. How could we have forgotten that map? I chided myself. The one we had didn't start until somewhere north of Venetie.

The Indians returned, swinging recklessly into the tethered boats which shied and bucked in ringing confusion. Isaiah turned contemptuously to stare at the fish wheel as it creaked through endless cycles.

"Why do they keep a fish wheel here?" I inquired of his austere back, my mind still on food. "If this isn't a good place?"

He glanced at me in amusement, then dropped his gaze. "Tourists."

Before long Phil returned, surprising me with an expensive cola and a drooping chocolate bar. Then he took my seat on the grass while I set off to explore.

It was a shanty town of variety: sagging cabins, oil drums, and new pickup trucks—despite the fact that there were only a few miles of road. A horse-drawn road grader rusted beside the pieces of a modern one. A discarded bicycle lay in a heap of cans and bottles. Racks of moose antlers were nailed over doorways. And everywhere were playing children and chained dogs.

A flavor of leisure wafted from the dusty roads. It seemed an easy integration of life styles and cultures. There were a few modern government buildings including a Native Center where people could wash clothes or see a movie, but the rest of the town lacked indoor plumbing. The town's electrical generator supplied power to homes, but water was delivered by truck to white and Native alike.

Thoughtfully I circled back to Phil, the canoe, and the shimmering plain of river.

"You look as melted as the chocolate," I said, coming up behind him.

"All done?" he asked, getting to his feet and brushing off his trousers. "Get some pictures?"

I nodded.

"Lets get going."

The Indians were still cavorting in the skittish boats. Standing there, I was inspired to sneak a photo of them. "Go ahead," I heard my mother's voice from somewhere in my past, "get the picture. You'll never see these people again." Covertly I aimed my telephoto in their direction only to confront a dark face scowling back up the lens at me. Unsteadily the men boiled from the boat and surged up the bank. A pockmarked face pushed close, raging, "Goddamn, smart-ass tourists!"

The man was short and heavy with a mop of coarse black hair overhanging scared, muddy eyes, bleary with drink. I caught a look of helpless anger as his face withdrew.

This was our introduction to Amos and Bertha Fred of Venetie. My mother was wrong about never seeing them again. I was to find that you never really leave your past behind.

The following morning I lay quietly under damp folds of down listening to the soft music of rain on the tent fly and ignoring the demands of my bladder. The light coming through the orange nylon tent was subdued by a low overcast. Phil, with his back to me, was propped on one elbow, leafing through our bird book.

"Well, it's ten o'clock," I said. "I suppose we ought to get up."

We were clothed in the night things we would wear all summer, I in light pajamas, he in a T-shirt and underpants. The cramped tent was humid from our breathing; the waterproof floor, cold and slippery where it protruded from under the ensolite pad. Phil stretched and slid his book into the journal box (an army ammunition box) and snapped the lid shut. Then he wriggled deep into our zipped-together sleeping bags and ran his cold hands up my back.

"Well, what do you want to do? Get wet or starve?" I asked.

He cocked his head and listened. "I really don't think it's raining as hard as it sounds."

"Maybe. But just think of the soggy bushes out there." I rolled over and snuggled my behind into the curve of his stomach and legs. My back ached from lying down. "What say you volunteer to go dig out the wool shirts?"

The day before we had entered a small winding slough that slithered for miles into the forest. Here we decided to try our gill net. After pitching camp, we had chosen a spot and (for want of a better idea) cut a pole, looping on as much of the net as it would hold, and hung the pole over the water.

"Come on. Here's your shirt," Phil said as he slid back into the bags and plastered his wet feet onto my calves. "Water's up since yesterday. Aren't you anxious to see if we caught any fish? Maybe the net's solid with them."

The warm scratchy wool felt good as I dressed in the confined tent and Phil curled down out of the way. Then I reached outside for my boots which were upended under a corner of the rain fly.

We emerged into a gray and scented world of bugs where bird calls

22

echoed between black-trunked trees. Clouds clung to the ground in tenuous trails, hiding even the direction of the sun. I sniffed deeply of dripping forest and poplar smoke as I knelt on the bit of sloping mud bank to start the fire. It was a good day to lay low for out in the channel small white caps crowded before a blustering wind.

There were indeed fish that morning: three scaly suckers. Flavorless, mushy creatures with numerous forked ribs, they nevertheless bolstered our spirits, being our first catch. Soon it began to rain again, cold drops splattering into our tin plates. We ate and returned to bed. Lying fitfully within the sticky bags, we read aloud until nearly midnight.

The following day was not favorable for travel either. A high overcast lent a chill to the drab sky from which a cold western wind descended to kick up waves. Still, we regretted every lost day. After another fishy breakfast we packed our outfit and set off.

Even on the slough, water slopped more than occasionally over the gunwale as we crept along. Although we had eaten some of our supplies, we were still riding dangerously low. When we reentered the main Yukon we motored quietly a few feet from shore. The sullen rushing river, as faceless as the gray sky, now seemed malevolent as big waves built up over miles of open water. The river was peppered with large islands, some distinguishable from the shore only at close range where narrow channels were sucked off between the trees. On the headlands of the islands smashed the relentless current, piling up debris in a deadly trap.

Again the shore opened ahead. Beset with indecision, we watched the crisis approaching. Which way? Should we risk a small channel that could meander for miles, perhaps losing itself in thickets and log jams? Or stick with the main river and chance missing the Chandalar? We had almost decided to avoid this little offshoot when Phil spotted geese. By the time he had photographed the departing birds, we found ourselves dragged sideways into the channel.

Thus two accidents, a stiff breeze and a flock of geese, charted our course. The river we sought collides with the Yukon in a confusion of arms, most of which would have added greatly to our journey (had we found them at all). But nature has provided a way, a wandering secret way, to enter miles above that tangle, and somehow we found it.

Our path snaked swiftly inland through fields of waving willows, green and gray in the shimmering wind. The mud strand was carpeted with the rich velvet of joint grass and the elaborate print of bird tracks. At our approach, startled ducks flung themselves into the air from hidden reed beds. We caught sliding glimpses of open areas, ponds and marshes, through the shifting trees. Within the cozy safety of the slough we began to relax.

We stopped for dinner at a confluence of waterways, building our fire atop a grassy cutbank. Nearby stood three or four deserted cabins. Below us the chocolate channel plowed into a small river. It had a friendly look, this river, not unlike the slough. But where the two swept together, a slight color change persisted. My heart lightened at this brave promise from snowy peaks hundreds of miles away. Our river! We had picked it from the map and now here it was: a real wilderness river! My gaze lingered on it affectionately.

We were waiting for the wind to drop, as it generally did at night, before trying our hand at upstream travel. Eventually we would need to "line" the canoe upstream, pulling it on foot, but now hoped to put that off awhile. This was the beginning of a hard and often discouraging chapter in our new existence. Our days of floating were over.

"Someone's coming," I said, cocking one ear into the wind. I tossed my fish bones into the fire and lumbered to my feet.

Behind us a boat suddenly materialized with Amos and Bertha Fred, two of my brief photographic acquaintances. With them was a proud and well-muscled young man, beaded headband holding back his shoulder-length black hair. They sighted us and swung toward shore, almost swamping Lady Grayling.

I climbed down the five-foot cutbank. It was flaking off and I jumped onto soggy tussocks of grass rooted in melting mud. "Would you like some tea?" I called out in greeting as I reached for their bow line.

"No, no. We gotta get back to Venetie tonight," returned Bertha. "We just stop to see are you okay." She was a well padded woman with short dark hair, a round face and intelligent eyes.

"Oh, we're fine!" I answered enthusiastically. "Sure you won't stop for some tea?"

Bertha shook her head resolutely. "No, we gotta get back to the village tonight." She studied our overloaded canoe in open skepticism. "You like, we can take something for you. We got lotta room. Wouldn't be no bother."

Amos said nothing.

Phil scanned our outfit with indecision. "Thanks for the offer," he replied politely, "but we'll do okay." We were beginning to tire of skeptical looks.

"You got plenty of food?" Bertha inquired with the same directness. We nodded. Amos pulled the starter rope and the young man shoved off with the butt of his rifle. I watched, intrigued as his new 30.30 sank into the ooze. Then the big engine caught with a rumble and the boat shot upstream and was gone.

That first evening was deceptively easy. By midnight the wind had stilled. We set out with our five-horse motor opening the wide bends before us. The water turned milky gray where our small bow wave broke the reflection of sky and trees as the Chandalar unrolled, taking on the look of a real river. Sitting in the front seat, I gazed at it with a new sense of excitement. There was promise on the early morning air and purpose in the smooth bends when, for the first time, we caught sight of the mountains clear and small ahead.

Cold dawn was upon us when we stopped on a sandbar to build a large driftwood fire. In the Arctic summer, the splender of sunset-sunrise may take several hours. This river wasn't so bad after all, we concurred as we sipped steaming mugs of spice tea and watched the brilliant morning fade into day. We had come quite a ways and seen the mountains: the great Brooks Range! Mud banks of the Yukon had given way to sand and gravel. We pitched our tent in that picture-book camp and headed for bed full of the happy miles we would make on the morrow.

A few hours later we woke to flapping nylon and blasting sand. Cold sheets of wind-borne sand thundered down the beach, obscuring the far shore and forming dunes. The stinging particles sifted into everything, filling our eyes, ears and sleeping bags. The tent billowed and strained at its moorings, frequently ripping free. Driven forth at last by hunger, we ate a gritty oatmeal breakfast, eyes squinted against the blast, and went back to bed.

When we emerged into the still amber of evening, our calm beach had returned.

For the next few days we traveled by night to avoid the wind. Every mile became tougher until each yard was a battle with the quickening river. We discontinued use of the motor except for occasional quieter stretches, and even then used it only at the loss of many shear pins, much gas, and the edges of our propeller. Our progress shrank to less than five miles a day as, on foot now, we hauled our stubborn canoe and her half ton of dreams up the rapids.

We became discouraged as plans of starting our cabin early withered and the elusive mountains slipped ever backward at our plodding. The longest day of the year came and went, marking the annual descent back into winter. And we weren't even to Venetie yet! "We have to get back tonight," they had said. "Chandalar very fast river." The memories lilted through my brain.

But there were good signs too, as we never tired of pointing out to each other. The Yukon jungle lay behind us now, mud and all. This country had an open, healthy feel. The living water was inlaid in bars of tawny sand and polished colored stones. Although we saw no game, the shore was often marked with the tracks of bear, beaver, wolf and moose. Trees were smaller here and spaced with patches of wild flowers: lupine, forget-me-not, fireweed, wild rose, and gentle gifts for which I have no names.

By now it was late June and the steadily dropping water was becoming clearer every day. New sandbars surfaced, growing up through the swift, shallow river like young plants. We feared that the canoe might escape while we slept, so each night she was firmly grounded out of the current and well shackled. And every morning found her high and dry. It always took considerable effort to badger her back in, but the peace of mind was worth it. This was big empty country. Phil now wore the .22 pistol, not for protection, but as a hedge against starvation should we ever lose the canoe, and we both carried matches in waterproof containers, mosquito repellent and our pocket knives.

Energy, I was thinking. So that's what it's all about. Living in a land of bulldozers, I had never realized how fragile yet tenacious our little selves are. Think of what it means to own a mule! To travel downstream instead of up! All the work of life must be done by something: the hauling of wood and water, the building, the growing of food, the travel from place to place. And mostly it was done like this, by human muscles. No wonder people wanted to take the load off their backs and put it on machines, I thought, looking upstream. But then, I admitted, glancing back the way we had come, progress certainly means more to you this way.

Early one morning found me immersed in icy water and chill dawn breeze, tired and discouraged. Minutes before we had broken a shear pin and, paddling furiously, come ashore at the base of a crumbling gravel cut-bank.

"What's taking you so long?" I snapped, holding to a sweeper with one hand, the canoe with the other. Beneath my numb feet, the relentless current sucked away the sand as I fought for balance, water to my waist.

"I dropped the goddamn shear pin!" Phil wailed. He disappeared from view and groped about blindly under water.

I shifted my grip, fighting the restless canoe. "Let's just camp. Maybe we can walk it over to that island." Together we scanned the whorls of morning-streaked river, oblivious to the song of sleepless Arctic summer. "I think we need to eat better," I said dully. "A person can't work like a mule on a handful of oatmeal." But we had caught no more fish and no rabbits.

We made camp on a flower-decked cutbank under shifting clouds. This was a young bank, composed of fine brown sand. Clumps of perennials laden with red blossoms were sprinkled between vigorous young balsam poplar trees and the tiny spruce that would eventually take over. When the first hardy plants invade a new sandbar, they transform it into a place where insects, small animals and slower growing trees can get a foothold. But now the capricious river wanted it back. That is what cutbank means.

We had finished our starchy meal when we caught the distinct buzz of an outboard. Very soon a river boat leapt into view, spinning down current. He spotted us and careened rashly shoreward, cutting the motor at the last instant. To my astonishment, the big boat settled gently beside our canoe.

"Difference between planing and displacement hulls," Phil answered my surprise. "Besides, he's not loaded."

It was Amos and Bertha out for an evening ride. They were bundled against the wind of travel and toiled stiffly up the bank while their handsome young friend fastened the boat. He was introduced to us as Johnny Albert, his long hair tied back this time with a pink silk scarf. He grinned as I handed him a cup of mint tea.

"We was a bit worried about you," Bertha stated, holding her chapped hands out to the blaze of our fire. "Our chief, even, Isaiah Daniel, he come lookin' for you last night."

"Oh, it takes us awhile." I smiled sheepishly. "Uh . . . how far is it from here?"

"I think maybe fifteen miles?" she turned to Johnny and he nodded.

Fifteen miles! That would take us days! My face fell.

I lifted our little blackened tea pot from the fire and squatted near the cups, steam drifting back over my hand as I poured. I was embarrassed by our apparent helplessness. "Sugar?" I asked, handing her a scalding mug.

She spooned it in. "I always like lotta sugar in my tea," she grinned. "You?" she handed me the bottle.

"I prefer mine plain," I lied, thinking about our diminishing supplies.

The clouds were once more closing in. I could feel a fine spray of mist hitting my face and soon big drops were dancing in the dust around the fire.

"We can give you a ride," Bertha offered, setting her empty cup on the lid of the grub box. "We got lotta room and we just put everything in, your little boat and all."

This time we accepted with gratitude and relief. Adding three quarters of a ton slowed their progress, but we sailed right over riffles and rapids at what seemed an incredible rate to me. I shouted a happy conversation with

Bertha above the roar of the engine. Already I had quite forgotten the river. It slipped by with such ease that I was surprised I had ever taken it seriously.

Morning sounds of Venetie, the discordant howl of two hundred chained dogs, woke us in our graveyard camp overlooking the village. Beginning like a distant wind, it swept upon us until all was drowned in a rush of voices.

We poked among the old grave markers for something to burn as the

first guests began to arrive, their trudge up the steep hill heralded by fresh dog song. We had been assured that it was okay to camp here, for the actual cemetery had been moved because of the encroaching river. Still, there were nervous titters from our visitors about ghosts.

Our first adult visitor was the ancient patriarch of the prolific Mark family. Slowly he topped the bluff, leaning on a walking stick. He had dressed to greet us in a rumpled white shirt, black tie and shiny black suit. He wore glasses and smoked a pipe. Atop his head was a quilted cap with a visor.

"Hi. I'm Jeanie and this is Phil," I said. I stuck out my hand and grinned. He touched it as if unaccustomed to shaking hands.

"Abraham Mark," announced the bandy-legged little man. He sat cross-legged in the dust, sipping sugary tea and conversing with Phil in broken English while his great-grandchildren swarmed about. The old fellow appeared oblivious to the shrills and giggles that engulfed us as he continued his stories.

He told us that few in the village had been far up the river, for as he explained it, "Nobody walk no more."

"Tell us about the river," I persisted.

"Many year now I have not go there." He brushed mosquitoes from his leathery neck with a small dark hand and smiled winningly. His worn suit seemed somehow in keeping with his personal dignity as he sat amicably in the dirt by our breakfast fire. "Too darn many rock, I tell you. Too fast that river." He shook his wrinkled head at some memory. "You can't take no boat there, I tell you that. Why you want go?"

"We like the woods," I answered.

He nodded eagerly in agreement. "Trap line. Lotta fur sometime. Sometime no good. That lynx, you catch him, maybe he plenty good sometime. Two year ago, rabbit everywhere," he extended his small arms to encompass the village. "Oh, plenty lynx that time," he beamed. "But nobody trap too much now. They just wait for native checks. No good, them people now days," he declared, clamping his jaw shut. "Drink, all the time drink! Venetie is a dry village. You know what that means? Nobody supposed to drink in the village. But they go down to Fort Yukon and bring it back, then everybody drink. Drink and fight! Drink and fight. No good. God as my witness, I never drink, not one time, and now I ninety-one years old. I work when I was young and I know what my life was for. What they live for? To drink and then shoot each other!"

"Gran'pa present," a child tugged at his sleeve. Old Abraham smiled angelically. "All my gran'kids love me and my great-grankids," he proclaimed modestly. From his pocket he fished out a crisp dollar bill. A rush ensued. Soon the kids were off down the hill to buy candy and tobacco at the village store. "My gran'son, you know him? He get lotta moose last winter with the snow-go. In the village, everybody eats lotta moose then. In Fort Yukon, they got freezers so they just keep their own moose, just hide it, put it away."

By our third day in the village we knew almost every adult on sight and a good many by name. There were perhaps 120 people in Venetie and they were friendly and curious about us. When we met Bertha returning from the airstrip where the daily mail plane had come in, Phil was carrying boxes of welfare food for one of the larger Mark families. Followed by skipping children, we dropped off the groceries and trailed after Bertha back to her cabin, each chewing on an apple.

As we passed the last cabin, old Sophie, bent double and nearly blind with the seasons, hailed us from her yard. "You want come in for whitefish? I just got good whitefish." Her cabin was large and well tended with wood stacked before her door by neighbors. The small village retained its sense of community: sometimes petty and gossipy perhaps, like any group of people living together, but still a unit that cared about its members.

"No thank you, Grandmother," I called to her. "I will come visit you this evening."

The path wound among broken and discarded equipment and the inevitable skinny dogs. Here was a culture that for years had been supported by the government. People who once lived happily with few possessions had discovered the toys of civilization. It seemed to me that by comparing themselves with others, they had also discovered poverty.

I knew that it was not a simple problem. The land once supported the Indians because they starved when game was scarce, keeping their numbers within the balance of nature. They can't go back, any more than we can return to the days of covered wagons, but if they move to cities they must give up the support of their village and their whole way of life.

My eyes lingered covetously on the boats tied along shore. How would we make it into the mountains before winter? We had offered to buy the needed fifty-five gallons of gas for anyone who would transport us upstream to the abandoned gold town of Caro beyond the first fork of the river. But no one stepped forward, and daily the river level dropped, making upstream travel more difficult.

The Freds' cabin was constructed of unpeeled, green-cut logs and papered inside with stained cardboard and pictures cut from magazines. The main room was divided by a high linoleum-topped counter. Behind the counter was a propane stove, cupboard, dish drainer, various pans and an open five-gallon slop bucket for dog feed. Across the room stood an oil heater, a sofa, several chairs and a gas-powered wringer washer. Over the stove rows of wires were strung for drying socks and mittens. Only the village school had electricity, and the people hauled water from the river in buckets.

Amos brooded in a corner of the dark cabin while Phil and I chatted with Bertha around the counter. Like most of the villagers, his days seemed spent in a tedium of inactivity. For hours he would sit beside the cabin, staring at the ground. He seemed a sad and lonely man and in poor health. I found the silences between us too great to span. But then I never tried.

Amos Fred, I thought, watching him covertly while I spoke with Bertha. Amos Fred, the early missionaries were wrong. A man should keep his own name.

"You want some fish?" Bertha asked, turning from the propane stove with a skillet of fried grayling. She had been more than generous, often feeding us meals or snacks of pilot bread and jam. In fact, although they seemed at a loss to understand us, the whole village treated us with kindness.

We ate in silence, each wondering what to say. Although her English was good, our backgrounds were so different that we often misunderstood one another.

"We caught some fish too," I boasted, "only they were suckers."

"Oh, we don't eat those," she told me seriously. "Too many bones."

My attention was drawn to something still bubbling mysteriously on the back burner. "Whitefish guts," she said, following my gaze. "Very good." She seemed defensive. "You try some?" So far we had eaten muskrats, boiled unskinned; and boiled geese, heads and all.

I walked over to the stove. "Sure . . ." Forking out a bit, I returned to the counter and gingerly tasted them. They were much the flavor of oysters.

"Is there anyone else we could ask?" I finally approached the subject that was on my mind.

"Maybe Bobby Mark takes you when he get back from drinkin' in Fort Yukon," Bertha replied irritably. "I worry about you," she said after a minute. "Maybe you get into lotta trouble. Two years back, this white man, he went and live by himself. We never see him again until the Trooper, he go back there in the wintertime, lookin' for him. That man, he builded himself a little house, so small he couldn't even stand up and with no real door, just canvas. And he didn't have no food. He eat up everything and then he shoot himself."

She got up and placed tea before us on the counter. "Even good Native boys, sometime they get killed. Last winter a Native boy (he know what he was doing too!) die when his snow-go break down not too far from the village." Bertha watched us, chin in hand, from her stool on the other side of the counter.

I knew that others were wondering too as they studied our little canoe or talked quietly with us. Some of the young men had borrowed Lady Graying for a frolic near the shore, for none had ever been in a canoe before. "We'll be okay," I smiled reassuringly. "Next spring we'll be fat as beaver. Just call us the upstream Indians."

She looked uncomfortable for a minute and then declared, "You aren't Indians."

The door of the cabin stood open and drugged mosquitoes drifted in and out of the punk smoke. The smell of the slowly burning insecticide coil tinged my thoughts, reminding me of the Mackenzie River and other people who had entered my life briefly along those far-away banks. Outside in the bright hot sunlight, flies buzzed about the dogs. Often sadly neglected, they are kept as status symbols, a cultural hangover from the days before snowmobiles. I remember Great Slave Lake in Canada where the dogs were abandoned on small islands to survive the summer or die. In the fall, they would be gathered and fattened up for winter work.

A dog was probably the last thing we needed, but watching them from the cabin, I decided I wanted one. Phil and I both loved dogs, and I missed that relationship. Seeing the ratio of dogs to humans, I assumed we were in the ideal location to acquire a pet. We followed one lead after another around the village. People were friendly and proud, bragging about their dogs, which were all shapes, colors and sizes, but no one wished to part with a single one.

By evening our quest brought us to young Johnny Albert.

"Just woke up," he said, swinging open the door of the small dark cabin reputed in old Abraham Mark's gossip to be the haunt of the undesirable.

"We're trying to buy a puppy," I began. "One to take up the river with us. Franky Jim told us you had some."

Reluctantly he led us around the corner of the cabin to a makeshift wire pen enclosing a dozen colorful balls of fur. "I had to put 'em in jail." He pointed to the tumbling puppies. "They broke into Isaiah Daniel's cache and ate up all his dry salmon. And he wanted that fish for himself."

I laughed and Johnny looked up in surprise from tying on his headband. I suddenly was aware that humor takes more than a common language: it takes shared assumptions.

"I'm gonna race these dogs," he finally stated, obviously embarrassed at the request. The spring inter-village dog races are a big social occasion. "I don't want to sell none of 'em."

That evening Bobby Mark returned from Fort Yukon, his boat laden with a cow moose that he had shot along the river. After we spoke with him, he agreed to take us up to the old abandoned gold town of Caro, which was probably as far as his boat could go.

It was sprinkling fitfully the next morning as Phil and I trudged up and down the hill behind town, lugging gasoline from the airstrip. There were no vehicles, or even any real roads in town. As we broke camp, Johnny Albert appeared unexpectedly with the runty mongrel puppy I had liked. He told us that he had dreamed he would be killed in a boat accident. To prevent this, he said, we should take the dog.

So for five dollars we acquired a bundle of problems which we named Net-Chet-Siil, or "Little Girl" in the Kuchin dialect of Athabascan. She was a pretty little thing, just weaned, all honey and cream with strawberry tongue and licorice-drop nose. Her coat was thick and soft, her tummy bald and freckled, fuzzy ears flopped over her puppy-blue eyes and her voice carried for miles.

As we loaded our outfit aboard the big river boat everyone in the village came down to see us off. With a wave of farewell we shoved into the current.

Go! Go! Go! Pleeeease! I pleaded silently as we crept up the tumbling river.

Bobby seemed surprised by our sluggish pace and I caught the words, "One time I got four moose in this boat! I chartered a plane on floats and just fly around and look for 'em!" as he shouted to Phil above the roar of the outboard. He was a fine looking, cheerful man of medium stature, about thirty and already head of a large family. Like many of his generation, tawny eyes, bronze skin and big bones told of the infusion of white blood. He motioned to his friend, Kevin, a slender youth of seventeen, and turned the motor over to him. Then settling his back to the wind, he cupped his hands about a cigarette and opened a can of coke.

I watched Kevin driving the powerful engine as he stood proudly in the stern, legs apart, eyes scanning the water, long black hair streaming.

Net-Chet-Siil burrowed under my red woolen coat, soft and wriggly next to my body, as I craned forward, urging the boat on. We plowed toward the foothills as rainbows and showers played over a landscape colored in nameless shades of velvet green. I saw Bobby shake his head as Kevin swung the motor up once again, avoiding sudden shelves of rock.

"I think I go back to the village and get more gas tonight," he shouted to Phil, flipping the empty coke can overboard. "We sure use it up this way." Phil reached into his pocket and drew out our remaining cash and handed it to him. It was the last money we had in the world. Finally I crawled under the overturned canoe to get out of the drizzle.

Then we were stopping. I stuck my head out as Phil ran nimbly forward and leapt ashore with the bow line. Two tiny old men greeted us and we arranged ourselves about their smoldering fire. Like other places we had noticed along the river, this was a well used camping spot for the Indians. It was situated on a small cutbank in the protection of mature spruce, many of which had been stripped of bark. The bark, which comes away easily in large sheets in the spring, is used like plywood to cover lean-to's.

After a brief conference in their own language, one of the old men, Matthew Fred, turned to Phil with a big smile and said, "This my lucky day! I see moose over there. I shoot 'em and he swim across and die on this side. I didn't have no boat. I was just gonna eat those little fishes and I don't like 'em." He pointed to a can of sardines.

The three young men unloaded the boat and set off to retrieve the skinned and disjointed carcass of a yearling bull. This they heaved onto a bed of willows in the shade. No one seemed concerned about the flies, which will lay their eggs on meat, converting it to maggots in a short while. The two old men stood quietly by as the quarters were hefted ashore. I thought of the skill that lay in those small, veiny hands. Butchering a moose is no small chore.

We ringed their smudge fire, sipping coffee while the Indians exchanged news. Finally Bobby turned to us in English saying, "Jeremiah Daniel, Isaiah his brother. He don't speak English good. His gran'son, Niel, he was supposed to take 'em up the East Fork to their cabin. But he run out of gas and went down to Fort Yukon to drink and just leave 'em here."

Jeremiah grinned and nodded, not understanding a word. There was something gentle about this man. Like his companion, he was of slight build, dark and weathered. His almost beardless face was carved by history, as were his small, gnarled hands. In the near blindness of age he wore thick glasses. He was dressed in baggy slacks, red checked flannel shirt and beaded moose-hide moccasins. His short-brim cap secured a flutter of gauzy material to protect his neck from bugs.

Matthew Fred offered us the interesting animal matter that was gurgling glutinously in a thick green soup over the fire. The Indians were already at work with their pocketknives stabbing long strings out of the five gallon can.

"Moose guts," said Bobby, glancing over his knife as he chewed. "The old people, they really like this stuff. They eat it when they was young." Matthew nodded and smiled.

Phil and I looked timidly at one another and dug out our knives. When in Rome. Phil leaned over and whispered, "They still have the shit in them!" I nodded and smiled. Rubbery, but not bad.

Next came boiled tenderloin. The backbone was severed with a knife at each vertebra and plunked into our large kettle. Most Native cooking seems to be geared to reducing preparation of the food, not a bad idea for people living a simple life outdoors. This was topped with the usual sugar-laced tea and the budding antlers of the young bull. Jeremiah singed the velvety skin and roasted them in the fire.

We spent the night there. After breakfast of boiled moose, I squatted on the bank, scraping the impervious tallow deposits from Mightypot with sand. Behind me, Jeremiah had a tape recorder going. It was playing Native chants sewn together with his fiddling. I listened, feeling across the cultural chasm that separated my world of science from this ancient heritage. I was intrigued and would have stayed awhile, but Bobby, who had taken most of the moose to the village and returned during the night with extra gasoline, considered the old folk dull company. He was anxious to be off.

So I hurried to pack up our camp gear and load the river boat while the recorder fiddled on and Jeremiah danced.

"You know," I said to Phil as we shoved off and the waving old men dwindled into the Arctic vastness, "in our culture we'd lock those two up someplace safe where they couldn't hurt themselves. Did you hear that old Jeremiah spends every winter alone up on the Wind River? As blind as he is too. I suppose some day he'll die out there and people will wonder why somebody didn't stop him. But he's alive now."

We hadn't been long underway when the East Fork veered off taking most of the water with it. Because of the shallows, I and half of the gear remained at the junction while Phil and the other half continued on up the diminished river.

As the sound of the engine melted into the river, I took a moment to look around. We were now actually in hilly country, able to glimpse mountains through breaks in the green. Underfoot spread a springy six- inch carpet of multi-colored sphagnum moss, lacy white reindeer lichen and dainty sprigs of lingonberry, also known as low bush or mountain cranberry. This intricate work was woven with minute flowers and inconspicuous plants of many varieties. The scattered trees, spindly and often draped in threads of gray moss, contrasted somberly with the bright ground cover. The land seemed brilliant and fresh after the dank Yukon and dusty village.

This new country pleased me. Its very openness should enhance our chances of seeing game, I decided. As if to prove me right, my eye caught the cautious hippity-hop of a feeding snowshoe hare, brown now in its summer attire. I unsheathed my old .22 rifle and soon was cleaning the luckless rabbit, our first game. A flash through the trees drew my attention to a hole in which a pair of yellow flickers tended a brood of demanding young. Everybody is busy this time of year. I rinsed the rabbit, very unimpressive now, and was saddened that it was a nursing mother. Guiltily I tasted the milk on my bloody fingers, then washed the fluids from my hands in the river.

When the boat returned to shuttle me upstream, I was ready. Phil had camp set up by the time we arrived, and a short while later I was preparing rabbit and dumplings. The Indians were tired of our slow travel and we did our best to make them comfortable. As we sat gnawing diminutive bones and glancing casually at one another, Bobby announced that he could take his boat no further. Tomorrow they would leave us and head happily downstream hunting.

As for us, we would be left entirely to our own strength and imagination. These were the last people we would see in almost a year.

Chapter 3

BEAUTIFUL AS THE WILDERNESS IS, I don't recall enjoying it that first summer. Somehow we had expected the sweetness of an extended hike and were unprepared for the continual stress that faced us. We found ourselves in the position of wild animals, dependent upon the land, but unlike them we were neither highly adapted nor specifically trained for this role.

I heard the Indians leave early, the guttural growl of their big engine hushing the woods. The sound faded as they slipped down current, and was lost in the song of the river. The day was July first.

It felt good to be alone. I lay still, listening to Phil's deep breathing. The ceaseless babble of water soothed me, tempting me back into the fairyland of sleep, where I had been doing . . . what? I couldn't quite remember. Closing my eyes, I shut out the day ahead and listened. The river sounded like people all talking at once, the pitch seeming to rise and fall. Sunlight dappled my face, teasing me. I rolled onto my elbows. The screen door of the tent was dotted with mosquitoes and I shook it before zipping down one corner to let Net-Chet-Siil out.

The Arctic was no longer in bloom. The succulent green of deep summer was swollen with mature plants coming to fruition. Many had burst from hidden roots, rocketing into the brief summer on energy stored the year before. I call this country Arctic because it is far north of the Arctic Circle, although the vegetation here is mostly boreal forest and not the tundra of the high Arctic.

We were camped atop a thinly spruced cutbank and I studied the bright ground cover a few inches from my face. Each curl of moss was perfect to its kind. A damp, earthy smell rose from the warm carpet to mingle with the spice of Labrador tea and the rich vanilla scent of spruce bark. The river had changed too. Semi-transparent like fine jade, it tumbled over large and slippery stones. Rolling green hills descended to gravel bars, obscuring the mountains beyond.

"They've gone?" Phil asked.

"Uh-huh." I dropped my gaze to his upturned face and kissed him on the lumpy bridge of his nose. "I was just contemplating getting up," I said. Even from the tent I could see that the flies were busy with our half-dried moose meat, tasting it with their feet for moist crevices in which to deposit eggs. It was a parting gift from Jeremiah. We had cut the meat into strips to hang near the fire the evening before.

Glancing back at Phil, I could see that he was already repacking in his mind. Net-Chet bounced forward at the sound of our voices, demanding to be readmitted.

"No!" I snapped, unhooking her sharp claws from the frail mosquito netting. "Now go on!"

"Looks like a nice day," Phil announced, sitting up and reaching for his red checked wool shirt. The faded blue T-shirt he slept in looked dingy. He stretched and glanced at his watch. Then he shook his wrist and listened a moment. "It's dead."

He looked at me and we both shrugged. "Who cares what time it is," I answered.

"Isn't it good to be here?" he grinned.

"I wish I knew where here was. When do we get on the map?"

"We'll just have to keep comparing the map with the country until we get them matched. Our map starts on this side of Caro, so if we find the town, we'll know exactly where we are."

"Bobby said Caro isn't really on the river," I reminded him. I was pulling on my jeans and I lay back to tug them up and fasten them. "We could miss it."

Phil unzipped the door and crawled out on hands and knees. "I'm going to start loading the canoe," he said over his shoulder.

"I want to do some laundry before we start out."

Had we known that we were scarcely half way from Venetie to the ghost town of Caro, perhaps things would have seemed different. But that morning we were full of hope.

Two hard days and five miles later, we stood panting in the shallows, leaning heavily against the tug of the canoe while white water boiled around our knees. We almost didn't make that one, I thought, staring back down the foaming trough.

The principle of lining a canoe upstream is simple. The craft is worked on a long rope, one end fastened to the bow, the other to the rear thwart (a brace across the canoe). When the stern is pulled in, the canoe pivots and ferries out from shore. A shifting balance of tension is maintained as conditions change. Lining works well with a moderate current and an even bottom. In rapids we needed direct contact with the craft to hold her and it often took all of our combined strength.

I caught Phil's glance and shook my head. "Not yet." My arms felt weak and my legs shook with fatigue. Overhead an afternoon thunderstorm growled and billowed darkly into the cobalt sky, mounting as we watched. The weather seemed to have changed as we neared the mountains, or perhaps it was only the advancing summer. A warning gust of wind swept upon us, kicking up spray and turning the river a flat, metallic gray as the sun blinked under.

"Well, here it comes," Phil stated as the first drops hit. He took a firmer grip on the bow decking. "I can handle it from here. Why don't you go on up to those spruce and get a fire started? Here, take the tea things."

I gave in too easily, and tucking Net-Chet under one arm, ran wobble-kneed over the rocks for the distant trees. My feet were numb from the cold water and my pants clung to my legs. Scattered sheets of blowing rain raked the willows that crowded the nearby bar and flattened the few pioneer weeds that poked between stones down on the beach. Ahead loomed the dark, thrashing spruce.

I entered the trees abruptly. Humming and swaying they wrapped privately about me, dense and secret. I cleared a space in the thick moss and kicked into the duff. Beneath the green feathers of sphagnum moss, the years had layered a deep pad of peat interlaced with twigs and punky logs. The flames took easily to the twigs, burrowing into the dry duff with alarming speed.

It was raining hard now. From the relative safety of the trees I could see a little figure out on the river struggling through the driving sheets. A mist rose from the rocks where the thundering rain exploded on impact. Phil became a shadow, a small toiling wraith in a world of gray. Stinging hail joined the deluge, and Net-Chet began to whine as a fine patter sifted through the needles of our shelter. By crouching against the trunk of a tree I managed to avoid most of the rain.

"Shut up, Net-Chet!" I turned on her. Phil was trying to beach the canoe, dragging it onto a rocky spit in search of something to tie to. I dared not leave the fire to help him. At last he was running up the beach, blindly, head down into the rain. Poor guy, couldn't get much wetter, I thought.

As he entered the forest, I seated him on a carpeted hummock of roots, close to the bole of an old spruce. He was soaked and shivering. I poured scalding water over the tea grounds in his stained enamel mug and crawled under the branches with him. His hair was plastered down and streaks of dirt drained into his beard, joining the trapped mosquitoes. Net-Chet was curled up on my only summer coat, so I squatted over the blaze warming my fingers.

"Have some almost jerky," I offered from a cloth sack. The mist sifting through the trees was becoming a drizzle punctuated with big drops. Lightning scared the gray world beyond the trees. "It tastes pretty good if you don't look too close. Hey, you know your shirt is running?" I fingered a red stain around his cold, dripping wrist where the dye had leached.

We crouched together, feeling the comfort of wet warmth pass between us, chewing raw rubbery moose while the storm raged. "Here's another batch," Phil said, precisely excising the wriggly pearl of a maggot with the point of his pocketknife.

"Just don't tell me about it. I'm not looking," I replied in disgust.

"More protein," he teased.

I shot him a sour glance. "The cycle is amazing when you think of it. Moose to maggot to fish food in a few weeks." I closed the cloth game bag and slid it behind us to keep dry. It was made from sewing two large kerchiefs together and served to allow air circulation while keeping out flies.

As the storm rode northward on the expanding evening sky, we gathered up our tea things and carried the squirming damp dog back to Lady Grayling. The clean land was tinted delicately tangerine by a low sun, and the air felt clammy on our cooled bodies. Cold water spilled into my boots as we pushed the canoe back into the current. Within fifty yards we hit a rapid that swamped her. Fighting for every foot of progress, we towed her ashore and unloaded everything, spreading our belongings on the stones to dry.

It was Phil's twenty-third birthday.

⋆

One drizzling afternoon a few days later we rounded a bend and stood before the mountains. For the first time no foothills blocked our view. We grounded the canoe and dropped onto the wet rocks to study the map.

"Where do you suppose Caro is?" I asked Phil. "We've got to be getting close. Do you think we could have missed it?" We glanced from map to mountains attempting to fit it together. Somewhere nearby was the abandoned gold town. Ahead were the dusky blue peaks, jagged and almost naked of trees. Behind us the shaggy, meandering shoreline was lost in a lush belt of foothills, dividing us from the past.

"About four miles to the inch : . ." he shook his head. "It's hard to tell. The creek we saw yesterday could be this one . . . or maybe this . . ." he traced a muddy finger along the map. "Hope it wasn't this one or we've missed it."

"Well, I'm not going back." It had started to rain again and Phil bent over the map, shielding it with his body. From her nest in the canoe, Net-

Chet was complaining ever more insistently. The bugs were vicious on the bar, stinging as they bit into my wet face. They seem to prefer rainy days as long as there is no wind. Irritably I shoved Lady Grayling, stern first, into the current, playing the rope through my chapped hands to adjust the pitch.

"I'll take it awhile," I said, glad for a chance to warm up. I threw my weight into the rope, running it over my right shoulder and using my left hand to control the angle. Water piled into the side of the canoe, forcing it out. The river was shallow and pebbly, hooking slowly into another broad curve. I relaxed, placing each foot with care. Feeling the thigh muscles tighten rhythmically, dependably, I straightened my leg. Step, splash. Step, splash. Slowly the bottom deteriorated into slippery rocks and rushing water. Step, jerk, stumble, tug. The canoe fought back, hanging up, yanking. Progress.

I peered ahead. Did a creek join at the bend? The ghost town would be difficult to find. Built near the water in the 1890s, it was left inland when the river changed course, willows reclaiming the abandoned channel.

"It's a stream," Phil called from the shore a little distance ahead. "Let's camp and see if we can locate the town in the morning."

"Got a place picked out?" I asked, my eyes searching the shore for a safe harbor for the canoe.

"This looks about as good as any."

Together we heaved the bow firmly aground. I reached into the front seat and pulled up my coat, setting the squalling pup ashore. Phil tied the painters to a large drift log embedded in gravel and fastened the cable around a boulder.

Minutes later I had the tent set up and sleeping bags spread out. Phil unloaded camp gear and lashed the fitted tarp back over the boat. Crawling inside just as the clouds opened, we stripped off our wet clothes and piled them under Net-Chet. From bed I stroked her delicate head and listened to the storm. We lay reading aloud while the rain drummed on the tent fly and fog built up inside the tent.

I tucked my hands between my legs to warm them and tried to forget my hunger. Concentrating on Phil's voice as he read, gradually I slipped into a dream. I was swimming after a drowning infant. I dove beneath a muddy current and pulled up the lifeless child. As I kicked for shore, I breathed into her lungs, perhaps too hard, for by the time I climbed the beach she had degenerated into two transparent balloons.

I woke in the stillness of gray midnight overcast. The tent was empty. I lay motionless, soaking in the silence as I sought out Phil's presence. I could feel the uneven press of stones against my spine and hear the distant murmur of the river to my right. To my left a soft twittering of sleepy birds delineated the edge of the forest. Then a slight shift in the air brought the scent of wood smoke and I relaxed.

I sat up and reached for the shirt I had used as a pillow. Shaking the dog's mud from my wet trousers, I forced my legs into them and hunched my way out of the tent. The Arctic had a somber look that evening, chill and drab. Across the rocks I could see the canoe, dark against the mottled water. Nearby a small fire added the only touch of color, the slight movement of a dark figure squatting over it the only sign of life.

Phil looked up at my approach and smiled. "I chopped up the last of the old moose ribs and boiled them," he said, giving the pot a last stir and replacing the lid. He ran a spoon under the bail and carefully lifted the blackened little pot from the coals. "See what you think of it. I put in some dried vegies and flour for thickening. Watch out for bone splinters."

He seated me on a log he had hauled to the fire. I could see the uneven drag marks trailing up the beach.

"Have you fed the dog?" I asked, placing the pot between my feet. I pried up the lid and a sour meaty smell assailed me in a billow of steam. Phil poured us each a cup of tea and squatted down on his haunches across from me.

"I gave her some of the soup." He hesitated a moment and then said, "I know we decided not to shoot the little tree squirrels, but we have to feed her something . . ."

"Okay," I answered, not looking up. The thick, grayish soup tasted good. "I guess bringing her was a mistake, wasn't it?"

He didn't answer. He dipped a twig into his tea and fished about. "The trouble with finding a mosquito leg in your tea," he said, changing the subject, "is you wonder where the rest of it went."

"Only one?" I smiled.

The next morning was sunny and warm. We discovered that the small stream had a dozen grayling living where it emptied into our river. Grayling are beautiful silver fish, twelve to fifteen inches long with big iridescent dorsal fins of turquoise blue. They live in clear water and are fun to catch, for you can see them. You often find several living together in some glass-clear "hole." Like children we played along the bank, catching fish and cooking them over the fire in the sunshine.

It was late afternoon before we set out on foot to look for Caro, and evening was again upon us when we discovered the old ghost town slumbering among the fireweed. The rotting cabins stood quietly, a part of the Nature from which they had been fashioned, and yet so totally different. Washed by three quarters of a century, there still lingered that strange ugliness that clings to abandoned human dwellings. Once there had been voices here: now only the song of the white-crowned sparrow, the tired creak of a spruce tree, the gentle quiver of wind in the tall weeds. Through the seasons it had remained here, this cluster of ancient log piles that had been the homes of men.

The cabins, their dirt floors now covered with wild flowers, seemed small and dank, mere holes to crawl into out of the snow. Trees sprouted in the narrow doorways and on the sagging sod roofs. Rotten wooden barrels that had contained flour or nails, treasures in a land of wilderness, lay scattered in the blooming fireweed. Fallen dog houses built in rows had once confined the hard but necessary lives of slave dogs, long dead and forgotten.

Many of the cabins were no longer standing. Most were rooflessly tumbling back into time. Perhaps thirty people had lived here. A red tree squirrel raced along a naked ridge pole, vibrating at our intrusion, his tail flicking in agitated little jerks with each "Chit! Chit! Chit!" Dreams were built here. The dark walls whispered of loneliness, of men living for the time when they could return home rich from their long winters in the gold fields. What becomes of men, I wondered, who search for the pot of gold only to miss the rainbow?

We rummaged through quaint old garbage: patent medicines, faded newspapers, tools of another era. These tools had made life possible in this land, and the land hasn't changed. After a long time in the dirty, dim interior of a cabin that still boasted a roof, I stepped into the lavender twilight and came face to face with a wolf. He didn't look startled or even impressed. He was tan in color with a black face. Standing perhaps three feet at the shoulder, he coolly returned my gaze a long moment before turning with indifference and trotting out of the clearing on long, silent legs. Net-Chet was engaged in searching for a vole and was blissfully ignorant of her close call.

Finding Caro had at last put us on the map, and we carefully marked each day's travel with little penciled lines. It was encouraging to see the daily change in the landscape that now marked our upstream progress. The river no longer rambled freely. Often the channel was bounded on one side or the other by a two hundred-foot cutbank, confining the river to a broad glacial cut where it swung from side to side as if seeking escape. I tried to imagine what the land looked like ten thousand years ago when a massive river of ice had carved out the valley.

At that time a people very much like ourselves hunted moose and bear here. In the fall they picked cranberries and blueberries with their children. In the spring they saw the ice go out and watched the birds return. They nursed their babies and cared for their old people and told stories around the night fires.

One day the Chandalar swung abruptly, butting into the bare bones of the mountain mass. For some time it had paralleled the range as if undecided. Now it turned resolutely northward, wedging open a wide valley into the secret heart of the mountains. Soon we were leaving our familiar gray crags behind for another set of landmarks.

As the river began its climb in earnest, we had to develop a different method for surmounting rapids. Here they were strewn with large boulders, "boat eaters" we called them, interspersed with deep holes. Water gushed over rocks the size of slippery basketballs. The high crumbling walls often dropped steeply into the river at a bend. In the past we had both grabbed the bow and muscled the canoe up the watery stairs. Now one of us braced against a boulder, holding her in the turbulence of its wake, while the other worked the rope upstream. Finding secure footing, the one on the rope would haul the canoe (and the person guiding it) hand-over-hand up the racing chute. Already behind us lay nearly a thousand feet of elevation.

We were approaching the last major fork in the river when we pitched camp on a sandy white beach late one afternoon. It was a clear, still day and the low-hanging sun gave the country that peculiar golden quality that outlines every detail in color. A few yards upstream a sandspit protruded into the current in graduating shades of blue, sheltering the canoe from the main stream.

There were few mosquitoes on the bar. Their numbers naturally diminish by mid summer, one of Nature's many cycles. We stripped off our clothes and hung them on small willow bushes to dry. A slight breeze tickled the naked hairs on my back and legs as I worked, but did nothing to deter several blood-sucking flies. They were as long as a finger joint with iridescent, rainbow eyes and sharp, triangular mouths.

I staked down the tent floor as Net-Chet circled my legs, whining. She was never happy until home was established. Pushing in the last peg, I tightened the nylon guy lines. Phil had plucked a small seagull and was heating water to cook it when I plopped down in the warm sand by the fire. A large spider danced away, lugging her egg sack.

"We need to refill Wonderbox," I said.

"Again?" Phil was squatting near the blaze, positioning the tea pot.

"Well, we're out of pancake mix, oatmeal, sugar, and powdered eggs."

He looked helplessly at me. "We've eaten a third of our supplies."

"I know it, but we have to eat something. And so does Net-Chet. In fact she eats almost as much as we do. If there were more small game or fish . . ." I trailed off. We both knew the problem. In the far north small animal populations are cyclic. We had seen only four rabbits all summer and no spruce grouse. Our attempts to fish on the main river had been fruitless. We now ate the tiny tree squirrels.

"Well, we may be hunting big game before too long," he stated.

"I haven't seen any of that either," I reminded him. We stared at one another in silence.

46

Phil poured boiling water into two mugs and added sand from a plastic bottle. I grinned at him. The day before I had spilled some sugar and he had saved it, dirt and all.

"To my golden retriever," he smiled, handing me a cup. "The way you jumped into the rapids after that gull I shot."

"A Bonapart's gull. Honestly, Phil. Next it'll be chickadees," I teased him. "Here's mud in your tea." We sipped in silence. "We might be better off if we ate more. As it is we are dull-witted and weak. Very ineffective."

"I guess any way you look at it, it's a gamble. Use up all our supplies and keep strong to find more, or ration food and starve longer," he answered.

A vague hunger had come to live with us, an uneasy craving that even a full belly could not quench. We had planned to depend on small game for protein, but instead found ourselves living on diminished servings of starch. A listless apathy haunted our movements and we found ourselves inclined to sleep away long hours, even entire days.

"I feel like I could eat a whole moose myself," Phil told me seriously. "Waiter! Bring me a moose, medium rare, and a bushel of apples." Phil was a big fan of apples. His mother used to buy them by the bushel. He would eat eight or ten a day regularly.

"If we do get a moose we'll sit and eat for a week." I grinned at the thought.

"Can you imagine drying a moose in the summer? Out here?"

I understood his point. Curing the horse had been hard even with a table, oven, and refrigerator. "I'd like a bacon, lettuce, and tomato sandwich," I said suddenly.

He leaned forward with a wicked grin. "Well I'd like a chocolate cream pie with a tender flaky crust and mounds of real whipped cream."

He had me there.

Net-Chet rose from her place on my coat and nosed into my lap. She really was a pretty little thing, I thought, stroking her silky ears. Similar to a gold collie in color, she had a white diamond on her forehead and snowy ruff and legs. Her tail had the curl of a husky, but her fine bones seemed to promise a smaller dog.

A coolness was settling over the beach, creeping up from the singing river and out of the nearby forest. In the evening breeze our empty clothing danced on the bushes. We three drew closer to the fire and one another as the blue silence filled our thoughts. I looked across the river and let in the presence of the wilderness. I could imagine viewing us from directly overhead and then pulling back until we disappeared in the landscape, further and further until even these mountains were lost in the Arctic. For a moment, I let go of my worries about tomorrow and sought to encompass the vast, interlocking beauty of this living country.

As if part of my thoughts, a cow and calf moose materialized from the willows on the far bank. Transfixed we watched this apparition. Often we had seen tracks, tangible evidence of the unseen denizens of this land, but they were the tracks of ghosts. The big timid animals emerged specter-like from the shadows, ears and noses questing the uncertainties of the bar. People who think that moose look awkward and clumsy have not watched them in their world or tried to follow them through thickets. Moose are big deer.

For a long moment they poised in frozen silence, their dark forms as motionless as the mountains. Perhaps these secret creatures sensed something amiss or maybe a whiff of smoke betrayed us. As if in slow motion, they shied and dissolved into the trees, leaving the land empty once more.

To celebrate the sighting, we ate our last two squares of chocolate.

✼

In mid-July we hit a solid spell of cold rain and wind, a change that reminded us soberly of autumn. Through days of icy clothes we trudged on as the river became a swollen torrent of liquid mud. Rain and increased melting of high snowfields turned the river into a frigid slurry. The water rapidly numbed our legs and sucked the warmth from our bodies.

As August neared, the nesting urge began to tug at us in earnest. We watched the country now with new intensity. I could feel the desire to be settled into a little cabin of our own, warm and well fed, almost as a physical ache. No longer adventurous, I felt like a child who is tired from play and seeks safety and rest. Like denning animals we studied the river banks, testing, sniffing, searching for the right combination. Not here, not this, but soon. . . . The presence of the Arctic was with us always now, like a giant third person, tireless, patient, uncaring.

We had planned to journey far upriver, to be free at last of the pressure of humanity that had defined our lives, to be on our own. I had even chosen a possible cabin site on the map that now looked depressingly far away in this world. The futility of our goal was becoming ever more apparent, but still we struggled towards it, the weight of its distance heavy upon us.

What difference did it make? I began to wonder. It took time for our isolation to penetrate: we were so accustomed to the signs of man. No trails, no tracks in the sand, no telephone wires. At first we didn't notice. Not a beer can, not a cigarette butt, not a gum wrapper. Our senses were slow to miss them.

We could feel the inescapable flood of Arctic winter already creeping down from the Pole. Soon it would become a white torrent, surging southward to reclaim the land it rightfully owns. At night now our fire had a cozy red glow in the waning daylight.

One day we decided that our outboard motor was of no further use, and built a cache for it and the gas tanks. Because of the rapids we hadn't used it for some time and wanted to lighten the load. We were in the mountains proper now. No foothills were these bald and silent observers of our nightly camps and small daily battles. It felt cozy in the mountains. True, over that peak lay another and still another, all wild and without the track of man, but there was security in being able to see the horizons of our world. This was our valley, our future home.

After a discouraging day and the usual fruitless hunt, we were sitting quietly by our fire, sharing a pot of cornmeal mush. We had given up plates, having neither the detergent nor energy to waste on them. There was only a quart of detergent for the entire year for clothes and dishes. We spoke less these days, our voices low as we enjoyed little jokes that no one else would think funny.

Our camp was perched on a slender strip of mud that separated the roaring brown river from the dark wet forest. A few feet away, the soiled and battered canoe was snugged up in a shoal, rocking slightly in the backwash of waves. Pools of rain sagged in the blue nylon tarp lashed over her load.

Water dripped from the end of my nose into the pot as I took my turn eating. There would have been little point in wearing rain apparel even if we had it, for much of our day was spent in the river. Our possessions were few and because we had no way to dry clothing, changing was useless. Like the moose, we got wet when it rained.

I breathed in the cool night smells and rocked forward on my sitting log to push a charred branch further into the fire. Across from me Phil squatted flat-footed on a rock like some great, hungry bird. He was comfortable in that position, although I have met few adults who are, and I secretly suspected some defect. Nearby Net-Chet was finishing off a tree squirrel, head, hide, guts, bones and all. Oblivious to the drizzle, she chomped, holding the gory remains with her front paws. I watched her work down the hind quarters, shearing the bones with a rhythmic crunch. She finished and sniffed about for missed tidbits.

Through a clean wet stillness, sounds dropped like pebbles: the bird songs, the drip of overhanging alders, the intimate crackle of fire and the torpid drone of a few chilled mosquitoes. Around us the rain was slackening. A breath of wind touched the saturated earth. Far beyond the clouds, the sun sloped northward into the summer night. As it reached the rim of mountains it seemed to gather strength. A small spot in the cloud cover began to fade, brightening at first to a light gray and then a pale yellow. There it smoldered as it slid along the peaks, fanned at last to an almost unbearable orange. Then for a moment it burned through, catching the ragged clouds afire before they closed back in.

I handed Phil the pot and spoon and got stiffly to my feet. I was still hungry. Steam drifted from my wet jeans as I presented my behind to the blaze. Slowly I rotated before the fire, roasting my cold limbs. The skin heated but the deep chill of my bones remained.

"The rain has almost stopped." I sniffed, staring up at the expressionless sky. "Perhaps tomorrow will be good."

I lifted the can of tea from Wonderbox and dropped the lid again. Then I squatted near the fire to pour hot water into our cups. When Phil leaned forward for his mug, I popped a vitamin into his mouth. My parents had lived for years at a time on nothing but meat, but it seemed that the small expense and weight of vitamins was worthwhile insurance. Phil's jaws opened with such innocence that I had to laugh.

"You're so trusting," I grinned. "Maybe some day I'll slip you a spider."

"Nope," he replied. "You're afraid to pick them up."

"Dig up any more birch bark recipes?" I kidded.

He made a face. We had spent one day collecting "edible" plants that Phil had read about, and nearly ruined our stomachs on such delicacies as powdered lichen "flour extender" and birch bark "spaghetti." The book said the lichen had a "slightly nauseous taste," something I can vouch for personally. Most of the recipes called for using a wild plant to spice some main dish. If I had the main dish, I wouldn't need the herb, I thought. The Arctic is a very poor place to be a vegetarian. The number of species is limited, and except for berries in the fall, there are not many plants that are fit for the human digestive tract, especially in the quantity necessary to survive on.

Methodically Phil scraped the pot, then rinsed it and drank the water. I watched him, wishing I had some special surprise up my sleeve. Of late he had been increasingly plagued with stomach cramps and it worried me.

Finally I broached the subject that had been on both our minds. "Phil, we've got to talk about the dog."

He looked uncomfortable, but said nothing.

"What's wrong with us?"

Still nothing.

"I've been thinking about this," I persevered. "We take everything she does as a personal threat."

"There's just no place out here for a spoiled pet," he answered defensively.

50

"That's what I had been thinking, that she's overly demanding. But is that the real problem? Think about it. Is she really that bad?"

He avoided my eyes and reached for his cup. "No," he said at length, his voice very quiet. "She's okay, I guess." He turned to face me a moment. "Is there something wrong with me?" He looked pained. "I'm not a dog beater! Dogs are my favorite people. I speak dog, remember?"

"What about me? I almost drowned her today!"

I had encouraged Phil to hunt while I handled the canoe alone. It seemed a quiet stretch of river, but I soon found myself bucking sweepers in a fast, deep current. Gradually the bottom dropped from beneath me. I worked my way along the cutbank, hanging onto the roots and thrashing branches with one hand, the canoe line with the other. It was raining and I felt half drowned, frightened and scratched as I fought the river. Through it all Net-Chet never ceased her piercing screech from the safety of the front seat. I thought she might be happier ashore so I worked the boat in and tossed her up on the broken bank. But no! In a fury I turned on her. Freeing one hand, I flung her into the water.

All my anger vanished in that instant. I watched in helpless horror as her little head disappeared under the flood. She bobbed up almost at once, shrunken and scared, swimming wildly for shore. Then she hit the canoe, struggled a moment, and was sucked under. Panic welled up in me and stunned remorse, but there was nothing I could do! A long time later she popped up at the stern and resumed her furious shoreward flailing.

I pulled the canoe up into the sweepers and tied it, then went after Net-Chet. Phil found us both soaked and crying when he returned.

"Phil," I continued insistently. "I'm not going to drop this. What does she do that's so terrible? She buries her food. Okay, to us that's a threat, but to a dog it's normal. Yesterday she refused to stay in the canoe, which she hates, and you became impatient. Then she got scared and hid, which made you angry. So when you found her, you beat her. Yes, it is ugly. Look at her. We are all she has in the world and she's afraid of us."

"I know." He was close to tears, head hung. "I've never had an animal fear me before."

I leaned sideways and put my arm about his shoulders, smelling the wet wool smell of him. "Don't you see? I've never even seen you mad before. Why, you get angry at the canoe lately! The canoe! An inanimate object!"

"The main thing that drives me crazy is her constant whining," he confessed. "If she would just SHUT UP!"

"Don't I know it!" Net-Chet had tremendous control. She could pitch a whine so that it was scarcely audible, like a single mosquito in the bedroom at night. But in the canoe her shrieks of loneliness carried above the loudest rapid, like a train whistle. "We can't beat it out of her. She'd rather be punished than ignored. Now look: here she is, alone in a wilderness, no home, no other dogs, no way to survive without us. She hates travel. She has nothing but the two of us, and we have nothing left over for her."

"I know," he said unhappily. "Sometimes I really love the little nuisance. Other times I almost hate her. How can we even hunt with that racket?"

"It was a mistake to bring her," I confessed. I looked at Net-Chet. She was sprawled on my coat, bare freckled tummy skyward in the trusting security of sleep. "But she doesn't deserve this. If we can't accept her for the puppy she is and cope somehow, we had better destroy her. Anything else would be unkind . . ." I let the thought trail off and it hung between us, unsettled. At least I brought it up, I thought, stirring the coals idly with a charred stick.

I stopped and glanced about. Across the river two wolves appeared. They had come down to drink and it was some moments before they too looked up in the watchful habit of wild things. They studied us awhile, a mated pair perhaps, black and white together. Our minds, like theirs, were intent on food, but our rifles lay in the canoe a few yards away. The two turned and vanished into the wall of spruce.

"If we're going to hunt we should keep the rifles with us," Phil said.

"What do you think they find to eat out here?" I wondered aloud.

"Same as us."

"I just don't see how they can catch enough to keep alive day by day. I know they're supposed to eat a lot of rodents this time of year. Still, it must be a full-time job."

For three days a storm raged. Water crept into camp, crowding us higher as the river became an angry sluice. The wind hurled itself into our frail tent, while clouds crashed blackly about us. We lay in our small buffeted refuge and read aloud from a novel. Why is it, I wondered, that people write about imaginary earth-shaking deeds? The real heroes are everywhere: people dieting, crippled children, old folks taking care of one another, middle-aged women going back to school, fathers holding down two jobs, single parents. Life is full of heroes.

During brief lulls we emerged like damp ground squirrels to sniff the weather. On the third day we returned to the river and spent an entire day making less than a mile in the icy torrent. It was one continuous rapid, a foaming sea of mud and tireless wind. Yet even above the wind and water we were tormented by piercing wails from the front seat where Net-Chet rode on my red wool coat.

When we woke the following morning to a gusting rain, we rolled over

52

in tandem and went back to sleep. We could sleep much of the twenty-four hours and still feel tired.

"Oh, Phil, how I hate to face it," I admitted about noon. I gazed out upon the endless boil of brown water through the tent screen. I felt drugged, stuporous almost. Our mud-splattered Lady Grayling waited patiently for the day's struggle. A cold breeze fingered the spruce trees, shaking off a patter of morning's rain. It hit the tent fly in a rattle of drops.

It was clearing off as we crawled into a day of liquid skies and soap-bubble clouds. We decided to take a look at the country instead of breaking camp. With the afternoon sun to our backs we set off together, unconsciously turning upstream into the future. Chet stayed with the tent, happy for a day in camp.

As we hiked, water wheezed out of holes in boots that were never meant for eternal soaking. The rich blue of my checkered wool shirt had faded to gray across the shoulders; Phil's red one was patched in several places, as were our ragged jeans. We had taken off perhaps twenty pounds apiece. My pants were held up at the waist with a hank of rope.

We followed the curve of river, the sandbar deteriorating into large stones. At the bend we climbed a cutbank ten feet above the river. Softly we walked between spruce trees searching for rabbits. Each of us carried a rifle, prepared for large or small game. Amid the woodland paths, distinct in the slow-growing lichens, we wandered through tunnels of sunlight, feeling the hum of growth about us. At one point I heard a rustle and handed Phil the .22. I sat on the lip of the bank, the 30.06 resting easily between my knees and watched the far shore where the trees were brushed with brilliance in the low afternoon sun.

I was day-dreaming again, pretending that caribou were silhouetted on that bank. Caribou were about the right size, around 300 pounds, and legal to shoot throughout the year. I had rehearsed the shot many times: just behind the elbow, a few inches up from the belly line, as my mother had taught me. I was like Kipling's mongoose, Rikki-tikki-tavi, who had never met a live cobra before, though his mother had fed him dead ones. I had already downed several hundred animals in this fashion, from every imaginable angle, using even the .22 and my pocketknife.

I heard the crunch of gravel as Phil rejoined me, squatting in his customary vulture position. We traded rifles then sat watching the far shore in comfortable silence. It was a wide bend, the bank obliquely across from us perhaps a hundred yards away. A rocky bar gave way abruptly to a forest of stunted black spruce and muskeg, that swampy broken land peculiar to the Arctic. My gaze flowed up the shore and scaled the luminous peaks beyond. Snow lingered among the high barren rocks and I watched the white patches intently to see if any were sheep. Then I dropped my eyes to the shore again.

"Phil! A moose!" My hand reached out to touch his leg.

On the beach across from us a big dark shape was just entering the bushes. It hesitated with its rump to us, half screened by foliage. Phil dropped to a sitting position and pumped a shell into the 30.06 chamber, looping his elbow through the leather sling to stabilize the rifle. But he could find no place to shoot. We held our breaths. Come down on the

JEANIE

© 1977

beach! Please come down on the beach! I intoned silently, as if I could move the animal with my will.

It was then I saw the other animal. Small and brown, it flitted into the trees in front of the moose.

"It's a cow and calf!" I whispered, urgently. "We don't want to shoot a cow with a calf!"

At that moment we spotted the wolf, gray and white, maneuvering out behind the moose. I was startled by the blast of the big rifle. The wolf leapt sideways and vanished. Phil rammed another shell in.

"Damn! Missed him!"

The moose hadn't moved. Now it backed out of the willows and down onto the beach. To the water it glided, shoulders rippling smoothly under the glossy dark hide. It stood a moment broadside in the mellow sunlight. Big velvety antlers sprayed back over the high shoulders as he poised at the water's edge.

"It's a bull! It's a bull!" I couldn't believe my eyes.

Phil sighted through his scope. The moose flinched as the bullet struck. I had a sinking feeling. We could not kill this forest spirit with a tiny flake of metal. He would dissolve away wounded into the jungle of bushes, leaving his tracks to fill with the river and melt into faceless sand.

"Shoot him again!" I urged.

Phil shot. The moose shivered and turned to disappear into the trees. Holding our rifles aloft, we plunged down the bank and into the muddy river. We gripped our free hands tightly to steady one another as, kicking against the broken bottom, we were swept toward the rapids below. Gradually the water became shallower and soon we were able to wade. The tension was unbearable as we walked back upstream towards the beach. Wet mud told the story in deep footprints. We skirted them, looking.

"Blood!" Phil whispered in relief, stooping to touch dark splashes on the rocks.

Then through the trees we saw him. He was lying in the moss, fuzzy antlers turning in stately dignity as he looked about. Phil fired a final shot from where we stood into the back of his splendid head. We took our time approaching the fallen specter, giving him time to die alone and in peace. My mother used to say that the animal should never know what hit him.

Studying the tracks, we pieced the story together. When the moose first hit the beach, both wolves were behind him. Then the one I had mistaken for a calf swung around to the front while the gray one crept close to his heels. At the first shot, the wolves dispersed and the moose turned for the safety of the river.

I have since seen moose do this many times. They are excellent swimmers and can leave their natural predators behind. Healthy adult moose stand their ground against wolves, and it is generally the old and sick that fall prey. The Eskimos used to say that wolves keep the caribou strong, recognizing them as two sides of the same energy, dependent on one another for survival.

"Here, give me a hand," Phil called. "Let's see if we can turn him on his back. My word but he's solid! Maybe a thousand pounds. Ought to last us awhile."

The moose was very deep through the chest and had long slender legs. While I balanced him on the ridge of his spine, Phil twisted the heavy neck backward, planting the spread of antlers in the moss. His coat was short and sleek with summer, a rich chocolate brown with cool blond legs and a warm gray belly. Like his upper legs and chest, his throat was black and from it dangled a shiny black "bell." The split hooves were small and neat for his size, deer feet of polished black with matching dew claws. The tail was tiny.

As I studied him it was his remarkable face that caught my attention. The nose was unusually long and slender, delicate almost. His long lips were sensuously soft; the nostrils elongated into slits that could be closed underwater. Big ears were placed near the top of his head and below these, a ridge of bone extended across his forehead. From either side of this grew the trunks of fuzzy new antlers. Beneath the antlers were large and gentle brown eyes, clear as glass and open in the vacant gaze of death.

I left Phil and his pocketknife to their task and started a fire of driftwood down on the rocky shoreline before heading back to camp for the canoe. Already it was chilly. The sun had gone and a purple twilight blanketed the once bright land.

I laughed as I splashed into the river and I emerged laughing on the far shore. Carelessly I skipped over the rocks in my squishy boots, oblivious to the unnecessary noise. How beautiful and gentle was the Arctic that evening! I arrived back at camp still laughing after my mile run.

By the time I returned to the moose, towing the empty canoe with Net-Chet aboard, the deep dusk of midnight covered the ground. The land seemed strangely quiet and empty. When Phil appeared out of the trees and came down to greet us, Chet sniffed him suspiciously. Feeling chilled and stiff, I sat down with a groan on the bare rocks to rebuild the dead fire. Phil hadn't taken a break since I left him and only a few scattered coals remained. He knelt and began to blow softly on the embers.

"Did you check where your bullets went?" I asked.

"They were within three inches of each other, so my shooting isn't off. It's the scope. They were both in the paunch. He could have lived for days.

Now I'm sure I missed the wolf."

"Wolf? You shot at the wolf? Why?"

"I couldn't have killed the moose at that angle," he reasoned. "Besides, we agreed not to shoot a mamma. But we had to get something."

"You look tired." I said. He didn't look up. "How about some dinner?"

Phil returned to the moose while I set a bucket of saltless muddy water on the fire to boil and dropped in pieces of meat and fat from the quarter he had hauled down to the beach. Then I climbed the twilit bank. Phil looked up from the steaming carcass. Knee-high piles of guts surrounded him and the ground was saturated with blood. A strong smell of hot meat and viscera hung in the chill air.

"How do you suppose we'll ever dry it all before the flies get it?" I asked.

"It'll be a job," he smiled wearily. "But it's worth it! Look!" He spread his arms. "No more worry about food." I looked instead at his gaunt face. "Glut yourself! No more wasting all day hunting for squirrels and gulls."

"Ours, all ours!" I gloated with him, still not believing it.

"Until the flies wake up," he replied soberly.

After a meal of tough boiled meat and tea, we finished cutting up the moose and together hauled the pieces down to the canoe. An early morning dampness hung in the misty air as we worked, heaving the slippery pieces aboard, one at a time. In went a five gallon bucket of organs and fat I had stripped from the intestines. In went the liver. Even the stomach found a place in our load.

When we had finished, we sat wearily by the dying coals a last minute, enjoying the warmth on our stiff, damp bodies. Chet lay nearby, groaning loudly from the pain in her distended belly. I felt like kicking her.

"He's pretty lean. Not compared to the horse perhaps, but lean anyway," Phil commented.

I had noticed that. My mother had told us that a person could starve to death on lean meat. The Eskimos call it "rabbit starvation." In civilization we never see truly lean meat, for domestic stock is bred to "marble" fat into the muscle layers. At best moose meat has less than half the calories of lean beef.

"Well, hopefully they will fatten up more by fall." I stretched my stiff legs out. "It'll be good to dry our clothes out tonight," I said, pulling at the blood-caked fabric of my pants.

"This morning," he corrected. Behind him a washed turquoise sky crept northward beyond the luminous yellow clouds, heralding a new day. I could see the lines of fatigue on his face by the growing light. Phil had always seemed so strong and dependable. I looked at him now, small and fallible, just like me. I had thought of him as older and stronger. I suddenly realized that he needed me as much as I did him if we were going to survive.

Chapter 4

I WAS PULLED from two hours of dreamless sleep into the frail pink dawn by the cries of birds. Families of gray jays descended from the woods, their dark forms gliding across the tinted river. The charcoal plumed juveniles floated in behind their grizzled parents, an urgency compelling them all as they carried our meat and fat back into the trees. Eagerly they ripped off chunks, filling their craws, then departed to disgorge into secret niches and return for more. Food is precious in nature and it belongs to the one who eats it. These persistent thieves can carry off an entire moose given the opportunity.

I shut my eyes, and sank into the sleeping bags seeking unconsciousness in the soothing whispers of the river. But the birds were still there. They were stealing my meat and I had to get up.

Jays were not our only guests. I crawled from the tent and pulled on my cold, stiff trousers. Three ravens were extending their wings for balance as they tore into the moose. Even a mew gull had joined the banquet. I stretched and shut my eyes. My head throbbed with fatigue and my eyelids felt like sandpaper. I pushed my contact lenses into place. Sleeping with them at the corners of my eyes was a trick I had learned years before on the Mackenzie River. It worked well when there was no clean way to handle them. I opened my eyes. The moose and birds were still there. Already the flies were waking up.

Slipping on my mildewed socks and boots, I left the laces to flop, and began to gather driftwood. The lower beach was swept clean, but higher the willows were matted with sticks. Further inland stood a spruce forest and from this came the sound of chopping. A sturdy frame of poles, perhaps eight feet high and ten on a side, was taking shape down near the canoe: a rack to dry meat on. Toward this I turned with my arms full of wood.

At my approach the ravens skipped back a pace, watching me with impatience. The disjointed carcass lay on a bed of cut willows, long legs arrayed to enhance air circulation. On the windward side I kindled a fire to discourage the flies, then squatted in the sand and began to skin the big furry head.

Resting on its own velvety stand of antlers, the head stared bleakly at the ground. Starting at the throat, I slit the thick hide down to the wiggly pad of his chin, then slipped the skin back from the long jaw bones. Here the lips confronted me. Like the chin, they seemed integral with the hide, whiskers growing from deep within the spongy, cream-colored tissue. The lips were covered inside with gray and white cone-shaped bumps about a quarter of an inch long. The bottom front teeth, long and loose, meshed with a hard pallet of gray and white scales. There were no upper front teeth. The mouth was still warm, and white fly eggs crusted the gums. I shook the head and irritable buzzes echoed from inside the cavernous nostrils and sinuses.

The day had emerged, bleached and flat without shadow or color. A haze from distant forest fires blanketed the valley, erasing the familiar marks from our mountains. Remote and aloof they seemed now in the bright, empty sky. The still air felt dense and sticky. Into the breathless heat of morning I worked skinning the head, adrift in the drone of countless flies.

Phil finished constructing the rack and lashed the poles together with wire, guying the structure with parachute cord. Over it he tied a big plastic tarp. We had brought it along to waterproof the sod roof of our cabin. This would hold smoke around the meat, protecting it from flies as well as rain. He raked coals from the fire and started two more. Then he sat nearby in the sand boning out the ribs.

"Where do they all come from?" I asked, shooing flies as I worked. "They must smell meat for miles." I had peeled the heavy hide down to the white sockets of the eyes and the base of the antlers. Kneeling next to the head, I tried to remove the jaw bones. I leaned back and wiped the sweat from my eyes. "I can't get the tongue out."

"Try cutting along the bottom of the jaw," Phil suggested, glancing up from his work. "Are you hungry?"

I nodded and paused to run the steel over my knife. Phil had taken a butchering course at the University our last semester and had purchased some good cutlery. A steel keeps a finished edge on the knife so that it doesn't need to be sharpened as often.

The day was turning hot. There was an uneasy, brooding feel to the sultry air. I set the steel on a pile of neck meat. The slender jaw bones extended about eighteen inches, gradually closing to join at the front teeth in a small arch of bone. I ran my pocket knife along the inside of each bone. Pulling the tongue out and back, I severed it near the neck, exposing the mouth cavity. The tongue, like the mouth, was a slate gray, its upper surface roughened while the bottom was smooth.

Phil was preparing breakfast, squatting by a cooking fire as he sliced meat on a piece of driftwood. I got stiffly to my feet and rinsed the tongue in the river. Filling a bucket with water I set the tongue on the fire to boil. Then I sat in the sand and accepted a cup of spice tea and a fork. The fork was crusted with grime and I wiped it on my pants, which were already stiff with gore from loading the great slippery quarters into the canoe the night before.

"We can cook the meat off the head if you can figure some way to chop it up," I said. "I've cut all I can from the outside. The quarters should keep several days, but the head and organs are going fast." Large pieces of meat skin over in the air and remain good for some time if kept relatively cool.

"What do you want to do about the liver?" he asked me. There was about twenty-five pounds of it.

"I thought we'd try drying it. Stomach too. If nothing else, we can use it for dog food. I want to save every morsel we can. We probably ought to render most of the fat down, but we can try drying some too. I don't know how well it'll dry. I suspect it'll turn rancid, but we can try. There really isn't much."

I forked a strip of fried tenderloin from the skillet and sat chewing. It was lean and dark. My gums were sore from poor diet, but I relaxed in contentment at the rich flavor. Phil was silent, also engrossed in chewing. Unless you have known hunger, you cannot know the simple joy of eating.

Behind him the rows of poles were already draped with thin strips of unsalted moose meat. The main reason that meat deteriorates is that it is good food for micro-organisms and insects. One method of preserving it is to remove water. We could have used salt or sugar in this process, but it's not necessary.

Phil and I worked together through the heat of the day and into evening, cutting and turning the strips as they crusted on one side. With the gradual descent of twilight, the birds and flies went to sleep, but we continued our labor, slicing meat and tending the fires in shifts throughout the long night hours.

On the second day a wind began and by the third we could hardly see through the blowing sand that swept over us, scouring the beach. Nearly blinded by the tireless cold blast, we sat and sliced, determined to save our meat. Wind ripped away the tarp, shredding it, and sand drifted over the falling jerky. Our eyes became swollen from smoke and sand as we clung to the fires for warmth. Day and night we took turns catching snatches of sleep as we worked.

We finished cutting the last quarter into strips on the fourth day, and began the process of breaking and boiling the long bones for their fat. The wind subsided and we started to take in dried meat, sorting and packing it away. Thicker pieces were sliced again and laid on a tarp. There were surprisingly few maggots, and aside from sand, we seemed to be getting things under control.

Then clouds drifted in, layer upon layer of dark ships, blotting out all hope. By evening of the fifth day it had started to drizzle. Perhaps we could have salvaged something, but our plastic tarp was in tatters and the job overwhelmed us. We were at the end of our endurance. Exhausted and defeated, we retreated into the tent. A quiet, drenching rain fell for twenty straight hours while we slept.

When the rain ceased we crawled out to survey the damage. Rows of foul-smelling rubbery jerky awaited us. Flies swarmed over the meat, depositing their ugly broods. We restarted the fires, determinedly picking up the cause after our long rest. I began by dragging the hide and bones back into the woods and washing down the beach with buckets of water. My liver-drying experiment had failed, and much of it too disappeared into the trees. The bed of willows had handfuls of fly eggs, and I gave it all to the fish. By afternoon a surprising amount of order had been restored.

Evening found me sitting cross-legged in the damp sand, munching raw kidney fat as I sliced the half-cured meat on my lap. Smoke swirled around me in the chill night air. Nearby in the tent, Phil was sleeping the first shift. With practiced ease I sorted the jerky, noting with satisfaction how rapidly it was redrying. My hands were tender from a dozen knife cuts. At intervals I would stretch them toward the flames.

We should be seeing stars soon, I thought as I watched a great golden moon rise out of the smoky blue north. It was the first full moon I had seen all summer. In the Arctic the moon is visible for two weeks and gone for two. One sees only the sliver phases during the summer and the fuller ones in winter.

August, the month the stars return, I thought. In more temperate climates, August is considered summer. But here we know that the earth is well past the solstice. Time for us to be underway; to find a place of our own.

Trees stood etched clear and distant on an eastern hill where a band of yellow bled into deep blue-gray. Rocking forward I sucked in the cold smell of autumn and exhaled it as steam. I reached for a piece of wood and cracked it over my knee before feeding it into the fragrant blaze. Slowly the fire tasted it, sending blue and yellow flames up from the coals.

Before me appeared a secret cabin, warm and candle-lit. It had a cozy stove in the middle and maybe a fireplace at one end. How could I manage a fireplace? Would mud and rocks work? In my mind I gathered and placed rocks. An open fire is very cheerful, but chimneys draw warm air out too, I considered. There were Plexiglas window panes and I arranged them all on the south side for maximum sunlight during the Arctic winter. If only I had some white paint to brighten up the interior. I could peal the logs, that would help.

I sniffed the hushed air and listened before continuing my dreams. It had to have a floor. Rock perhaps, but that seemed as cold and unappealing as dirt. My parents had a dirt floor on the Alatna River. Most of the old places did. Moose hide stretched over poles maybe? If only we had a way to rip-saw lumber . . .

I glanced up again and scanned the dark bushes, feeling suddenly vulnerable. Their outlines were uncertain and seemed to shift and fade, strangely alien and remote. I'm just not accustomed to darkness, I assured myself, returning to my work. After a summer of constant light, the falling twilight seemed to brood with unseen menace.

My little cabin failed to reappear. I could not shake the feeling that someone was watching me. A cold sensation crept up the back of my neck. To hell with it, I decided at last. It may be silly, but I'm going to bed. With a last look at the dark woods, I joined Phil in the tent, zipping the fragile screen door shut against the night.

In the morning, while scouring the beach for wood, I found the grizzly tracks, big as dinner plates. He had come upon us in the dusk, a shadow among shadows, to linger at the forest edge. As in a half-remembered dream, I traced the silent footprints to the bone pile, sensing each one materialize before me in the sand. Appearing out of nothing, one by one, they drifted back into the trees and dissolved in the moss.

Eleven days after we killed the moose, we were back on the river again. I hopped over the stones with Net-Chet tucked under one arm until camp was left behind. She hadn't wanted to come. We were stronger now and rested. The river pouring endlessly by our familiar bank was clear once more and a deep green. Off shore, Phil strained with the canoe. The river had dropped and rocks peppered the rapids. Two wooden crates and a duffel bag of dried meat rose from the canoe seats.

It was evening, calm and cool, and a light sprinkle pattered occasionally over the wet stones, squeezed from an expanding sky. The day had been one of clean-up and repair. I boiled our stale clothing while we bathed and played in the clear water. It had rained off and on all day as we sorted and packed the moose, now reduced to perhaps 250 pounds of jerky, and rendered tallow. Tallow is a hard form of body fat. Pigs, bears and people have the softer, greasy lard. Cattle, sheep and moose have tallow.

At the bend we loaded the dog into the canoe, and straddling the boxes of meat, paddled hard for the far shore. Here I left Phil and a disconsolate Net-Chet with the slow upstream labor and walked inland to check the kill site. The area had been a scene of great activity. Everything was gone. Even the ground was scraped bare and embossed with the teeth marks of wolves.

Taking a last look, I ran to catch up with the canoe, settling into an awkward trot over the stones. I could see Phil plodding into the distance, small in the gathering dusk. From atop the load intermittent screeches of loneliness drifted from Net-Chet's little backward-facing figure.

"We repaid the wolves," I said, slowing to a walk beside the canoe. "They returned with their pups. Or else a small army of foxes," I grinned and handed him the black tail feather of a raven. "Everyone was there, even our bear." We walked for a time in silence, me on shore, Phil a few yards out in the current. "Moose guts are what we need this fall to attract a bear," I decided. "Bears have fat on them.

Phil's patched boots made sucking sounds in the soft wet gravel. He looked older in his shaggy beard. His big green eyes seemed strangely hawk-like, offset in a lean face by the jutting nose and predatory brows. His lips were chapped and weathered. The muscles in his neck and forearms knotted in cords as he threw his weight into the rope. If Phil were a tree, I decided, watching him, he would be a spruce: somber, slow to change, dependable, strong. I'd probably be a birch or aspen: spontaneous, sun-dappled in summer, full of life and color; withdrawn into my roots in winter. I wondered suddenly how I looked now.

Three days of travel passed and discouragement settled upon us again. It was as hard as ever. We were checking another river bend for possible cabin sites. Somewhere above me I could hear Phil traversing the scantily forested hillside. Steeply below, our evening camp punctuated the wilderness with a small splash of orange. Next to it a singing rapid, white and emerald, caught the late evening sun. Already the gray shoreline sank into shade. Emerging sheer and dark from the waves a great stone monolith, perhaps a hundred feet high, split the bright current. It was a memorable and awesome sight, its sides dropping sheer into the river, though enough soil had formed along the top to support a few trees.

I knotted a strip of rope about my waist securing my pants, and tucked my hankerchief into a back pocket. We had only ten rolls of toilet paper to last a year and needed to use them sparingly. Early in the trip I had adopted this method, washing my special kerchief in the river frequently.

It worked far better than sticks and moss. I did have a year's supply of tampons. My mother had had to wash out old socks on her expeditions.

I scanned the hill restlessly. The cabin needed to be high enough to avoid flooding and on relatively level, firm ground. We wanted a southern-facing location to catch the winter sun. There should be enough dead-standing timber nearby. As we progressed northward and climbed into the mountains, good trees became scarce. We were at 1400 feet and tree line was around 2000, but there was a great deal of variation in timber due to drainage and soil conditions. At best this country sported crooked flag poles, often only muskeg. From a distance muskeg may look like firm ground, for it can be found on the side of a hill where one would not expect bog. But the ground is broken and fissured by frost.

Phil appeared above me, working his way down the uneven slope. He shook his head. "Nothing here."

On the sandbar below us the small wailing figure of Net-Chet shrilly proclaimed her loneliness to the world.

Phil was studying the map. "Tomorrow let's see if we can find the old trail that's supposed to cut from here over to the creek," he said pointing northward along the base of the mountains. "There should be an old cabin or two, and maybe we will find something useful." Ahead the river swung to the other side of the wide valley. There it traveled for some miles, snugged against foothills, before angling back at the junction of a creek. The valley between the bends looked swampy.

I nodded and Phil started down through the trees. Soon we were in deeply rutted muskeg. Under the thin mat of vegetation, melting pockets of ice, remnants of glaciation, left the ground in chaotic collapse. The river bank itself was greatly undercut. As I lowered myself carefully over the tangle of mud and branches to the sandbar, I could see dirty ice beneath it, ice that was thousands of years old.

Net-Chet was overjoyed at our return, wagging and circling our legs in delight. While Phil set the tea pot on, I lifted a bucket of boiled "drymeat," our standard meal, from the coals and sat down on a log.

"My jaws are sore," I grumbled, chewing monotonously. "You'd think it would soften some." My gums were tender too. Phil joined me, stabbing into the pot with his pocketknife for the dark leathery strips.

"How about a treat?" I suggested. "We haven't had one in quite awhile."

"Treat?" He turned slowly toward me, making his eyes go wide.

I had to laugh at his little boy act. "Sure. Maybe some oatmeal." This was a thin oatmeal gravy sweetened with saccharin. Sometimes I would add a handful of the ripening blueberries and call it "pudding."

Tonight I made pudding. We ate in silence for a time. I was lost in a

65

dream of the cabin, still unable to construct a floor. I slipped from my sitting log onto the sand and began tracing the floor plan. Phil scooted around to watch.

"How big a structure do you have in mind?" he asked presently.

"Big," I answered. "Big enough to live in all winter."

"I had thought to put up a little cabin, say eight by ten and four and a half feet high, and at least have a home before snow falls," he suggested.

"That's what all these old places look like," I countered, already defensive. "Holes to crawl into out of the weather. I want a real home. I want book shelves so we can look at our books whenever we want to, and a kitchen table, and a high snug bed, and most of all I want a floor."

He just shook his head. We both knew the trees were too twisted to split and that we had no way to rip-saw boards. We are tuning in to one another, I thought, watching him as he studied my drawing: relinquishing the snappy comeback to listen to the other's thoughts.

"It's so difficult to get a foothold," I admitted. "So incredibly hard. Like drying the moose without even a table. Maybe what we need is to set up some sort of a shed roof first so we can at least stand up on rainy days. Just being able to keep dry would make such a difference."

"I like that idea," he answered. "I must admit I'm burned out on this traveling."

"What do you think we'll find at those old cabins?" I asked casually. I had been daydreaming about a cast-iron skillet. It was a silly dream and embarrassed me. We would be lucky to salvage a few nails or old tin cans for scrap metal. "Maybe we'll find a new skillet," I hinted.

Phil looked sheepish. "How about a big can of strawberry jam?" he asked innocently. "That's the sort of thing that people leave behind, isn't it?"

I had to laugh. So he'd been dreaming too.

"Right! And some white paint for the walls. I want our home to be airy and light inside. And lumber."

"Crackers and canned milk."

"Your mind is on food," I teased. "What about a sled?"

"More tools . . ."

"A cast iron stove with an oven. What I wouldn't give for a good stove. I know our little folding steel one will work, but wouldn't it be grand if we found a good one?" We had purchased a fifty-five gallon drum to make into a stove, but left it with the truck for lack of space.

"Think we could carry it away if we found one?"

"If we find it, I'll find a way to carry it," he assured me.

Next morning we were on our way early and found the old trail without too much difficulty. The dim path was rough and game-maintained but carried the decisive bent of human thought. Straight and single-mindedly it ran, slicing above the two mile loop of river. It kept to the marginal fringe of stunted spruce that separated the mountain from the lower muskeg. As we climbed, a wild land of lakes and nesting ducks spread below us, already yellowing with autumn. The trail formed a zigzag slot where our unseen feet groped and slid in black mire, for even here the muskeg encroached. Wobbly tussocks of cotton grass protruded from an icy bog. These sprouted so thickly in spots that we could not see the "ground." Beneath the chocolate ooze was often the slick hardness of ice.

Net-Chet had a wonderful time, burrowing along or leaping atop the deceptive hummocks, her nose quivering with news of other animals. It was good to see her having fun. Into the tunnel she plunged to emerge crunching a rabbit's foot, leavings of some hunter. A young junco flitted unsteadily to a twig before her, his little body bristling with half-grown feathers. But Chet was unaware, nose in the grass, furry bottom wagging at the sky.

The trail nestled into the mountain, becoming drier as we climbed. We found ourselves traversing splashes of birch between mature stands of spruce, their red-brown bark smelling of vanilla in the warm morning sunlight. Moss replaced the muskeg, and shiny red cranberries popped underfoot as softly we trod the pile carpet. A cold, crisp smell of fall washed down from the nearby peaks, mingling with the scent of Labrador tea and blueberries. Birch trees fluttered, shaking the light from their leaves. Birds that had been silent with the care of nestlings now called repeatedly to fledglings that darted clumsily before us.

As we curled into the mountain cleft, we came suddenly upon the remnants of an old garden. It was choked with alder, and its split-wood fence was returning to soil. Inside were a homemade wheelbarrow and a hoe. A few more steps brought us to the rotting abutments of a log bridge.

We hopped the creek on stones and spent some time scouting around for the cabin. Animals had confused the trails. Moose tracks stabbed deeply into the sod, and bear diggings obscured the old ruts. Then, through the trees I spied a gold and purple swath of fireweed, which always seems to grow where man has been.

We broke into the clearing and stood for a moment in silence. There was something secret about the place, a sheltered sense of care. Unlike Caro, this fragile bubble of history had been lost in the timeless wilderness and forgotten. No human voice had disturbed the memories here for forty years. No alien thought had violated the spell. Even as we stepped forward, time seemed to seep into the glade, and a sigh whispered past us as the memories began to fade.

Before us were several structures in various stages of decay. Between them stood a sturdy little cache, untouched by decades of rain and snow. It was about eight feet square and firmly rooted on four-foot posts. The logs were peeled and neatly dove-tailed at the joints. From its sod roof, half-grown trees sprouted. Still solid and snug it stood, the work of a man who understood wood and enjoyed it.

We spent the day there forming a strange friendship with the past. It was indeed a strawberry jam day. Here were the tools we had thought to do without. Here too were ideas from one who had known and loved this land. We collected the scattered utensils, bottles, nails and cans from about the clearing and carefully stashed them in the little cache. While I watched anxiously, Phil wriggled into the wreckage of the cabin to hand out still other treasures. Gradually we pieced together the life of Chris Olsen, for this was his name, as we discovered from labels on crates. People reveal themselves through their possessions. He was special to us, and much of our well-being we came to owe to that long-ago person.

Chris Olsen was a man who enjoyed the North. It was during the Depression, and there were other men in the woods then, men looking for a way to endure hard times. But Chris was different. He made this country his home. It was evident by his garden and make-shift inventions. He was a man who took care of his tools. He kept sled dogs, and when they died he buried them in little graves covered with rocks and surrounded by tiny fences. He ate moose and caribou. In winter he trapped, forging miles of trails up and down the creek for his sled. He wore shovels and picks down to stubs, one swing at a time, looking for gold along his stream. I could almost see him there, digging, as I peered into the cavernous hole over which an outhouse teetered, the hand carved seat worn smooth by use.

Chris was old when he built this cabin, though he had been in the valley for years. He left a few white hairs caught inside the cache, metal rim spectacles by his bed, and medicine bottles. He lived alone, sleeping in a wooden frame filled with dried grass. He was a big man (or at least he had big feet). He shaved with a soap stick and straightedge razor. He didn't read much, maybe he couldn't, but he had a collection of 78 records and a wind-up Victrola.

It was winter when Chris Olsen died. He put his snowshoes by the door, his handmade skis in the cabin and his tools down in the midst of daily living. On his sled a load of firewood remained, dissolving gradually into moss. Perhaps he weakened slowly, using up supplies. Maybe death came upon him suddenly, a heart attack or an accident. His chained dogs starved in their houses, dwindling to piles of bones. A quiet settled over the clearing.

A friend came by one summer and buried Chris in the little fenced plot of flowers or vegetables before his cabin door, covering the grave with stones from the creek. He took those things he needed and could carry back across the mountains. So the records stayed and the Victrola went and perhaps an ax or auger or maul. Years later I met a State Trooper who had known the man that found Chris, and all that we had supposed was true.

Chris Olsen left us wooden kegs for storing berries and clean tin cans. Here were axes, shovels, and picks. There was a mattock, a sledge, a vice, a maul, an anvil, hammers, planes, a bucksaw. There was even a Yukon stove, larger and of better quality than ours, with a stove-pipe oven and cake pans to fit. He had tools for working wood and metal. There were enamel dishes, silverware, cooking pots, a dishpan, a ceramic bean pot, a glass kerosene lantern and a big tea kettle. It was Chris Olsen who gave us our floor.

To other eyes, these gifts might have seemed shabby. They were worn by use and weather, caked with mud, mildew, and rust. But in a land of trees and rocks, a nail, no matter how bent, is a nail. We laughed and grubbed, oblivious to the sinking sun, until twilight overtook us.

It was dusk when we left the clearing, descending along a ridge that paralleled the stream. My arms were laden with tools that I hoped soon to use: a shovel and a mattock, a heavy hoe with an ax on one side of the head. Somewhere during the afternoon, clouds had drifted in unnoticed, and a fine drizzle now narrowed our darkening world. Net-Chet, cold and weary, waddled gamely along, staying close to my legs. An old trail, wet and rutted with moose tracks, led down the ridge toward the river. This route, if it were passable, would take us some miles out of our way, but give us added knowledge of the country. We hesitated a moment at the fork, then committed ourselves to the strange course.

We made good time until the path topped a rocky knoll and disappeared. Below us, the creek dropped sharply, and we could hear it cascading into the gloom several hundred feet down to our right. Ahead, the gray evening sky melted into the valley floor. Finding no trail in the eerie half-light, we cut for the river, cleaving off the crest into a thicket of aspen. As we descended with our tools, clanking and thrashing through branches, the night seemed to listen. Driven back by our stumbling, silence flowed in behind us, drawing up the shadows. I thought suddenly of wolves. Hair prickled on my neck, and I fought back the fear of being lost in this unfamiliar darkness.

Finally we blundered from the steep hillside into a dense, black forest. Between the spruce we once more picked up a scanty path overhung by dripping foliage. Our feet sought out the faint trail that our eyes could not see, seeking the packed ground in the dark. Our pants became soaked by bushes. At last the big trees opened and our path slid from the timber down to the foggy river.

"We've got no one to miss us," I stated, dropping my load on the wet rocks of the river bar. I was relieved to be in the open, away from the brooding trees. Soon a bright circle of warmth enclosed us, pushing back the night. Fog rising from the river into the chill air drifted eerily over us. We sat on the slick rocks chewing jerky, our first meal since breakfast. I held the tired, wet puppy on my lap, turning and fluffing her before the blaze until she stopped shivering.

Net-Chet slept in Phil's arms the last miles as we plodded beside the familiar sounds of the river, adrift in a shifting world of darkness and mist. Through a strange land we followed the shaggy, meandering shoreline, buried under cold, stifling fog. Morning was stealing upon us when our little pile of belongings appeared unharmed out of the gray wilderness ahead.

Two days later we passed the confluence of Olsen Creek on the river. The water was very shallow and swift now, gushing mint green over shelving gray slate bedrock. A chill north wind whipped sheets of sand toward us, blistering our faces and gritting teeth and eyeballs.

"Nothing," I said under my breath as I paused to study the shore for cabin sites. We had discussed building near Chris Olsen's cabin, but decided against it. It was nearly a mile from the river and the canoe, and we felt we would have a better chance of seeing game where the country was more open. And old cabins have too many memories around them; we wanted our own place.

We were almost a mile above the creek junction. I tucked my numb fingers under my armpits and glanced at Phil, trying to keep the despair from my eyes. "Let's cross to the island."

Net-Chet plunged bravely through the current as we crossed the channel, her head pressed to my knees to keep from being swept downstream. She seemed unhappy most of the time, poor little beast, whining even to herself.

The island had a good stand of mature spruce. "Lot of trees," I said hopefully. I grabbed the bow and hauled Lady Grayling firmly aground on a sloping sandbar at the tail of the island. "At least it's solid."

Phil met my gaze a moment and then pointed to the driftwood lodged back in the trees.

"It can't be too bad or the trees wouldn't grow." Angry tears filled my eyes. "Next year isn't likely to be the fifty-year flood, is it?"

"If we're going to build a cabin, it may as well last," he insisted, always so damn patient.

We traversed the island, emerging from the woods on the far side. Another island rose nearby, as well forested as the first. We waded a narrow, swift channel and paced to its head and out onto a long gravel beach.

"Phil, we've gotta find someplace soon!" I blurted out, my eyes flooding with misery. I sank down onto the rocks and put my head in my hands. Net-Chet edged wettly into my lap, shivering. "The further we get from Chris's the harder it will be. We won't even get our floor!"

He sat quietly beside me and reached out to stroke my hair. "We'll find just the right place," he assured me. "You wait and see."

The river beyond was still and deep, an unusual sight. A string of five islands spread the river, damming it with a connecting ridge of submerged rock. This created a lake of quiet water that stretched away to the north and east reflecting the long sweep of hill and cliff, bounded perhaps a mile away by a white ribbon of rapids.

My attention was drawn to another island on which several ravens rested. They are larger than crows and can be surprisingly musical. Ravens are very intelligent and are often associated with magic in Native folk lore. These seemed to be involved in a ritual dance. I had never seen anything like it. They would draw together, raising their wings, then bounce upward to come fluttering down like leaves. We watched, transfixed by the odd ceremony.

"Come on," Phil roused me at last, "the west shore looks good from here. I think we can wade back along these rocks."

The reef led us diagonally upstream, rapids below, still pool above. As we came dripping ashore, a large white wolf flushed into the woods. From the gentle bank, a carpet of sphagnum moss and cranberries climbed smoothly between mature spruce trees up the knees of a large hill. There was a safe boat landing and a broad southern exposure with a clear view of the islands and the mountains beyond. Twenty feet above the water, a narrow bench cut the slope, not actually level, but useable.

We criss-crossed the hill, calling out excitedly to one another as we explored it. Here at last was home, overlooking the five islands and quiet stretch of water. Abruptly our journey had ended. Satisfied and exalted, we retraced our steps for the canoe.

After all the miles we drew our load up snug against this shore. Once these belongings had littered our living room floor in Tucson. Now they were here: down parkas, sugar, fish net, gas lantern, snowshoes, books, flour, backpacks, underwear, rifles, traps, camera, toilet paper. How precious and small it all looked as we unloaded it onto the bank in the late afternoon sunlight.

That night I dreamed I was in a large school trying to find the right classroom. I was late and didn't know where to go. I ran down the hall, past rows of lockers. All the doors were closing and in desperation I chose one and entered. It was a calculus class and I sat in terror, unable to remember any calculus, knowing that soon I would be called upon.

For two days we worked, axes flashing in the sun with renewed vigor. We left the trees and ground cover alone as we cleared away thickets of alder and willow. While Phil started laying out the cabin foundation, I brushed a trail to the toilet hole and began to dig. We didn't build an outhouse. There was no need to screen ourselves from the view, and squatting by the hole was more comfortable in freezing weather than sitting. There were plenty of small trees to hold on to.

Nights were getting dark now, and cold. The second evening I startled a large black wolf behind camp. That night they started to sing, their wild spirits claiming the blackness. We could hear the older wolf voices, the parents, mingled with the young sing-song of adolescents in the pride of their first fall. Net-Chet whimpered while I thought of cabin walls. It was a beautiful and haunting sound, deep and melodic. These were not my small desert coyotes, but powerful carnivores weighing as much as I do and standing close to three feet at the shoulder. This was their valley. I knew that there were no documented cases of the North American wolf ever attacking man, but under the night sky I felt very small and vulnerable.

By unspoken agreement, Phil cleared back the brush behind the tent the next morning.

The third night we spotted our first stars. Dusk came gliding into the clearing, stealing over the calm water and down out of the woods. I sat cross-legged on the cold ground, reading aloud by firelight. Near me Phil looked worn but happy. His callused hands were carefully mending my frayed boots by the flickering light. Net-Chet rolled closer to the fire, whining irritably in her sleep as a faraway owl hooted.

Suddenly the shore seemed alive with wolves! The first we knew of them was Chet's startled "Woof!" They had not stumbled upon us, but circled down from three directions, pinning us against the river.

"Good heavens!" I whispered, grabbing the puppy. I leapt to my bare feet as Phil unzipped the tent for a rifle. It was too dark to see, but he fired a warning. A wolf just behind the tent moved nervously, and Net-Chet let fly, soaking my leg.

"They're all over the place!" I whispered, feeling conspicuous in the firelight. A powerful and ancient fear awoke in me. The hair rose along my neck as sleeping racial memories stirred. I was a child again facing the jaws of a doberman. I was a primitive man in a world of big carnivores. I was barefooted. I was afraid.

The second shot slammed into a wolf a few feet away. The others circled further up the hill, retreating slowly with forlorn cries. Still we did not approach the fallen animal. It lay just beyond the fire light, ominous and

73

black. Finally Phil handed me the rifle and cautiously moved toward the carcass.

It was a young male, a puppy of Chet's age. Although the size of an adult german shepherd, he still had his milk teeth. He was gray with a dark muzzle and very large paws. He had died suddenly, a big hole blown through his thin chest and a look of surprise in his golden eyes.

"Why, he's only a puppy, just hide and bone," Phil said, stroking the long, scanty fur. "I wonder what they were doing?" He took out his pocketknife and began to slip off the skin, bending low in the flickering light.

I watched the shadows uneasily, hoping nothing would appear. A last grieving call drifted down the hillside and floated out across the river.

Fear, like frost, melts in the morning sun. We awoke to a crisp August day. Buttermilk clouds printed the pale blue sky. But Net-Chet had not forgotten. Perhaps she had never really believed in wolves, but the stories in the grass had come true. She screamed in horror whenever she was startled and refused to leave my side. For his part, Phil tanked up on tea and set about marking our boundaries, wolf-style.

I fried wolf liver for breakfast. Phil finished skinning the head and extracting the brains to use in tanning. The stomach was nearly empty, containing two mice and some blueberries, leaves and all. When food is scarce, wild animals eat what they can find. The meat was the light pink of a young animal. It had very little smell, but tasted much as you might expect wolf to taste, slightly musky. Net-Chet refused to touch it and went hungry.

Days passed in toil. Phil lined out the cabin using a plumb bob made from a 30.06 bullet. His level, known as "Phil's almost level," was a medicine bottle full of water tied to a stick. He cut and removed sods from the site, thankful for the heavy mattock and shovel. These we stacked out of the way to be planted later on the cabin roof. We dug into the hill, leveling the bare earth and setting large stones as a foundation. I made numerous cross-country trips to Chris Olsen's cache for tools and dug on the toilet. At three feet I hit what I thought was solid slate rock. But it thawed into mud within a few days and I realized that it was "permafrost," the permanently frozen ground of the Arctic.

Blueberries were ripe, and I spent much time collecting winter stores. Cranberries were more numerous and would withstand frost, so I left them for later. Chet often accompanied me, complaining of our slow progress: berry-picking bored her. On my frequent trips to the cache, I started a trail, running it straight up the hill away from the river. Then it would run southwest to "Cranberry Hill," the ridge overlooking Olsen Creek, where I could pick up Chris's trail. The land between was rough and deceptive.

Then the autumn rains began. Somewhere we had lost the violent storms of summer. For days the soft, drenching rains fell until the thick ground was a sponge to the foot and every ring of the ax brought cascades of ice water out of the gray trees. Streams appeared everywhere, excess water on its way through our camp to the sullen brown river. Day after day our little pile of belongings sat drearily in the soaking rain.

We spent the time lying in our damp little tent listening to the drum of rain on the tarp and reading aloud from Michener's *Hawaii*. All about us the trees were turning gold and the tannic acid smell of fallen leaves lingered between the silent black trunks of spruce. Nowhere else was there a nook for us. We had no warmth, no place to dry wet clothes, except next to our skins inside those clammy sleeping bags. We felt panic at the slipping days, but gained nothing by exhausting our cold bodies in the rain. So we lay in the bags, often fully clothed except for boots, and read. Our breath condensed and ran down the walls forming puddles, and the rain beat endlessly down. We didn't even rise to cook, for it was nearly impossible to start a fire, and we would only end up soaked. We drank cold, muddy water from a bottle in the tent and chewed damp jerky and dreamed about Hawaii.

We were grateful not to be on the river. Where once it had been a sunny stream, now it was cold and bleak. Even camped it was difficult to keep anything dry. Phil had almost finished tanning the wolf hide for winter mittens, but in the steamy dampness it began to mildew and became laced with maggots. The jerky turned sour and slimy, and we were plagued with diarrhea. It could have been caused by rabbit starvation, but at the time we thought it was the spoiled meat. Phil's stomach bothered him constantly, waking him in the night with pain.

I put away the book in the dim light and hunched further into the smelly down, tucking my cold hands between my legs. "It's too dark," I said. "I can't see the words." My body was sore from lying inert and the thought of another endless night made me irritable. "We should move the tent to give our backs a new set of lumps."

The monotonous patter of rain had lost its music. An odor of wet feathers and wool saturated the tent. Phil sat munching crumbs of jerky and lint from the cloth bag, his bearded head touching the roof while frigid air seeped into the bags. He looked thin in his dirty T-shirt. I ought to dig out our longhandles someday soon, I thought. Everything seemed too much effort.

It was evident that we would consume the entire moose in less than six weeks. How many moose would we need to kill to see us through the winter? And where were they?

Phil stashed the jerky sack and slid back under the covers.

"Did you ever think how much we take food for granted?" I asked. "I have memories of supermarket aisles, food everywhere. Do you realize there is NOTHING you could do right now to get an apple?"

He groaned.

I was thinking that the "starving people of India" were always such a long ways off. Unreal. What was it like to watch your child starve?

We were silent awhile. "I have really enjoyed my dreams lately," I told him suddenly. I smiled and rolled close, wrapping myself about his bony body, smelling the familiar unwashed whiskers. "Lately it's great gooey pastries, chocolate eclairs, donuts, apple turnovers and strawberry short-cake with mountains of whipped cream. It's as if my brain is escaping the only way it can."

Net-Chet shifted in her sleep, pushing in the tent wall. She was prepar-ing for winter with a downy set of underwear about an inch long. We hoped the guard hairs would come in later. She was dry under the tent fly, but insecure and unhappy to be out of the tent. Perhaps some old memory told her of the coming winter.

"That was some dream you had last night," Phil reminded me. He flopped onto his side and pounded his moist clothes into a pillow, and grinned, waiting for me to remember. His haggard face was strangely foreign in the gloom.

I frowned. "Yes . . . I was being attacked by wolves. One leaped at me and I shoved him onto his back. He was struggling and I could only hold his head back, my hands around his great furry throat . . ."

"My great furry throat!"

"That's right! That's right! Well what about the night you woke up chewing on my bra while dreaming about the world's toughest jerky?"

"Oh, I dreamed I conquered the Arctic in my chewed up bra!" he sang out into the evening. His thin voice was swallowed up in the great drip-ping land.

Chet curled more tightly, whining in her sleep, her little body almost collapsing the tent wall. Outside I heard the rain stop and a soft wind be-gin. My intestines suddenly called and I bolted from bed. Grabbing the shovel, for the toilet hole was not yet finished, I set rapidly off up the beach. My pink and white pajamas were now a uniform gray, worn through at the bunny feet and knees. I shivered in the wet sedge grasses over my hastily constructed hole as a shower of drops spattered from an overhanging tree. Across the river the leaves were suddenly gold and the grass was streaked yellow.

Over the dusky water the sky was clearing. A single star shimmered in that deep patch of faraway blue. I covered the hole and started back. Phil met me going out in his bare feet, T-shirt and ragged underwear. Silently I handed him the shovel.

The next morning we woke early to an icy south wind that smelled of snow. The sky was clear. Phil decided to use my new trail to cut trees at a place we called the "Cathedral Grove." It was a lovely group of trees up on the hill, almost parklike, with mature spruce and open spaces where we had removed dead ones.

It is dangerous to fell timber in a wind, but every day was precious. Taking his double bit ax comfortably in one hand, he draped the hauling slings over his shoulder and called Net-Chet. She had grown over the summer and was now a fifteen-pound beauty with a soft showy coat. She had large perky ears and a curly tail. She was beginning to lose her baby teeth and her baby shape. Cavorting on long slender legs, she danced after him.

I finished digging the thawed mud out of the toilet and spread it on the trail. Taking my ax and berry pail, I grabbed a pocket full of jerky and set out for the day. Picking lint and sand from the drymeat, I ate as I climbed the hill.

Already the voles were depleting my berries, leaving little piles of husks. I fell to grazing near the path, cranberries springing up under my fingers. The lacy leaves were fresh with dew, and a rich earth smell enveloped me as the ground began to warm.

I picked contentedly beneath the shifting flutter of yellow birch leaves. From my hill I overlooked a turquoise river adrift in autumn colors. The naked high country had turned to brilliant red where arctic birch and blueberry bushes were brushed by frost. On the peaks a dusting of new snow touched the liquid sky.

Time is somehow different here, I thought, gazing over the valley. To say it is 9 o'clock is meaningless. With the passing days, the jumble and trivia were fading from my mind. At first it was replaced by memory flashes, trite and forgotten episodes from that other world, exercises of an idle brain. Then fantasies appeared. Thoughts became as real as spoken words. Often Phil and I would work all day in near silence, each within his own world.

I was dreaming of moose meat and Thanksgiving. If only I could get two spruce chickens and hide them away, I would plan a grand surprise. Cotton clouds rolled past in the Indian summer sky. A squirrel was busy drying mushrooms for winter, hanging them in a nearby tree. Now what could I use for stuffing? Oatmeal, of course! And powdered onions, eggs, and sage. Yes, I would really prepare a feast, if only I could find those grouse.

I could hear Phil at work below me, the rhythmic knock of his ax carried distantly on the breeze, mingled with an occasional loud complaint from Chet. About noon I heard a prolonged shriek. It continued for some time and I concluded it must be a bird. Cranberry sauce, I thought. I would make cranberry sauce. I listened again, strangely uneasy.

I filled my berry bucket and left it by the trail as I continued on with my ax. I was learning not to fear a double bit and had become quite proficient with it. In work I discover my strength, listening to the repetitive swing of my body. By evening my trail extended half way up the hill, a hard-won ribbon of space, gliding through the trees behind me. Aldo Leopold wrote that each man kills the thing he loves. Perhaps it is true. I had debated over every twig cut.

It was too dark to swing an ax when I started homeward over my trail. How beautiful it looked in the twilight, that smooth snaking path; how differently it organized the hill.

A flurry of startled white erupted before me, a wolf. I broke into the Cathedral Grove and saw that Phil had been hard at work, felling and hauling. From there to the river a little trough was gouged in the trail telling of the hours of lugging, sometimes with pulleys. How frail our little efforts, but how persistent. The real triumph of life is persistence.

I entered camp to find Phil in tears.

"We have a problem," he said miserably. Net-Chet took one step towards me and fell to screaming.

"I didn't mean to do it!" he sobbed. "She wouldn't stay put when I was dropping a tree and I just gave her a toss. Nothing, just tossed her . . ."

I hugged him until he could talk.

"I tried to examine her," he told me, "but she's just in too much pain. I gave her one of those codeine capsules and then another later, but it didn't help."

I sat in the damp moss and carefully lifted the trembling puppy. She convulsed in pain and terror, lolling stupefied in the urine that soaked my lap. I began to cry too.

A great gray owl swooped low out of the trees to survey us and glide on, noiseless wings pumping the heavy body out over the water. Every predator within miles would come to the sound of a wounded animal. It was cold in the gathering dusk as we sat helplessly with our little bundle of misery.

"Maybe we should shoot her," Phil suggested in desperation. New tears filled his eyes. We both had grown to love her. "She hasn't had much of a life so far, has she?"

"No," I said, taking charge. "First bring me my medical kit."

Phil set to work on the splint I ordered, glad for something to do. I filled a syringe with Novocaine and injected it into the left hind leg until the muscles relaxed. Gently I examined the leg. I could feel the slender bone ends grate together as the foot moved. Only one of the two parallel bones was broken and we could use its neighbor to help hold it in place. When he finished whittling the splint, we stretched her leg out and tied it down. Unfortunately we had no plaster, and a dog's foot isn't built for traction.

For three days we struggled, trying to keep Chet quiet and her leg immobile. But the traumatized muscles contracted relentlessly, pulling the poor little foot up and out. Her body was wracked with tremors and chills. Our bedding became soaked with urine. We even tried a modified sprained ankle bandage around her hock, but the pressure necessary for traction soon cut off circulation and the foot began to swell. Our hours were filled with the sounds of her misery, compounding our own anxiety.

As a last effort, we taped the hock, laying a strip of nylon cloth under the adhesive. This was tied to wire that bound the end of the willow splint. The top of the splint was forked and braced into a sling about her hip. If this failed, we would have to kill her. We moved her out of the tent and onto a clean bed of spruce boughs under a tarp. It was all we could do for her.

We sought our bags early that night. The air had that cold, crystal quality that promises frost, stinging into the nostrils even before the sun faded. About midnight we woke with our usual need to visit the outdoors, and discovered the northern lights. At first appearing as a green-white luminous cloud, the bright curtain crept towards us, poised and then lunged across the sky, trailing green fire in cold, aloof splendor.

Together we stood, shivering and hugging one another against the night, reluctant to retreat into the closeness of the tent. How expansive and glorious it seemed, that silken display put on for no one at all.

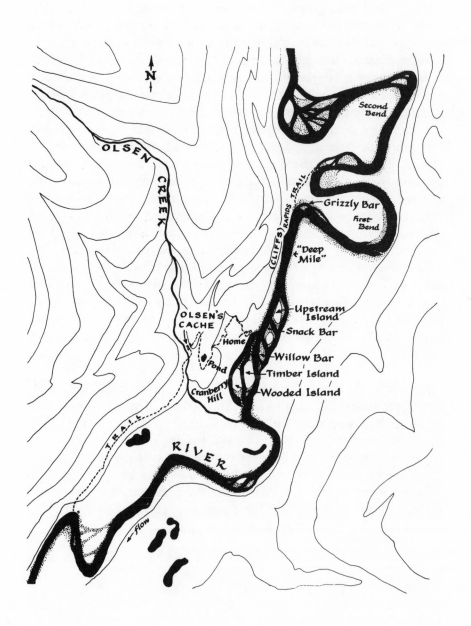

Chapter 5

SEPTEMBER CAME in cold rains and overcast skies. A few hardy mosquitoes remained, although less active. Occasionally we found cold and stiff caterpillars, hatched perhaps too late. Around our camp there was a brief frenzied activity of gnats mating in the ashes of our fire, drawn to the warmth. Spider backs were furry with their many-legged young. Soon all were gone, vanished with the summer.

I think I secretly hoped that winter would pass us by this year. How could it snow after the tropical days on the Yukon when my hair bleached white and my face burned brown under that endless summer sun? Now ice crept out at night, skinning over puddles.

The birds grew restless, gathering in flocks, talking excitedly of far-away southern places. They made trial runs up and down the beaches, testing themselves against the long miles ahead. No longer did the Bohemian waxwings dot the exposed river rocks in the evening. The bright and noisy kingfishers were gone too, as was their faithful enemy, the Swainson's hawk. One day a great band of small birds raced twittering through the yellow trees and out over the water. It seemed to me that I detected a new note in their voices. With a sense of loss I watched them disappear into the southern sky. A longing stole over me: we too should be winging our way southward with the birds.

Hunting took on a new urgency for us. Soon the moose would begin to rut, running off their summer fat in search of mates. From dawn to dusk I wandered through the falling leaves, rifle in hand, praying for food. It seemed somehow wrong that I should ask the Creator for the death of another living being, but I did. The largest animal I had ever killed before was a rabbit.

To our great relief, Net-Chet began to recover, but we had lost precious time in her care. She learned to walk again, using the splint as a crutch, screaming whenever she entangled it in brush. We knew she would make it when she reinstated her old whining, picky, nagging, complaining ways. Dogs have individual personalities, just like people. I must admit a grudging admiration for her tenacity. I have never met a more stubborn dog. She always had to have the last word.

It was a bleak and windy afternoon and I was cold. I had been walking all day, following the river, looking for game. Moose season was open, and we could legally take two apiece, including one cow. We could kill six black bears at any time of the year and unlimited caribou. I reached into my wool coat pocket for crumbs of jerky, which I sucked with satisfaction, chewing them slowly to savor the taste.

I emerged from the horseshoe swamp onto the beach. The swamp was an old river bend, now partly silted in, stubbled with cotton grass and sedges. The mud of the shore was imprinted with my old tracks. I found them everywhere, hopeful wandering feet. Sniffing the icy wind, I looked upstream and down. Might as well cross the river, I decided. I trudged into the crystal water, feeling it tug at my knees. Cold billowed sharply to my waist.

I climbed the cliff above the rapids and sat searching the colorful terrain. Across from me a yellow expanse of willows and muskeg butted into the mountain feet, clear and perfect across the distance. I leaned my rifle against my knees and watched, wondering if I had knocked the sights out of alignment in my travels.

Scanning the thickets, I pretended to see big dark forms moving in the brush. I sighted at my imaginary moose, thinking how I would shoot it in just the right place. Then I would swim the river above the rapids . . . there . . . and, let's see, how would I gut him? I would have to gut him of course, to surprise Phil. I smiled privately.

It was almost dark when I plodded into camp. Phil was bent over his logs in the fading light, skinning off the bark with a drawknife. He smiled when he saw me and stuck the blade into the butt of a log. He greeted me by bounding down the hill like a puppy. I had to laugh. Phil could be very silly and it was nice. Net-Chet sniffed cautiously, then broke into a little dance of her own, dragging the splint loudly over the rocks. Phil took my hand and pulled me up the bank to the campfire. Gently he pushed me onto my sitting log and handed me a steaming mug of tea. Then he knelt and began to remove my soaking boots.

"Oh, Phil, you don't have to do that," I protested.

"Hush, now. My hard working L'ammal deserves a little care," he answered using a nickname we had started calling one another.

I dug into my trouser pocket and found a brightly colored stone. He received it like a treasure, turning it to study the markings. We often brought one another such gifts.

"See the red vein?" I pointed out. He licked the stone and rubbed it with his thumb. "I watched a wolf hunting across the river today. I sighted on him for some time. But he seemed to be having such a hard time, I felt bad. He was checking all the ground squirrel holes and not catching anything. How would you like to hunt ground squirrels with your teeth?"

Phil wrung out my shapeless socks and flopped them limply over willow twigs near the fire. We hadn't washed our socks all summer, merely wringing them out evenings. In fact they rarely dried. I wriggled my bleached and wrinkled toes over the flames. I was tired and discouraged. Phil had a pot of jerky on, and steam filled the air as he lifted the lid with the point of his knife and set it before me.

"Last squeezings of the moose," he said cheerfully.

"It's getting pretty grim," I acknowledged. "An old trapper once told me that the difference between what he would and wouldn't eat was twenty-four hours. I hate to bring this up, but if we don't find something soon, we may have to eat Chet. Not that she'd make much of a meal, but not having to feed her would buy us time. Starving won't be any fun for her either. I love her too, but we need to be realistic." I stroked the soft trusting head that pressed into my lap. Phil glanced away.

"If we don't start getting a lot of something soon, we're in big trouble," he agreed. "We can't make it on small game. It just takes too much energy hunting, and there's no fat on any of it."

"It's not fair to her either," I continued. "She's trying to grow up on a poor diet. No wonder her little legs are brittle."

Phil sighed deeply. "Well, maybe the moose will start moving soon and . . ."

He stopped in mid sentence, following my gaze across the darkening river.

"That rock . . . " I whispered, pointing. "I don't remember a rock there, do you?"

"Could be a bear!" He grabbed his rifle and sighted through the scope at a sandspit island we called the "Snackbar." We planned to put moose guts there, when we shot one, to attract a black bear.

An explosion startled me as Phil fired his 30.06. Before my eyes the dim shape melted in the gloom and sank to the ground. That was all.

Phil grinned, exaulted.

"Think he's dead?" I could hardly make out the spot in the shifting gray light. I blinked and squinted.

He peered through his scope a long moment. A scope concentrates light. "Hasn't moved. L'ammal, I think we got ourselves a bear!"

I danced around Phil in my cold bare feet, then snatched my freezing socks from their sticks, all weariness forgotten in a rush of sheer happiness. There is no feeling to compare with a reprieve, even if temporary, from starvation. Impatiently I thawed the socks over the blaze.

Phil was already loading the tethered canoe with tea pot, skillet, knives, steel, whet stone, buckets, tarp and pack frame. I could hear the metallic thump as he set them into the empty craft. "I think Chet better stay here," he said over his shoulder. "She'll just be miserable over there and we'll be back soon enough." He paused a moment and gave me a triumphant hug. "We got one!"

Within minutes we were underway, skimming easily across the glassy river in the empty canoe. Behind us, Chet set up a howl of protest. I leapt ashore with the bow line as the boat grated to a halt in the shallows. Phil followed, his arms loaded. Together we pulled the Lady far onto the gravel. No moon tonight, I thought: it would be very dark. From out of the blackness overhead came a first soft whisper of snowflakes.

We were reluctant to approach the silent form, that ominous lump on the beach, black within the blackness. "He can wait," I assured Phil. "Let's build a fire." We had no flashlight, it being another item we decided to do without. It is surprising how rapidly darkness claims this land once it arrives. Only a brief time since we had seen our first stars and already there were several hours of real night.

Across the river Net-Chet wailed her loneliness. I grubbed about in the dark, searching for something to burn on the barren island, and with difficulty kindled a fire. A dry wind froze my wet jeans stiffly about my calves and kicked sparks into the rattling sedges. My feet hurt and I stamped them and bent low over the flames to warm my fingers. Steam rose from my thawing trousers.

The bear was dead. Phil began skinning and gutting him while I scrounged for firewood. Watching Phil, illuminated by the flickering, I felt suddenly weary. Behind him the circle of light was swallowed up by the night. I should be over there helping, I thought guiltily. Only a moment longer near the fire.

There is something spooky about bears. He was powerfully built, the snout and teeth menacing even in death. His claws and thick arms seemed almost human as we bent over him in the darkness. He was a small animal, perhaps only 350 pounds, but rounded with fat for the winter. Here was the energy we needed to get our moose. A sweet, cloying smell rose from his open belly like fermenting blueberries. The stomach was full of berries, branches and all. The meat was dark and greasy. His lovely golden coat gleamed in the firelight. A grizzly!

We hadn't known, of course, but I think we would have killed him anyway. We were beginning to feel endangered ourselves. Grizzlies are rare and not generally considered good to eat. The season for hunting them was a single month in the spring. They, like the wolf, are one of the last vestiges of truly wild country. Neither can survive crowding by humans. Grizzlies and wolves need big, healthy tracts of land. A world without either of them would be an impoverished place.

"Want some liver?" I asked, looking up from stripping the congealing fat from the intestines. I longed for an excuse to return to the warmth of the fire.

"Good idea. And some tea. Think you can find the river and fill the teapot?" he asked. It certainly was black out, not even stars. Suddenly a chorus of deep answers broke Chet's mournful soprano in mid-screech.

"Now see what she's stirred up," I said wryly. "I hope nothing gets her."

We worked through the night. Gray streaks of dawn lined Phil's face as together we loaded the canoe, heaving aboard the icy bear meat, buckets of organs, and hide. To the north the morning star glimmered in fading velvet-purple. Gradually we pushed the craft out from shore as the weight increased.

Lady Grayling slipped over the dawning water, our paddles dispersing the mirror of autumn mountains as we glided across the stillness. Strands of fog lingered, snagged in tree tops beneath a clearing sky. We scraped bottom over the shelf into our harbor, leaving silver streaks on the rocks.

It was the fifth of September, a cold and misty morning with fine snow powdering the frozen mud where intricate patterns of ice had formed during the night. We blew life into the coals of our home fire and squatted near it in the growing light, frying bear liver and fat while we comforted Net-Chet. Liver doesn't keep well and we planned to eat it up first.

Phil sat on my log. He had his boots off and was flexing his stiff toes over the blaze. I could sleep for a week, I thought. My body was sore, my pants caked with blood. I glanced fondly down at the loaded canoe a few feet away. The first jays were arriving. Groaning upright, I knocked Phil's rifle over with a thud and hobbled toward the river to toss the nylon canoe cover over the meat. I spun back in surprise. A moose!

Chet saw him at almost the same moment I did and began a frantic baying. Phil was instantly up, grabbing his rifle from where it had fallen. His bare feet flew up the beach, leaving no trace in the frozen mud. I crammed on my socks, ice and all. In panic I closed my hands around Chet's muzzle to shut in the noise. Damn her! Damn! Damn!

I galloped after Phil, boot laces dancing, rifle bouncing on my shoulder. Far upstream a great dark wraith stepped from the misty river. He poised a moment on the far bank, looking back, and Phil shot. Four rounds I counted as the specter slid into the willows. I was praying and running as fast as I could. Phil came panting back, cold and sore footed.

"Go up to the lookout rocks at the bend and see if you can spot him! I'm not sure if I hit him. I think the scope is off again!"

"Get your boots on and cross over," I answered back. "Work up the far side!"

"Okay!" He was off in one direction, me in the other. Chet was still shrilling the alarm.

I rushed wheezing over the mile of broken ground, scrambled up the cliff at the river bend and stood gasping. Rapidly I scanned the land across the river, seeking out a big dark carcass back in the bushes. Then I ran on. Around the cliff tops I scurried, knowing every step, through the bushes and now down the rock slide, stones scattering beneath my feet and . . . then! I stopped. My mind came sharply into focus. Directly below me was a bull moose.

Unafraid he stood, knee-deep in the rapids, watching me from fifty feet away. His body was massive and strong, a yard across at the rump, his shoulders close to seven feet high. From just above each eye a great antler curved outward forming a vast spread of flowing bone. There was a sense of power and majesty in his presence that altered the very scenery for me. This was no longer my familiar river bend. How often I had imagined this meeting, but how different it was! I had been looking for a big brown target browsing in the bushes. Now I confronted this mighty being.

I slipped to a sitting position, sending another shower of rocks down the slide. My rifle heaved with each breath and heartbeat, and shook violently to the tremble of my hands. Calm down, I commanded myself. There is time. Don't shoot him in the water. My mother had drilled it into me: never shoot a moose in the water.

He turned and slid from me, cleaving through the roaring current of the rapids like a long-legged ship. Where shall I shoot? I looked down on the smooth ripple of his great shoulders and back. I had never thought of this position. He's going! He's going! My mind cried out as I wavered in indecision, frozen. He clattered out on the far shore and flashed between the high bushes, floating easily away, leaving only a memory.

Stupid! Stupid! I grieved in silent rage. He was everything, and now he's gone! I scrambled down, knees still shaking, and cut above the rapids, wading the river. How slow and clumsy I seemed compared to him. On the far shore I thrashed through the dense brush, sweeping back and forth to check for tracks. You would think that tracks as large and deep as a moose would be easy to follow, but it isn't always so. Heartbroken and exhausted, I started back for the river in the vain hope of seeing him once more.

I was flailing through a willow thicket when a rifle went off a few yards away. I wanted to scream, "Don't shoot!" but clung to the knowledge that Phil would not fire unless he had a clear view of the animal. I pushed through to the river bar. Phil was there. He waved me towards him and then plunged into the water. The moose had crossed back over. Ice water plowed into my chest, dragging me downstream as I fought for the far bank. Phil was ahead and vanished into the forest before I reached shore. Then came another shot. And another. Oh, please God! Don't let him get away wounded! I prayed silently.

At length Phil reappeared, a big grin splitting his tired face. He spread his hands like antlers, fingers sprouting from his scalp, and stamped his feet, grunting.

"You got him!? You got him!?"

"The biggest bull moose you ever saw! Twice the size of the other one!"

"I want to see," I insisted.

I followed him through a jungle of alders and into a sudden clearing where a deep pond and muskeg pushed back the trees. There, on the only piece of dry land, lay an enormous animal, his belly as high as my waist. He was still breathing, shuddering founts of steam into the air. Looking queasy, Phil fired into the back of his massive head. The long legs thrashed a moment, then the thick neck relaxed. Smoke blew out one ear and drifted into the morning.

I went for the canoe, leaving Phil to begin butchering. First I unloaded the bear, heaving the heavy pieces onto the hide, fur side down, and covering them with the tarp. I could feel fatigue in every muscle of my body, my movements slow and leaden. It was almost noon by the time I lined the canoe upstream to the moose. I axed a trail through the dense alders and found Phil bent over the giant carcass. A wholesome, almost milky smell filled the clearing. Sunlight had burned away the morning mist, and fluffy clouds scudded in a rich blue sky. The sun was warm and in the dazzling light, the mountains stood forth in purest colors, brilliant with fall.

Despite our weariness, we were festive. Here was meat in plenty, and Phil gaily pointed out the two-inch blanket of fat over the haunches and the lacy caul fat about the paunch. White and brown velvet still hung in tatters from his antlers and the full stomach showed that he was not yet in rut. I built a fire and fried another breakfast of liver sautéed with generous white nuggets of kidney fat.

Butchering an animal of this size is a big job. First we had to heave him onto his back, which took all of our combined strength. We skinned the hide back from the belly and carefully slit the abdomen, allowing the contents to billow out. Opening the rib cage at the brisket (breast bone), we

87

cut the ligaments that attached the internal organs to the spine, and severed the intestinal tract at both ends. Only then could we drag the voluminous stomach, or "paunch," out, taking care not to rupture it or the attached intestines.

We ran a seam up the inside of each leg, and worked the heavy hide down the animal's sides until he lay naked on his own skin. The front legs were removed by slicing the muscle between the armpit and the ribs. The hind quarters were heavier, perhaps 175 pounds each, but the ball joint was pulled open as we severed the muscles at the groin. The trunk proved harder to section, but we cut it into four pieces using only our pocketknives: the pelvis, two rib sections (one attached to the backbone), the neck, and the head. We then had nine pieces weighing from 100 to 180 pounds, plus the hide and assorted organs.

It was growing dark once more as I lugged Mightypot full of liver, heart, and kidneys to the water's edge. Dully I dropped to a boulder and gazed back into the woods. Phil emerged, slid down the short cutbank and started over the rocky beach. He had a five gallon bucket of blood in one hand, one of gut fat in the other. I had stripped the intestines of fat. He moved like a sleepwalker, stumbling over the stones.

"Hi," I said.

"Waste not, want not," he answered, settling the blood-bucket in the canoe. "For Chet."

I struggled to my feet, and picked up the pack frame. Phil took my free hand and plodded wordlessly beside me. It was two hundred yards to the moose. We made the trip fifteen horrible times, stumbling along through muskeg. Supporting the slippery meat between us on a pack frame, we crashed through bushes in pitch darkness, caught in an endless nightmare. We would rest a moment and start back for more to the squish, squish, squish of sodden boots, our clothes drenched in freezing blood.

The last thing we took was the hundred pound hide. Hauling its stretchy bulk into the river, we secured it by rope to the canoe. The entire moose weighed perhaps 1500 pounds alive, and our load floated very low in the water.

The route home was hazardous even by daylight. We had to run the rapids before we would reach our still mile of water. In total blackness, we walked the sagging craft out from shore, then climbed aboard and paddled frantically for midstream. We could see nothing as we spun along in the quickening current, wincing when we slammed into rocks. The roar increased as we shot into the main channel, alone and adrift in the night. We were in deep water now, funneled into a narrow shoot. Waves smacked into the bow and coursed into my lap as we swept through.

Then we were past it, the sounds diminishing behind us. Soon we floated homeward on a quiet ghostly river, lost in the daze of our own fatigue.

❄

Now that we were fed, we seemed to reach a slump. Like runners who have sprinted the last mile, we had no more to give. We had perhaps three months food, but our "cabin" remained a pile of skinned logs. We moved slowly, as if in a dream. It took a long time to get anything done. We were indecisive and spiritless—no longer able to think clearly, to act, to choose. Winter was coming. Daily we watched it close upon us, hypnotized by its rapid descent. Still we floundered, unable to help ourselves.

Why hadn't we put up the shed roof as planned, or even unpacked our warm clothes? All I can say is that prolonged stress, like semi-starvation, both of which we had known, undermines judgment and ability. These conditions also bring about a state of apathy. We didn't realize this at the time, but we knew that something was wrong.

I worked quietly rendering gut fat, cooking it until the water was gone. Then the oil emerged, floating the dry "cracklings" to the surface. I poured the golden liquid into five gallon cans, moose tallow in one, bear lard in another, where it quickly cooled in smooth white layers. I munched raw moose fat as I sliced and stirred, sitting cross-legged on the freezing ground before the fire. I had craved fat all summer and it tasted wonderful.

The wind hadn't stopped in days, blasting endlessly across the fire where Mightypot bubbled. Our cabin site was set back in the protection of the trees a few yards up the hill, but camp was on the river bank. The ground was steep and there really was no other place to pitch a tent.

We had lost all interest in spicing our food. Too much bother. After a diet of drymeat, we were accustomed to doing without salt. Sugar tasted almost bitter. Our urine turned green from a diet of liver, and still we had not finished it all. Organ meats differ from muscle, containing concentrations of vitamins. In fact, large quantities of liver can even be toxic, something we didn't know then.

The time for hunting was quickly passing. It had been four days since we brought home the moose. Every night the ground froze. The river temperature plunged to just above freezing. Within three weeks, the moose population would be done rutting. Thin and stationary, they would settle back into the brush where we could not see them.

We had counted on Net-Chet developing a thick winter coat while sleeping outside. But again that night I was awakened by her shivers. I reached out and stroked the trembling bulge in the tent wall.

"Phil?" I said softly.

"Ummm . . . ?"

"I can't sleep thinking of her out there night after night, shaking like that."

"If she were still in Venetie . . . " he started.

I cut him short. "Maybe so, but she's our dog now."

"Don't you think we should give her a little more time?"

"No. Look at her. She's so skinny and she has her little broken leg. She can't even curl up properly. It isn't fair."

"She needs to be cold to grow good fur," he insisted.

"What if she doesn't grow any more?" I asked. "There was quite a mixture of dogs in the village. No telling what her ancestry is."

"All right," he gave in. I was already half out of the bags, pulling the surprised puppy into the tent. "But she sleeps at the foot of the bags."

"Now, you slept with Junior for eight years," I teased him, making Chet comfortable. "Your mother even had special sheets for your bed."

"That was different," he retorted. "Junior was a house dog. Chet is a work dog."

Net-Chet snuggled happily beside my feet as I dove under the covers. The pale gray sky outside promised another overcast day. It was still windy. The tent rustled and popped while the black trees sang to themselves.

"I'm going to zero my rifle today," Phil told me, peering out. Our heads were close to the open door. "May as well be ready." We rolled over together and he curled around my back. I slid my foot between his knees and pulled them tight against the back of my legs. "We have a great start, but at the rate we eat, we'll be starving by mid-winter when it's cold and dark."

I knew he was right. "My parents ate three moose, a bear, and a whole pile of caribou one winter and still were starving before March," I reiterated. "Spring is the hungry time. The snow is deep and animals are hard to approach."

"I sure hope the caribou come through here this winter," he said, "but we can't count on it. From what I've heard, we're on the very edge of their migration route."

Chet had begun a slow upward migration of her own, creeping onto the sleeping bags and crowding my feet. "They still had meat in March," I continued, "but were starving for lack of fat. Like us on dried moose."

"Which is another reason we need to push ourselves now. Those moose are getting skinnier by the minute." He was beginning to rummage for his clothes in the growing light. Chet, already accustomed to her new status as tent dog, complained as he pulled his trousers from beneath her.

"I'm going to check the overlook and then pace off a range to zero my

90

rifle at the river bend," he said. He was sitting with his feet out the door, lacing his boots. "I'll eat later."

I watched him disappear up the beach, red checked mackinaw closed tightly against the biting wind. Slowly I groped about for my clothes and began to dress in the bag. Then fully clothed, I drifted back to sleep.

Some time later I was startled by Chet's vigilant "Woof!" She was very bright, if stubborn. After the episode with the moose, she never barked at game again, giving only a single low note to alert us. I grabbed my rifle and bolted upright. A cold, plaintive "meow" drifted from the Snackbar, and there stood Phil. He stomped his feet and made antlers of his hands.

"You gotta be kidding!" I yelled across the river.

"Big as the last one!" he called back. "Come and get me."

Poor Phil is wet, I thought as I paddled. The empty canoe was unwieldly for one person in the wind. My teeth were chattering. Behind me, Chet started to wail. I hoped the moose was near the river.

The canoe grated in a shoal and Phil waded out. Shoving us back into the current, he grabbed a paddle and pulled for home. He looked cold, his lips thin and blue.

"Well, tell me!" I sang out as I jumped onto our two foot cutbank, pulling the bow line ashore. I began to search through storage cans for dry clothes and long underwear. It was high time we got them out, having worn the same outfits all summer. It was turning into a bitter day, a good day to switch from levis to wool pants. The water measured thirty-six degrees, and a strong south wind gusted past at twenty to thirty-five miles per hour.

"I was up on the cliff when I saw the flash of antlers near the far mountains across the river," he started excitedly.

I groaned. Two miles of leg-breaking muskeg: it might as well be on the moon.

"Now wait," he commanded, enjoying his story.

I had finally located the can with the wool caps. I stuffed the other contents back in and pushed the lid down.

"I swam the river and stalked him, unable to get close enough to trust my rifle," he continued. "Then I lost him and cut back to the river bend, looking. I peeked through the willows and there he was getting ready to cross. He gave a grunt when he saw me, and started for the water. I nailed him behind the head and he went down like a rock. Then I saw that he was actually in the river, about eighteen inches of it." He shrugged.

The chill wind whipped our light canoe upstream at a good rate as we paddled. This moose lay above the rapids, directly across from the last one. The shoreline, a long muddy bar, sloped from a yellow thicket of willows into the channel. There, a dark form protruded from the gray river. The icy stream flowed steadily over his submerged head and neck, around his belly and away. There was nothing to do but butcher him where he lay in the cold rushing current.

All day the wind blew wearily, kicking spray over us as we worked. Feet and hands burning with cold, we sliced away underwater, blood from our nerveless fingers often washing downstream with that of the moose. We tied the canoe to the inverted head, using his big antlers as an anchor, and loaded the quarters as we cut them free.

He was a big bull, perhaps a bit younger than the last, judging by his teeth and antlers. He had less fat across the rump, but more gut fat: individual variation. His antlers were free of velvet, polished and dry, but his stomach was still full, showing that he hadn't started to rut.

Cold dusk fingered us while I held the straining canoe and Phil heaved the head aboard. It was an awkward thing, antlers jutting like wings from either side of the craft. At the stern, the guts and hide floated in the river, tugging on their ropes.

Gingerly we walked the craft downstream over the riffles, hauling her through the shallows around the outside of the rapids. No point in running them if we could avoid it. They were becoming more difficult each day. If the water dropped much more we would have a hard time getting a moose down from above. The upper river was peppered with large submerged rocks.

We arrived home in the purple of evening. Tying the canoe securely in her harbor, we left the moose aboard, and rekindled our campfire. When we thawed our feet over a blistering fire, we found them drawn up in unyielding tension, almost as if the tendons had shrunk in the cold.

I was concerned as I massaged my rigid feet. "Do you think we are damaging them in some way?" I asked Phil. They looked unpleasantly white and wrinkled.

"We've had them in cold water all summer," he reasoned.

"Yeah, but not this cold. That water is almost freezing."

"But it isn't. You can't get frostbite above freezing," he reassured me. "Moose do it all the time."

I wasn't so sure, even though at the time I didn't know about the counter-current heat exchange in moose legs. Arteries running to the feet heat blood returning to the body cavity, conserving energy while maintaining proper circulation.

Years later I learned that cold can injure people even at temperatures well above freezing, especially if combined with dampness. Called immersion or trench foot, extreme cases may even lead to gangrene. Unlike the moose, our blood vessels close down, for the human body must sacrifice circulation in the limb to preserve core heat.

After a big meal of rib steak, we hobbled off to bed, leaving our boots, socks and pants to freeze by the fire.

✴

Dry leaves whispered past as I sat on the frozen earth and sliced fat for rendering. Two days before, we had unloaded the latest moose, hanging the water-bleached quarters with lengths of rope on a log propped between two stout tripods. We no longer feared spoilage or flies, and merely tacked the hides on the south exposure to exclude direct sunlight. Now we had food into the new year.

"I'm really going to zero my rifle today," Phil announced, untying the canoe. It was late afternoon and the sky was clear despite a nagging wind. He hopped aboard sending the slender craft over the water.

"Just don't shoot any moose," I joked.

"I'll be over on the Snackbar," he called back, paddle flashing.

I had done most of the hunting and he all the shooting, which was fine. It was the food that mattered. My mother told us that when you are in the country you are always hunting. The game is moving and sooner or later it comes to you. This was why we brought two large rifles, even though we had left out rain gear and flashlights.

I sat stirring the fat and skinning leg bones. We wanted to make mukluks from this slick-furred hide. We had no winter boots, having planned to make them, a bad mistake, I could now see. I laid aside a cold shin bone and foot, stacking it with seven others, and flopped the hide onto a pile. Across the river I could hear the thundering boom of a heavy rifle and I automatically counted the shots to myself. Every animal within miles is leaving, I thought sourly.

When Phil appeared on the far shore bellowing and making with the antlers, I didn't believe him. Curiously I watched him paddle home.

"I really did!" he said defensively. "I shot another bull."

"I don't believe it," I replied flatly.

"I can't either!" He laughed aloud and snatched up Chet to dance a little jig with her. "We're all going to make it! We're really going to live through the winter!"

I was gathering up buckets, dumping the fat and livers on the moss. My feet were still sore, and I hobbled happily about, filled with a sense of thanksgiving. Another moose!

Phil grabbed me up in a hug for a moment. "I paced off a seventy-yard range and lay down to shoot, using the cutbank as a back stop," he said ex-

93

citedly. He stooped to fish the pack frame out of the river where it had been soaking the gore off, secured by a rope. "After a few rounds, I reloaded. When I pulled the rifle down on the target, through the sights, mind you! I saw this set of brown legs!"

"Just walking?" I asked incredulously.

"Trotting! I was so surprised I completely missed the first shot. He broke into a run and the second round caught him in the diaphragm. The third one broke his back."

"Phil, nobody, but nobody, fires six shots at a target and then has a moose walk in front of it!" I danced him about. "Oh, L'ammal, we're almost home free! Three moose. How good the wilderness is to us. Is he big? Is he still fat?"

He grinned happily. "Sure looks it to me."

Evening was rapidly overtaking us as we started out. The water was very low, and we couldn't get clear across the river. We pulled the canoe up on the Snackbar and waded the freezing shallows, splashing over the rocks the last fifty yards to the mainland. The moose carcass was atop a four-foot cutbank and stood out plainly on the exposed yellow muskeg.

We gutted him by firelight, releasing his warmth to the frosty air. Even in sub-zero temperatures, an ungutted animal of this size will begin to rot overnight. We worked by feel, reaching into the cavernous belly in the dark. Thank you, thank you, I silently told the moose and the spirit of the land that had raised him and given him to us.

All this killing may seem greedy or uncaring, but it wasn't. I felt akin to the land and, like the wolf, entitled to its life. But not thoughtlessly. When we killed a moose, we saw the price that another paid that we might live. It is right that life gives to life, but not to be taken for granted. When I open a package of hamburger, it is anonymous and sterile. There is no opportunity to thank that life or acknowledge its contribution to me. We say grace over our meals, but have lost touch with what it means. I learned the meaning with my hands in blood.

This time we brought the tent along and pitched it nearby. I could hear Net-Chet making herself comfortable by the door as we ate a midnight meal of boiled tongue, brought from home. She wasn't allowed in the tent without us, and an occasional loud moan issued from her direction, urging us to come to bed.

"I think he'll cool all right now," Phil said, accepting a mug of tea. "What say we hit the sack?" Another insistent groan came from the tent, and we grinned at one another.

"Why don't you get out of those wet socks and give your feet a chance to thaw?" I suggested. I already had mine off.

"I broke the bladder in the dark and I want to rinse him out before we turn in. May as well do that before I get too comfortable."

This isn't much fun for him either, I thought as I cut off a piece of tongue and held it on my knife to cool. "I don't think he's quite as fat as the others," I said. "But it's hard to tell with his stomach empty. Notice the smell?"

A faint odor, like fallen willow leaves, still clung to the surrounding night. "That must be rut," Phil answered.

"It's not a bad smell." We had been told that a rutting moose was almost inedible.

"I think he's an old man moose," he continued, taking a long pull on his tea. "He has spinal arthritis or something. Anyway, the disks are solid. I couldn't get my knife between them. His hooves are worn through on the bottom, holes in his shoes. Also there is a healed broken rib, did you notice?"

I shook my head no. "Old battle scar, I suppose." I could just make out the stiff form a few feet away, legs up. "You know, all the time I spent hunting and praying, Phil, guess I thought I'd get my orders in early. Then, here it is as fast as we can handle it. Rags to riches in eight days! A week earlier and the meat might have spoiled. Two weeks later and the moose would have been thin."

He smiled at me. His face was haggard in the firelight, almost eerie. He put his dirty mug down in the withered cotton grass and got painfully to his feet.

This cold water is crippling us, I thought, watching him disappear in the night. I heard him stumble down the cutbank, and then the crunch of ice when he broke the water free. I stared quietly at my stiff fingers, caked with blood, sore from numerous cuts, ugly slashes in my flesh. They hurt less than it appeared, as if my body had forgotten them with its attention on survival. The little diamond hung loosely under my finger. No sparkle. Were these the soft, plump hands I remembered? Alligator hide.

Rags to riches, I mused. We were down to squirrels and dead mice. Now look at us. How wonderful life is. Of course, it is a matter of perspective. Most people wouldn't have envied me just now. But being wealthy and not knowing it is a form of spiritual poverty. Being down to basics puts things in perspective.

From the Snackbar sixty yards away came the long low call of a wolf. We had left moose guts there days before, but they had just discovered them. A higher voice answered from upstream and the first one repeated its message.

Phil appeared, squatting quietly down beside me. I heard Chet retreat further under the rain fly. The stillness was broken again as others arrived. We could clearly hear the young voices exclaiming over our treat, punctuated by the deeper tones of adults. Wolves live in highly social family groups. A single mated pair have pups within a territory, older animals often helping to raise them. I felt guilty that we had murdered one. They had undoubtedly never seen people before.

"The neighbors," I whispered, as we listened into their darkness.

"Hope nobody raids camp while we're over here guarding this one," Phil said in a low voice.

"Spooky, isn't it? They know we're here, of course."

"It's their night and their valley," he replied quietly.

That night I dreamed I was trying to cut my way out of a cavernous corpse. I was smothering in folds of fat. Pushing upward in a struggle to breath, I sliced and hacked in mounting panic. I awoke bolt upright in the little tent. Phil had his arms about me in the cold air saying over and over, "Shush, L'ammal, it's okay now. Shush."

Two days later I was back out hunting. Almost home free was not good enough. We might not get another chance before spring. Once the river froze, as it would any night, there would be no way out until breakup.

I stepped softly, rifle slung over my shoulder, my mind as hushed as the swirling snow. All day I had traveled a shifting land of black and white and gray. I searched the bleak water, the drifting flakes, the dark trees. Only I, in my red wool coat and blue cap, was in color. The only sound was my breathing and the muffled tread of my feet. A few withered leaves rattled against the bare alder bones, slapped by the drifting air, but this too was sucked up into the great whispering silence.

I cut quietly through the horseshoe swamp, frozen yellow tussocks hard beneath my boots. Vole trails stood out under the dead sedges, vulnerable in the scanty new snow. Ahead the river bent back upon itself and I turned to follow it homeward.

A dark phantom stood suddenly before me, stepping from the falling snow. He was talking to himself, grunting softly as he drifted towards me on the far side of the river. I dropped to my bottom, looping my elbow through the rifle sling to steady it. But my hands were shaking. Traitors! I thought desperately. Calm down now. Sight. Now again. Take your time, I told myself. But the moose turned and entered the river, perferring the icy swim to sharp rocks along the bank.

I galloped forward, bent double, hidden by branches. My side of the river was a willow bar into which he would vanish the moment he touched shore. I dropped down and fired. On he sailed with graceful strides. Again!

Water sprayed up and he jumped. Then he was ashore and gone. I crept through the dense brush, seeing nothing. God, no! I thought in panic. Oh, please, NO!

Look back on the beach, came a small voice within. I emerged to see him seventy yards away, standing indecisively near the river. Down I plunked and fired. And over he went. So easy. "Take your time and let him die quietly," my mother's voice admonished me. "It takes awhile."

Carefully I crept over the rocks, my eyes always on the moose. But no! He began struggling, long legs flailing the air. He would be up any moment! I sat, grabbing bullets from my pants pocket, dropping them in the sand and snow. My bolt jammed! Why won't it . . . ?! There's an empty shell in the chamber! I pumped it free. Stop shaking! I commanded my hands. Jam in the shells, dirt and all.

Damn! Damn! He's swimming. Shoot! Shoot! Why won't he die? Blindly I tried to knock him over. See? I thought miserably. I knew mere bullets wouldn't kill a real moose. Again I shot into the chest. Hadn't I always imagined bringing him down with a single shot? Just like big rabbits, my mother had told me.

But he plowed steadily on. I knew he would reach shore and dissolve into the afternoon, leaving only footprints. Or do phantoms leave footprints?

Then it was suddenly over. In slow motion the big animal pitched forward into the river and was still. I had forgotten the freezing water. I traveled slowly upstream in search of a shallow place, looking always backward at him. But he was dead. In my mind I saw a living moose, talking to himself, lovesick. My world had been brushed by magic for that moment, and now in my triumph I knew a great loss. I had killed the thing I loved and in some way that I could not define, I would never be the same.

I crossed the river, holding my rifle over my head. Down the beach loomed a dark carcass: carrion. A raven swooped from the gray sky, then fluttered away with a musical "Plunk!" I waded out, my sore feet burning as the thin shore-fast ice crunched against my shins. He was sprawled in shallow water ten feet from shore.

He was not a large moose, and younger than the others. From him rose the autumn smell of willows, that now familiar scent of rut. His velvet nose lay in the mud, eyes open. I touched his head and wiggled an ear. They let you down, fellow, I thought. Tears seeped through my lashes. I must build a fire, I told myself. Looking around I saw only soggy driftwood frozen in mud. I decided to skip the fire. My teeth were chattering loudly.

I wrestled the big head, turning it to plant the antlers. I could not roll him alone, but tied his front leg back to an antler, exposing the deep chest. Then I heaved the dripping hind leg over my shoulder. Moose have cold legs. His abdomen was soft and warm. I pulled my large jackknife from its holster, working the blade up with stiff fingers, and made a timid slice. Cutting into a newly dead animal was different from helping Phil with one already in the process of being butchered. The chest muscles quivered as I made the incision.

It was nearly dark when I left the gutted moose to cool. He had not eaten on his journey, and his stomach was empty, reducing my task considerably. I swam the river, ice water to my chest, and took the shortest route home, pounding my feet over the rocks. I began to warm a bit, pain returning slowly to my feet as I hobbled. Water spurted rhythmically from the holes in my boots. Before me, fresh wolf tracks dotted the new snow, and I quickened my pace.

At camp, Phil hurried about, building up the fire, making tea and fussing over me. I savored the moment, and when he started to strip off my wet boots, I said casually, "No, we have to get back to the moose." We laughed and hugged one another in chilled delight. How often I had planned that!

First we needed to unload the last moose, pulling the rigid pieces from the frozen blood in the bottom of the canoe onto the hide. The moon had returned, and by its half-light, we toiled slowly upstream lining the canoe until after midnight. We pitched camp in the snow and went to bed, too tired to eat. Unable to get warm, we chattered together through the endless hours until dawn, a tense knot of misery and muscle cramps.

In the morning we squatted over our breakfast fire, grimly appraising the day's task and chewing boiled flank. Flank is tough but easy to get at. It had taken me much time and pain to force my tender feet into frozen boots. They were hard as steel and would not bend at all. I thawed Phil's over a sluggish fire that I managed to start with the available wood.

It was snowing lightly. Already an inch of white had sifted onto the exposed bar, smoothing out the wrinkles, and frosting the stiff and twisted carcass of the moose. He was frozen into a thin film of ice that had grown out from shore. The mountains were lost in gray, the trees faint and unreal.

"What time do you think it is?" Phil asked. He was squatting by the fire, hands cupped around a mug of mint tea.

Not even a bright spot betrayed the position of the sun. I studied the sky a moment. "Morning."

"Shall we?" he asked, indicating the moose.

I shrugged. "May as well." I set the pot back on to boil and stood up. My knees were stiff from squatting, but there was no place to sit. "How long do you think we can stand in freezing water?"

"Until the pain gets too great," he answered, starting for the river.

"Won't our feet freeze or something?"

"Not before the river does."

Things are the way they are, I thought. There's no point in resisting them or wishing they were different.

Snow fell softly all day. I might have smiled at the thought of us, ice freezing around our shins as we struggled with that stiff carcass. Moose revenge. But it wasn't funny.

The work went slowly. We left the water frequently to gallop clumsily along the beach gathering the sparse fire wood and restoring pain to our feet. We kept the pot boiling and devoured quantities of meat and broth while thawing our numb fingers. By late afternoon we were ready to load the moose.

Phil started with the canoe, dragging it along the freezing channels. Chet and I plodded beside the river with the camp gear. As he dwindled into the mist, Phil seemed to shrink before my eyes, adrift in the falling snow on a black river. Alone he fought the canoe, helplessly splashing through the water, yanking the bow, slipping on the rocks.

He could hardly move when I pulled him from the slowly drifting craft and pointed him to shore. Numbly I climbed aboard. The river was unbelievably shallow and sluggish. At once the canoe grated to a halt and I leapt over, smashing my nerveless legs into boulders. Water seethed around my knees. Phil stumped up and down the beach, trying to restore circulation. I was misery beyond all misery. I had never been so cold. My legs were asleep to the thigh, my hands useless, my feet dead. Time lost all meaning. I was emptied, sucked down and down until nothing remained but that terrible cold.

Just above the rapids the canoe hung up badly, water driving her sideways onto the rocks.

"I hate it! I hate it!" I screamed into the evening, my voice lost in the roar of the water. I could see myself as if from a great distance, jerking at the bow line, sobbing hysterically, but no tears. Dimly I saw Phil drop the pack and begin splashing toward me, scrambling awkwardly over the slippery stones. But I couldn't control myself.

"I hate it! I hate it!" I kept shrieking repetitively.

Phil ordered me to shore. No legs. Where were my legs? They had lost all sensation. Violent shivers wracked my whole body. Phil was in the rapids now, the water rushing over him as the canoe jammed sideways onto the boulders. I stumped out to help, pitching into the swift current to my waist, smashing into rocks. He was fighting vainly, waves cascading into the swamped canoe, rolling her and spilling the meat out. He yelled at me above the roar. I strained with all my strength, praying. Slowly the craft pivoted.

"Get on! Get on!" I shouted. "She's moving!"

"I lost a quarter!"

So what's a quarter? I thought. "Never mind! Jump!"

It was too late. As the canoe picked up momentum, he was dragged down through the rapids like a sea anchor, directing his course by snagging on boulders. The trailing moose hide whipped around my legs, yanking me under.

"Here it is!" he yelled, gesturing at the quarter.

I was washed down after Phil. The water looked black in the fading light. It doesn't feel cold, I thought as it swept me through the foaming shoot. An odd light spot appeared just below me, and I tried to kick as I was carried upon it. I couldn't feel my leg connect, but my body slowed and the quarter lifted and moved in the current with me. Slowly I worked it to shore. In quiet water now, I ducked down and encircled the meat with my arms, my nerveless hands useless, and tugged it onto the rocks. Then I pulled myself from the river and started back for the pack, spasms convulsing me.

Phil deserted the swamped canoe, leaving it to drift down the deep mile alone. Together we stumbled homeward, hurrying as best we could, holding to one another for balance. At camp, he grabbed the other pack frame and started back in the darkness for the lost front quarter.

"Get into dry clothes," he told me, hobbling out of sight. "I'll be back in time to catch the canoe."

I nodded numbly. But how? I couldn't get my wet clothes off, working with fingers like sticks. My hands were useless and my body was shaking violently as I fumbled in the dark. A fire! First a fire, I thought. The coals had gone out in our absence. How I chattered and blew to start it as I knelt shaking in the blackness, matches grasped clumsily between my palms! I would have tea for Phil, dinner for my brave Phil.

"Get off me!" I yelled at Chet.

I held the matches until my nerveless hands were burnt. Finally the damp spruce twigs began to catch, smoke billowing harshly into my face. I pressed my mouth close and blew softly until a healthy blaze crept up. It was life to me.

Within minutes I was able to slowly pull off my clothes, standing naked in the freezing night. Shivering violently, I crouched next to the fire, hoping to warm enough to be able to dress myself. I was chilled to the bone, my core temperature dangerously low.

Then out of the night sailed the canoe. I could see its half-submerged form drifting relentlessly toward me in the starlight. I fought free of the shirt I had pulled about my shoulders. A breeze played over the little hairs on my back. I stuffed my dead feet into wet boots and wrapped the laces around my ankles, unable to tie them. Naked, I entered the freezing water again.

Phil rushed into camp as the laden craft collided with the reef. I was holding the bow, but couldn't see to maneuver into our harbor. I backed it up, fighting the current. He dropped the pack and stumbled into the black water to help me. Together we hauled her over the rocks and safely to shore.

He was bruised from falling down with the quarter in the dark. He had tried to run on numb feet, fearing that the canoe would escape into the night, with our final moose. But we had made it, somehow.

The next morning the river was running ice.

Chapter 6

IT WAS CLEAR BLUE OUT, and the bright morning sun streamed into the entrance of the tent as I dozed in the warmth of compressed bodies. It had taken us nearly all night to regain normal body heat after the cold water. I was dreaming of food, reluctant to awaken, but a nagging sound pulled at my consciousness. I opened my eyes, visions of pudding dissolving into the orange nylon walls, and listened. A merry tinkling of tiny bells was followed by a grating sound, then a swish and more bells. I pulled my shoulders from the bag for a look outside.

"Phil! You've got to see this!"

The yellow sunlight had already driven yesterday's snow into hiding behind rocks and under trees, but the river was a dazzling sea of moving ice, the rich blue water offset with sun diamonds. Big islands of ice drifted silently up and grumbled to a halt on our exposed reef, where slush piled until it was forced musically over the barrier.

The first chore of the day was to dry our clothes. My feet were blanched and badly swollen. With pain and difficulty I finally crammed them into my thawing boots. Phil was no better off. In flimsy night things we limped about camp, gathering our frozen clothes and propping them by the fire. The day was beautiful, not a breath of wind, and seemed warm despite the twenty-four degrees F temperature.

Camp was cluttered with animal parts. In ten days we had cut up and carted home almost three tons of live animal, or about 3000 pounds of food, figuring that half of an animal is guts, bone, and hide. Aside from the hanging sections and two moose still unhung, we had buckets of fat and organs, sixteen lower legs, twelve shinbone skins, various cans of tallow, four antlered moose heads, and sacks of cracklings. Of the heads, one still had a tongue, two had noses, and one had been cut up for boiling. We had eight kidneys left, four and a half hearts, one hundred pounds of liver, and five large hides. At least it wasn't likely to rain again, I thought, but the meat was beginning to drip in the gentle sun.

Fondly I patted the big cold slabs. I haggled a neck into thirds and put one into Mightypot to boil, then settled myself near the fire for a day of moose-sorting. About me a chaos of caked and filthy utensils were scattered. I had already rendered over a hundred pounds of tallow, insurance against winter.

During the fall rains, the mud bank behind our cabin foundation had caved in. Phil started fires to thaw the hummocky ground in order to dig drainage ditches and fill them with rock. Soon we would begin transforming our accumultation of crooked logs into a home.

The following day was also sunny, but the river was slushed over and no more rafts of ice came down. The next day it froze. A sparkling road now joined the two lands. Only the rapids remained open, pouring dark blue from under the white ice. After breakfast that morning I decided to visit the cache for a load of tools.

The country was beautiful as I hiked along, the red autumn peaks now capped with white, the ground strewn with birch leaves. Muskeg potholes were covered with ice as clear as glass and dusted with snow. The twigs and leaves encased beneath the surface stood out in color against the black water.

It was warm when I reached Chris Olsen's place, and I spent some time going through the cache to see what we needed. His creek was a fairyland of sculptured ice where spray from the tumbling current had coated the shoreline in a fantasy of white. A lazy trickle still gurgled unseen beneath the ice. The frosted cranberries edging the stream tasted delicious, and soon my fingers and mouth were stained red as I poked about the ruined structures.

I glanced up from time to time while tying things on my pack frame, half expecting old Chris. The clearing was haunted by his work and dreams, and I felt somehow an intruder, even a thief. Finally I hoisted up my pack and started for home. On it were strapped the stove, stovepipe oven, and assorted tools. As I reached the edge of the clearing, I stopped and turned around. "Thank you," I said softly into the still air. "You don't need these things anymore, and they mean a great deal to us. Thank you."

I covered the mile home in good time. Phil bounced up the trail to greet me, pulling the awkward pack from my shoulders.

"Gee, you've done a lot," I said, looking around. Neither of us had ever built a cabin before. (My mother's advice wouldn't have helped us much in this, for she was remarkably helpless in some things, for an Arctic explorer.) Phil had examined several, and his general experience with tools put him in charge of construction. We designed it together and he figured out how best to build it.

The cabin sill logs were in place, saddle notched together in a rectangle and firmly planted on a foundation of rocks. It was easier to visualize now, laid out neat and square. I thought it looked odd, that one spot in the wilderness so defined.

"I'm starting to notch the floor joists into the sills," he told me proudly, as we headed for the fire. "We'll nail the boards to them after the cabin is up. Here, sit down and have some hot soup. I put dried vegetables in for a special treat. To celebrate the sills. What do you think?" He scooped two mugs into the small cooking pot and handed me one. We walked back up to the cabin and sat astride a sill, basking in the afternoon sun. Below us gleamed the strange white river.

"Thank you for making the cabin larger than you planned," I said. It would be twelve by fifteen feet inside and at least six feet from floor to roof, so that we would be able to stand upright "in the warm," as we called it.

"I think we'll be glad we did," he answered. We sipped our soup in silence, admiring the sills. "We're a few logs short. I'm going to cut some green ones. There just aren't any more dead trees worth taking close by. I'd rather put them on the bottom. They're twice as heavy and they'll drip sap. They'll shrink some too as they dry out."

"They're a pretty twisted lot," I said, looking over the pile. "And small."

"I thought we could put every other row in with scrap pieces on the side with the door. They'll be doweled to regular ones to hold them in place. It won't matter because we'll saw out the door hole. A lot of these old places fall down because they aren't doweled under the eves or by the door and window openings. The guys who built them just framed in the door to hold the walls straight."

"Tomorrow I should start gathering moss to chink with," I said, draining my cup and fishing out the last pea.

"We'll need it under the floor too," he told me. "I'm banking the sills with dirt on the outside to keep the wind out, but we'll need insulation from the ground below."

"It'll help keep the permafrost intact," I said, "so we don't melt into the mud." After a moment I went on, "Maybe a moosehide rug is in order."

The sun was sinking and already an evening chill began to settle in. "Let's continue this celebration down by the fire," Phil suggested. He stood up and began to coil the hauling rope, slinging it over a branch. "I'll cut some tenderloin and we'll have a feast. With salt and pepper," he grinned wickedly.

I smiled and got stiffly to my feet. They were very sore and inflexible. Phil took my hand and together we hobbled down to camp.

"I think we should have treats every Sunday once we're in the cabin," I said as I started to build up the fire, blowing gently on the embers.

"Treat? Treat??" Phil went wide-eyed, making me laugh. "Treat!" he demanded, pretending to shake me. Chet caught the mood and began to sing shrilly. She never really learned to bark.

"Hush!" we snarled in unison.

Phil picked her up a moment and petted her. "Now that's a good girl."

I settled on my sitting log and Phil squatted flat-footed by the fire. We were eating our fourth course of fried meat and fat as twilight dampened the woods. I stopped chewing and extended my greasy hands to the flames.

"It'll be such a dream getting into the cabin," I said, shifting my weight to the other icy cheek. The temperature had dropped to around zero the moment the sun was gone. Only six weeks after our first star and now we had thirteen hours of darkness. "Just think what it will be like getting dressed in 'the warm.'"

"I want to place the stove so that we can light it from bed," Phil told me.

"Maybe in the middle of the cabin," I suggested. Arranging the cabin was a major topic of our conversation lately.

He tossed a bone to Chet and reached into the skillet for a fresh helping. She withdrew her nose from under her tail and sat quietly gnawing. She had recently been liberated from her splint, having outgrown two of them. The fracture site was a large bony lump and the foot was on a bit crooked, but it had healed. Her leg had atrophied and she ran with a funny little hop. To sit she would swing her foot up in the air as if still wearing a splint, a habit she was to keep for life.

"You can always tell when Chet's around," Phil observed with a grin, "by the smell of singed fur." At her name, Net-Chet thumped her tail twice over the coals. A flame flicked along it and Phil reached over and patted it out. She sniffed. "I spend more time beating out smoldering dogs around here," he continued. "She won't have a hair left by the time we get into the cabin."

"I don't think she feels it through her fur." I reached across and stroked her. She looked up with her lovely slanted brown eyes. "Do you know that she sometimes digs up the coals and sleeps on them when the fire dies down? Not that I blame her any." I hugged my knees.

All that remained of day was a lingering yellow streak over the southern peaks. The stars had appeared like jewels on the deep velvet blue of the sky. Life is good when the wind drops and you're well fed.

Phil licked his fingers and wiped his knife on his pants. "I'll go first," he offered, rising. While he arranged himself in the tent, I squatted over the embers, roasting my haunches. My rear was chilled to the bone, as dead as moose meat. He called, "Ready," and I gave my left side one last turn and bolted for the tent. Away from the fire the below-zero air bit sharply.

Net-Chet whimpered miserably while I slipped off my boots and stowed them under the tent fly. My teeth clashing together, I pulled off my clothes and fumbled into the thin, ragged pajamas that Phil had warmed next to his bare skin. I spread out my clothing and called the grateful dog onto them then partly zipped up the door. In cold weather, an enclosed tent condenses your breath and snows on you. Submerging in the icy folds, I balled up near the bottom of the sleeping bag, where I found Phil. Net-Chet began to creep upward from the foot almost at once.

ᕁ

Phil's patience was beginning to pay off as we fitted the twisted logs together. We had to customize each one. First we would lift it into place to measure and mark. Because the curves gravitated downward, I held it, clamped between my legs, while he cut the notch. We pinned the tiers together on either side of the door, solidifying the otherwise frail front wall by drilling down with a T-handle auger and driving in inch-and-a-half pegs made from small dead spruce. It was a cold, tedious job, and the auger jammed easily, filling the space between the logs with chips. Many hours were spent twisting it down through the logs.

At night our sleeping bags became rimed with ice. Crystals grew down the tent walls, cascading upon us when we moved. We ate enormously as autumn yawned, but far from gaining weight, we were still on the decline. At least now that we had fresh fat meat, our diarrhea had gone.

For a week winter relaxed its grip, gathering force for the final onslaught. We worked always under the weight of it, afraid of the cold and dark as we watched the snow creep down the barren peaks. The leaves and gay colors were suddenly gone, the willows transformed into lifeless sticks in the frozen mud.

With freeze-up, our last door had slammed shut. We were truly committed now. No longer could the river carry us downstream to safety. The ice was never really silent. Occasional slow motion waves rumbled through it, buckling the surface as pressure ridges stirred momentarily to life. We became almost accustomed to the startling groan and snap of the river resisting its bonds.

And then the snow came. For two days it piled steadily upon our icy corral of logs, accumulating as we worked. The familiar outlines of camp vanished under inch after inch of fluff.

It was September 29th. I huddled in the sleeping bag, writing in my journal with numb fingers, reluctant to rise. Nearby, Phil wrestled the rock-like quarters, trying to saw off a slab for breakfast. It was ridiculous to be surrounded by tons of meat and be unable to eat it. He gave up and set Mightypot full of meat on the sputtering fire to thaw.

At last I could put off getting up no longer. The temperature had risen to fifteen degrees F, but a wind was picking up. Cold need not be extreme for a person to suffer severe exposure. Even a relatively mild temperature coupled with wetness or wind has great chilling potential. It seemed too cold even for breakfast. My feet were soon numb in their worn summer boots. I shouldered my pack and set out at once for Chris Olsen's to get floor boards.

By noon snow was falling thickly. Wind whipped it up my sleeves and down my neck as I trudged homeward, trailing the boards. My world faded to a few yards and I fought along beneath the swaying trees, Net-Chet close to my side. One end of the lumber was lashed to the pack frame, but the other end dragged behind me, snagging on every lump. It would catch and then snap forward, driving the load into the back of my head. A human pack mule, that's what I'm becoming, I thought as I staggered along.

I left the trail just before Cranberry Hill, taking a short cut across a frozen pond. Away from the trees, all was silent but the hiss of wind and the bat of snowflakes against my stinging cheeks. I reached home to find Phil thoroughly chilled. Falling snow obscured the river beyond, leaving him adrift atop the unfinished walls. There he sat in his own little world of wind and white, faithfully twisting the auger.

We adjourned to the tent away from the pitiless wind, taking Net-Chet and a steaming pot of moose neck. There we crouched, the center of all things, the three of us alone in the world, and gnawed bones while reading aloud about ballooning in Africa. Outside the wind increased, shaking the tent as the snow streaked by.

A sober, very quiet feeling invaded our buffeted little shelter as darkness settled and the snow continued endlessly. Gradually we came to realize that here, at last, was winter.

Morning light came dimly into our tent, for we were snowed under. The wind had stopped, but falling flakes continued to rush out of the colorless sky. The nearby spruce stood in ghostly silhouette. All was silent, except for the lonely groan of trees settling under their burdens. Outside lay an alien land, lost in formless gray, an eerie world without dimension, no up or down, only falling snow.

What a beautiful world to play in, I thought as I dislodged the smothering blanket of snow from our sagging tent. This is a day to be a child and run through fluffy mountains of white. I reached through the doorway and dug for my boots. I had placed them beneath the fly, but it too was buried, collapsed under the weight of snow. A day to come inside laughing and red-cheeked, stamping feet and shaking soft hair. A day to sit by a crackling fireplace and drink hot chocolate. I kicked at the impossibly soft drift that blocked the entrance. The flakes were almost half an inch across, six-sided and as perfect as pictures. No way to avoid getting wet.

I waded to the fireplace and fished around for lost pots and utensils. We could lose things, I realized. From the trunk of a nearby spruce, I snapped off dead twigs for tinder. Buckets of snow emptied from the patient tree with each one plucked.

Snow woman. Icicle lady.

Already my feet were cold and wet, the new snow melting into the leather of my boots. I sniffed the thick morning air, my thoughts fingering the sleeping land, feeling the slowing pulse of life as blankets of winter were pulled on. I listened into the stillness. After the throb of summer and the autumn battles of wind and ice, this was something new. It wasn't the silence of a void, but the minute whisper of countless hurrying snowflakes. Every noise was sucked up and swallowed by this imperceptible rustle of stillness.

And where are all the people? I wondered, gazing into the empty gray valley. It was a dream world. The far shore drifted momentarily before me in the soup. My eyes could not focus on the featureless ice and it seemed to shift and change as I stared. I stood knee-deep in powder, twigs grasped in my bare red hands. Strange to be so alone after a life built around people, defined by people, hemmed in by people. And where are they now? I stamped out a small circle and squatted to light the tinder. People are my boundaries, I realized, my points of reference. I could be anywhere. It really didn't matter in a land of no people.

Above me on the hill was our unborn cabin, an illusion of warmth and comfort. I studied it as I fed the small fire, seeing only a lonesome pile of logs, half-buried in snow. I shuffled and slipped my way through billowing clouds of powder, climbing the slope to stare into the bleak structure: a three-foot corral with joists. Net-Chet burrowed unhappily up beside me, tail drooping. She climbed through the door hole, her thin legs resentful of the deep snow, and sat in anxious confusion, looking at this thing that demanded all my time. I know how it is supposed to look, I thought wretchedly, but I just can't picture it.

Phil was bent dejectedly over the sputtering fire, blowing, as I skidded back down the hill. "You don't like snow?" I asked him. Steamy smoke marred the snow, dissolving it like cotton candy.

"Not to work in," he replied. He was rearranging the damp sticks. The snow was too deep even for squatting, like knee-high feathers.

"I remember how we loved it as kids," I told him. "It so rarely snowed that any flake was cause for joyous celebration. Then the adults would grump."

"Now you know why."

"Because they were grownups," I stated flatly. "Is it really necessary to become so joyless? To lose your sense of play as you age?"

"Well, grownups have to work in snow," he answered me.

I stooped to remove the little tea pot that was suddenly boiling over, and poured tea for both of us. The pot was blackened and dented. "The first snow I remember was when I was six years old. I was spending a month or two with a sitter, a strict Baptist, while my mother was on a lecture tour. It was Sunday. I looked out and saw tiny flakes in the rain. It was snowing! Really snowing! She simply couldn't understand how important that was. For her it was just something that happened. By the time she herded me into that bleak old church, the snowflakes were streaming down. All I remember is looking back at the glorious snow as those heavy doors closed behind me."

Phil took another pull on his tea. Despite the new food, he seemed somehow gaunt and frail, back-lit in white. "When I was in high school it snowed once. They turned the sprinklers on and melted it all."

"Joyless creatures."

"And now you're a grownup," he finished mischievously.

"What could be more important than enjoying our glorious planet?" I answered, ignoring his comment. The love of life as an adventure was a gift from my mother. For her, life was a smorgasbord, a banquet of opportunities. The only thing it was good for was to be eaten up and enjoyed.

It snowed all day. We worked quietly, Phil on the cabin, me unearthing the sphagnum moss to chink with. Moss was plentiful and thick, and it would have been an easy job without the snow. Now it was getting hard to find. The last thing we talked about as we drifted off to sleep was our first Sunday celebration in the cabin, planning the menu in detail. The snow was still coming down.

The following morning the sky was clear but the temperature had dropped below zero. A numbing wind sprayed powder through the air in a stinging blast. Snow had melted into our summer boots and they froze into grotesque shapes during the night. I peeked from beneath the stiff folds of down, watching Phil struggle with his boots. I could see his red chapped hands strain with the unyielding leather, and I knew that his feet, like mine, were tender and swollen. Our feet never really warmed, but when sensation returned during the long night hours, they ached and itched unbearably. To add to our nighttime misery, we were now beset with muscle cramps.

I ran my fingers down my contracted legs and gently twisted one foot. It had lost much of its flex, and the skin protruded in painful lumps over the joints. I hadn't seen it in days, for I dressed in bed. I pulled it up for inspection. It looked pale and bruised and I kissed it tenderly before tucking it back under the covers, acutely aware of the love I have for my body and all its familiar parts. How unkind, I thought, to send my feet forth in frozen boots for yet another day.

In the tent entrance Phil was working with growing despair, forcing his wretched foot at the frozen boot. I knew he was wasting precious heat in this twenty-minute ordeal, but could offer nothing. Finally, one at a time, the poor extremities were crammed into the unyielding leather and he hobbled off to build a fire. Before I had completed dressing, he returned with my boots, damp but pliable, from the fire.

I was lame and my feet were cold almost at once. I hurried to the wind blasted fire and squatted over it in the bright, frigid sunlight. The flames gusted to and fro, singeing the hairs from my numb fingers but warming them little. Phil looked the picture of misery. His eyes had a lusterless, sunken quality in a dark, weathered face. His nose was running into his mustache, freezing icicles above the cracked lips.

"L'ammal, you go back to the tent," I said. "I'll finish breakfast. There's no sense in both of us being out here."

Phil nodded unhappily and handed me the warped Teflon skillet. He fumbled his pocket knife from the meat he had been trying to pry apart and finally snapped it shut against his leg.

"It's so frustrating to order your fingers to do something and they don't," he apologized, turning for the tent. I watched his woolen back recede, so vulnerable. He was staring at his feet as he placed them cautiously. They looked stiff and wooden. We have to finish the cabin! I thought desperately. Then everything will be okay. Yet I knew in the dark unspoken back of my mind that not all stories have happy endings. When you're young you feel invincible, but it's an illusion.

I scurried to the tent with a smoking skillet of meat. Phil was buried in the sleeping bags, his boots tucked beneath him to keep them from freezing. I zipped the tent shut behind me and pulled the bags over my lap. The tent snapped about me in the wind. Phil raised up on one elbow.

"Hurry now," I said, pushing a filthy fork into his hand. "The fat is already solidifying." My feet were in agony. I loosened the boot laces and worked them free. My socks were frozen inside the boots and I pulled to

111

get them out. Phil put my stiff feet through his shirt and pressed them against his bare stomach.

"I wonder how our meat will hold out at the rate we're eating it," I said. We were wolfing the meal, careful to share the fat chunks that made up a third of its volume. "I bet we each eat 6000 calories a day."

"Don't cut against the skillet," Phil intoned as usual. "I don't know how we'll sharpen the knives. I tried this morning, but ice sheeted over the stone too fast to work. And the ax stone has shattered from water frozen into the pores."

I was eyeing the last piece of fat. "Go ahead," he told me, receding into the covers, still chewing. "It's yours."

I finished and began scraping the burned grease from the pan, eating it off my knife. "I always wanted to be thin," I complained, "and now I don't enjoy it. It's uncomfortable. Even sleeping. Sitting on logs while you chop a notch is bone-shattering. Every time I slip in the snow, I fall on one skinny hip or the other. I'm bruised all over. My butt and legs are black and blue. I almost wonder if I haven't frosted the skin or something."

"Can't you squat? That would be warmer than sitting."

"Not while drilling holes and holding logs. The circulation in my behind has always seemed poor anyway. Remember how cold it got even in mild weather? Now the old body is shutting off service to the suburbs. Well . . ." I decided reluctantly. "I'll go fry us a couple more pans of meat and then we'd better get to work. The cabin won't build itself."

I pulled on my frosty boots and crawled from the tent, zipping it behind me. Our precious structure loomed above, completely uninhabitable. It was colder inside than out because of the shadowing walls. I dreaded another day of digging through the snow for chinking moss or straddling the icy wall, drilling holes for pegs. I hate it, I thought resentfully. If I ever get out of here, I'm going to spend my life inside, warm and well fed. I used to think of myself as the outdoors type. But I'm not!

"I agree with you, if that helps any," Phil told me as we once again gulped the unattractive food. It had cooled on top while the blasting fire burned the bottom. "This is the sort of 'character building' experience that I would like to have had long ago. I think it will be good for us . . . if we live through it."

I understood what he meant. "Hardship puts life in perspective," I decided. "It knocks the pickiness out of you and teaches you how strong you really are. You can quit almost anything for a price. You can drop out of school, get divorced, go AWOL from the service, run away from home, give up your job. But we can't quit. We have to finish that cabin."

"Oh, I suppose we could just die," he answered. He looked so lost that I

112

studied him awhile, thinking.

"No," I said at last. "There have been times in the past that I considered suicide, when I felt overwhelmed by the complexities of modern life and my relationships with people. But this is different. My body was designed to survive, honed by conditions like these through millions of years. It won't give up without a good fight. It's interesting to see, when really threatened, how hard I will fight. That's something I didn't know about myself until now."

The sun had almost reached the zenith of its low swing across the southern sky before we left the tent. Daylight was sliding rapidly now, deserting us more each day.

What followed were perhaps the most difficult and miserable days of my life. We felt a desperation waking each morning in frozen sleeping bags to temperatures of fifteen and twenty below zero and another endless day of toiling in wind and cold.

The cabin walls became more stubborn as they rose. First we would wrestle a log into place for fitting. Then, gripping it with icy thigh bones, I straddled it in the proper position while Phil sat astride a side wall and chopped the notch. Turning and shaping the logs, we settled them one by one into place. Then I would chink the cracks, using one frozen hand and then the other to pack moss between the logs, pounding it snug with a chip of wood. But the hardest task was to sit astraddle the frosty wall, slowly turning the auger down through the layers of logs and jamming chips. When we reached window height, there were five holes to drill with each tier.

Looking back it seems strange that we did not get out our winter clothing. True, there was little to be done for our feet, yet long after the rains ceased, we continued in our summer woolens. Our down parkas and pants remained in five-gallon cans, buried under the snow beside the tent. We didn't even sleep in long underwear. We knew enough to remove our damp day clothes, but night after night we chattered into filmy night things and rattled bones together in the middle of the sleeping bag. And bones they were. Although Phil was bundled in wool by day, at night I could feel sharp ribs and shoulder blades protruding through his thin T-shirt.

We were obsessed with the cabin and nothing else mattered. All our thoughts were of warmth and shelter. All our sentences began with "When we get into the cabin. . . ." Just as our numerous knife cuts from butchering were nothing in our fight for food, now other pain was ignored by brains engrossed in staying alive.

The hardest thing I have ever done was to face those mornings, putting on my twenty-below-zero clothes and frozen boots and climbing out of the tent. I remembered my previous life of comfort and plenty as in a dream, a fairy tale from another century. How had I ever taken such abundance for granted? This was the natural state of existence. This was the way it had always been. My world narrowed to the moment. Past and future dissolved as I struggled through the eternal present, caught up in an endless reality of pain and cold.

Each night, chilled and exhausted, we crawled into our sleeping bags and shivered together in the blackness beneath frozen layers of nylon. Seldom did we move, reluctant to waste heat despite the discomfort of the hard lumpy ground. We developed sleeping postures that gave maximum body contact. Phil would curl around my back, folding one arm under his neck and wrapping the upper arm and leg about me. Sometimes I slept on top of him, chest to chest, braced off the ground on my knees and elbows.

During the night layers of ice from our breath formed on the sleeping bags. Frost rained from the ceiling each time one of us rose to pee, chattering barefooted in the snow beside the tent entrance. In the cold dry air, we were tormented with thirst and consumed great quantities of hot broth during the day. We kept water in the tent by sleeping with an old syrup bottle from Venetie, until it froze and shattered one night. Then we took turns when we woke at night, melting snow in our hands for one another.

Net-Chet crept resolutely upward until the three of us were condensed in a tight little knot in the center of the tent. By midnight, thanks to the gift of Phil's stomach and legs, my feet and behind would begin to warm. How wonderful to be warm! We had one place to crawl into and raise our body temperatures, one place in all this frozen, uncaring world. How good the comfortable smells of our own unwashed bodies, the warm smells of life!

Net-Chet was miserable too. She spent most of each day curled wretchedly against the south wall of the cabin, out of the wind. Although she had put on a few guard hairs, she was slender of build, thin and unhappy with her Arctic lot in life. Her pretty, curly tail hung limply between her legs and though she seldom whined now, she was not doing well. It hurt to see her silent misery, but we could no more help her than ourselves.

The strain was showing on both of us. Phil looked thin and pinched, his great green eyes pits above his ragged beard and its mask of icicles. We wore our wool caps continually. Every few days I discarded mine to brush out my long, matted hair, which came out in handfuls. All this, and I'm going bald too! I thought in desperation. But it didn't matter anymore. Only the cabin mattered, that cold, useless edifice to toil, our haven to be.

We gave up trying to saw the iron-hard meat into pieces to fry. I chopped a hole in the ice and filled Mightypot with gallons of water and big hunks of frozen meat and fat. This bubbled all day over a listless fire. We ate continually and without interest, replenishing the pot as we worked. We even gave up tea as too much to bother with.

Work on the gables seemed to go slowest of all. They were high and exposed to wind. It took effort to climb up, and balance to hold the short, loose logs in place while securing them with pins. We counted our progress in two or three logs a day. But gradually the gables grew. We rolled the first purlin into place and then the second. A purlin is a roof support log, similar to the ridge pole, but not at the peak. Our roof was constructed off center, its peak four feet from the long south wall where the windows would be and eight feet from the darker north wall. The windows all faced south to catch the winter sun.

One afternoon we set Chris Olsen's sheet metal stove up on coffee cans balanced over the joists and built a fire, abandoning the windy fireplace down by the river for good. We should have moved long before. The cabin remained a roofless ice cave, impossible to heat, but now we could easily break from a task to stand for a moment out of the wind, drinking hot broth and warming our hands. Snow hissed upon the stove top as it fell. To celebrate the installation of the second purlin and the stove, I sawed a giant round steak for dinner and fried it up "inside."

The following day, Phil finished drilling and placing the last two gable logs while I cut and hauled rafter poles for the roof. We would need over a hundred, but some long-ago fire had left us acres of small dead trees standing between the ranks of mature hardier ones: nature's way of pruning.

By evening we were ready for our triumphant placement of the ridge pole, a great log that would form the peak of the cabin and extend beyond in a meat rack. A tree grew eight feet from the east wall and would support the far end of the log.

We heaved the heavy ridge pole onto the butt ends of the plate logs that capped the main structure under the gables. Then slowly we rolled it up the gables and into position. It was hard and dangerous work, balancing up there as we carefully notched and fitted the log. When it was done, Phil cut the top from the nearby tree, and we scooted the end of the ridge pole over the high stump and secured it in place with a metal strap.

Our cabin suddenly looked real. We measured the walls. Phil's "almost level" had broken weeks before when the water in the little bottle froze, but despite this, the cabin was accurate on every measurement to within a quarter of an inch.

Infused with new hope, we retreated to the tent for only a brief foot warming session. Then while Phil chopped the gable logs to pitch, I set off up the hill to the Cathedral Grove for more rafters. My skid trail was now a smooth chute of packed snow, worn slick by the passage of many logs.

We missed the deadline to celebrate Sunday in our new home. Still, it was with much enthusiasm that we attacked our growing roof the next morning. Phil pinned a rafter-retaining log over the butt ends of the plates and sawed my poles to fit, laying them side by side over the purlins. I felled trees as fast as I could haul them. Gradually the sky disappeared from inside our home. At last! The cabin was becoming a shelter! By mid-week, a pole ceiling spread over the entire cabin.

When we finished it was late, but we set off together for the cache and more boards. This was Phil's first trip over my route. Despite a new snow-fall, the trail I had broken two days before made the going easy. The temperature was below zero and my feet were numb, my body tired from the long labor. Still the woods were beautiful, a wonderland where every creature left its story in the snow. Here a lynx caught a luckless rabbit, discarding the hide and feet for Net-Chet. A squirrel had eaten a spruce cone, scattering the reddish scales over the snow. And there was the squirrel. He churred sleepily at us, flipping his tail as he cocked his head for a better look. I watched him a moment, grateful that I no longer needed to eat little squirrels.

Net-Chet bounded ahead while we wallowed through the knee-high snow. The bushes were loaded with snow, and cascades of it dumped down my back as I passed beneath them. It is hard to pick a straight trail through the timber, but now that snow marked my passage, I would blaze a trail and then clear it.

By the time we reached the cache, snow was falling thickly through the purple of evening. We wasted no time in dismantling the crumbling out-house, nailing the boards together in packets. They were rotten and warped, stained and dirty. And beautiful. We helped each other into our cumbersome packs and, trailing bundles of boards, we set out for home.

We trudged up the ridge, lurching through the mist and thickening darkness, pulling our boards. What if we should lose the path, I wondered suddenly. Ahead of me, Phil plodded like a patient shadow, only a dark form in the falling snow. The familiar mountains were gone. Strange creatures of the twilight we seemed as we thrashed through the silent, fuzzy world.

I was drenched with sweat and melted snow when the lone spruce that marked the home trail materialized from the gloom. Eagerly the boards followed our striding legs down the packed chute into camp.

We helped each other unsaddle. I propped my pack against the front wall and ducked through the door hole. Inside it was dark. Slits of gray light beamed between the rafter poles. The door and two front window holes were winter-evening gray.

"Look Phil, a real house!" I spread my arms. My shoulders ached with released strain. "Hey, the meat I left on the stove is thawed."

"Watch your step," he warned. Between the joists, the frozen mud was slippery with snow. We stepped over the knee-high joists as we moved about the room. "I think I'll light the lantern."

We had a single can of white gas for special occasions. It took time to find and fill the little lantern in the dark. I prepared dinner in that unreal white glow, and we ate sitting on the joists as the snow sifted between the rafter poles. The door and window holes loomed ominously black in the strange glare that now separated us from the rest of the Arctic. In camp I had always sensed the land about me, but now I was limited by these walls and cut off from the night by my dulled perceptions.

After dinner we turned off the lantern and sat by the glow of the stove. It was cracked and had bolt holes through which a dancing light and occasional showers of sparks came. I stood up to warm my bottom, as I had seen my mother do since childhood. She would pull her skirt up and, with her hands behind her back, toast her fanny near any stove or fireplace.

"Have you noticed the way Chet's new teeth are popping in?" I asked. "Our little girl is growing up."

She was snuggled in Phil's lap as he leaned back against one wall, cleaning his teeth with dental floss. He always kept a string of it in the compass case he still wore in his shirt pocket, using it until it was frayed. Dental floss is important to meat-eaters, we had found.

"Oh, she's a clever one," he laughed. It sounded good and I realized that it had been a long time since I'd heard him laugh. He pulled on the end of Chet's nose and she rolled her belly up, bicycling with her legs. "And hair! She just wanted to be a house dog. She waited until we let her into the tent," he accused. It was true. She had turned hairy overnight, submerging beneath luxurious blankets.

"Maybe she lost faith in our cabin," I suggested, rotating before the heat. My feet were cold in the mud and ice a foot below floor level. "I did myself."

"She's just stubborn," he countered.

"Really now, can you actually imagine our little family alone here, with you and me inside and her out?"

Phil was noisily driving the end of Chet's nose, her "squelch knob" he called it, and shifting gears with her legs. She rolled and growled happily. It was good to see them play.

117

"With her shiny new teeth and winter outfit, all she needs is a furry squelch knob, don't you think?" he asked. "How would you like to have that cold wet thing on the end of your face all winter? Ouch! Don't touch me with that thing!"

"You're silly," I said, watching them fondly.

⚹

When we woke the next morning in a dripping mess of sagging tent and melting snow, we abandoned camp for good. We left it frozen sadly under a burden of new snow and hauled our soggy sleeping bags into the cabin, where we spread them on boards laid over the joists. Winter had abated. The temperature soared to thirty-four degrees F. Falling snow melted into our clothes on contact, and the meat began to thaw. We were better off when it was cold.

There was compensation, however. The stockpiled dirt from under the cabin was soft enough to hack into lumps and shovel onto the roof. Phil tacked the tattered plastic tarp over the rafters, and the cabin began to warm almost at once. I could hear the rhythmic thumps of falling clods as I prepared breakfast. I nailed plastic flaps over the door and window holes, and soon water dripped from the frosted walls. Warm! I took off my wool coat and rolled up my sleeves.

We worked together into the half-light of a snowy afternoon, lifting the stacked sods and placing them on the roof. With the sealing of the roof, peace settled upon us. We wanted to stay inside, but there was still much to do. The cabin had no floor, windows, or door, and the upper half had yet to be chinked.

After a brief rest, I set out into the late afternoon to grub up more moss. It eventually required forty-four duffel bags, or about 120 cubic feet of sphagnum moss, to insulate us from winter. This may seem like a lot, but the following spring I couldn't even find where I had gathered it. With my shovel I rummaged through the snow and when my bags at last were full, turned for home. How strange it was to see a cabin perched there where none had been before. It was the same beach, same trees, same hill, same forlorn little tent. But there was the cabin!

As I mounted the hill, Phil met me and took my bags. "Wait'll you see how it looks with a floor!" he exalted, swinging the plastic door flap out of the way for me. The doorway was tiny, only four and a half feet high, made to conserve heat and boards. I ducked through, stepping over the sill log. Inside Phil had been laying out boards, patching them together into a floor. He came in behind me, rearranging the flap, and dumped the moss between two joists.

I held my cold fingers out to the stove and looked about. Our very own floor! For half a year we had lived outdoors. Now the whole world was snowed under, but we had a floor, flat and clean and warm. It was hard to believe. I hugged myself like a child opening a present. I would bathe and wash dishes and someday have a table to cook on. Erecting these logs between ourselves and the Arctic had made all the difference.

"Only about three more loads for the floor," Phil said, dropping the empty duffel bags by the doorway. He bent over and smoothed the moss between the joists.

I groaned and reached for the bags.

"No, wait and warm up a bit," he suggested, putting his arm about me.

I smiled and shook my head. "I want a floor for our first Sunday. We still need to bring up all our supplies tonight." Everything we owned was in a pile by the overturned canoe. "I'm going to clean out the plastic bucket and fill it with water. I don't want anything to ruin tomorrow." I grinned. "I want to fondle all our possessions in comfort."

Phil was carefully straightening rusty old nails as I dropped the door flap and plodded out into the snow. The world was the soft blue-gray of snowy evening as I stepped noiselessly along the familiar beach, headed upstream. As I passed the forlorn tent, a bird called from the spruce above me, strange and wild in the twilight. I listened, caught by a remembered tone from my childhood. I knew that bird . . .

The roar of wings startled me. Then I placed it. "Phil! Bring the .22!" I called out.

He appeared beside me, unlaced boots filling with snow, eyes alert.

"Up there." I pointed. "A spruce chicken. You can see the dark outline near the trunk. Want me to shoot?"

"No. I see him," he whispered.

The short "twhinggg!" of the .22 was swallowed in the flutter of wings as the heavy body plummeted. Phil started forward.

"Wait!" I called in surprise. "My bird is still up there!" I could see the shadowy form turning its head in agitation. The movement caught Phil's eye and there was a second echoless shot. Two spruce chickens for Thanksgiving dinner!

An hour later we were sitting on our partial floor, savoring chocolate pudding, our first treat in weeks, by the light of the open stove door. "Did you ever taste anything so good?" I asked.

"Never." Phil had his eyes closed as he rolled the pudding slowly around in his mouth. In the darkness I had used cornmeal instead of sugar, but what did it matter?

The glow of the fire cast strange shadows on the walls and my eyes danced over the logs, flicking from wall to wall in childish awe. How had we come to be here? I couldn't quite remember. Something about walking and wind and cold. A dream, I thought. A beautiful dream. My home.

"Just look! Oh, not you, Chet," I chided, stroking the basking dog. She was enjoying the cabin as much as we were.

"You have to be careful around a dog that speaks people," Phil told me in a serious aside.

It was true. Chet followed our conversations carefully and was able to pick out a good many key words. Perhaps she was unusual in this, certainly our circumstances were unusual. But I believe animals are often underestimated.

Chet settled her golden head sleepily into my lap, stretching her toes luxuriously. "Our cabin," I whispered.

Phil looked about the room. "You were right about making it big," he told me. "There were times I had my doubts." He took my hand and we laughed in delight. Our cabin! Every log was cut and dragged here with our muscles; we had shaped each pole just so. How solid and strong it looked, this product of a dream, this triumph.

I touched a log, fingers sliding over the smooth, cool wood. "Remember?" I asked. The log had once looked like a caterpillar.

He nodded. It was hard to see the crooked dead tree anymore. How well it carried the hours invested in it! He was glancing around now too, eyes caressing the wood, remembering the struggle.

Suddenly we were both laughing. We toppled backwards onto the sleeping bags, giggling and pointing out logs that we recalled. Each had its story. Overhead the sturdy rafters flickered in the amber light, and joy welled up within me, pure childish joy. How lucky we are, I kept thinking. How wonderfully privileged. Not just to have food and shelter, but to know what it is worth.

Later I lay comfortably half awake, stretched full length in our warm bags beneath Phil's arm. It been a long time since I had stretched out.

"Phil . . . ?"

"Uhmmm . . . "

"I had a fantasy of spruce hens for Thanksgiving dinner. And now we have them. Just like that. I don't know why I worry so much. When the time comes, we always have what we need. Do you notice? Like the floor. Or moose. Phil . . . ?"

"Uhmmm . . . ?"

"There really aren't any accidents. Phil . . . ? Are you awake?"

"Uh huh."

"Then why are you snoring?"

My only answer was a gentle snore. His arm twitched a moment, drawing me in. The stove on its cans sent a lovely red glow and occasional sparks from the vent. The walls danced in the light of the dying fire.

Outside I felt the weight of winter wind, black against the cabin, laden with big flying flakes. They swam through my sleepy imagination in flurries half seen, tons of frozen water. On they came, a white flood pouring southward over the drowsy land, pulling me with them. Flung onto my well known river, I became a snowflake . . . no . . . a leaf! A dried alder leaf. Lightly I danced, skipping and skating over the wind-rippled snow.

How different things were out here. How vast! Dried leaves don't mind the cold. And the music! I paused against a dune to listen to the tinkle and whisper of crystals, but the next gust threw me upward, twirled on the singing wind. On I shot, past the burl tree, past the large white rock that looked like a molar, past the deserted little tent. I caught a glimpse of the cabin as I hurled into the bigger world, tumbled southward on the rising crest of winter. I lost my vision somewhere in the mountains as sleep claimed me.

I woke the next morning with a feeling of complete peace. Gradually my surfacing mind constructed the cabin about me, and I opened my eyes and stretched. No icy tent walls.

"It's Sunday!" I remembered, sitting up.

"Hi, sleepy head." Phil had a fire going and was reading a book on tanning hides, his head pillowed beside me on his old, patched boots.

I slipped from bed, feeling the forgotten sensation of warm air on my skin.

> "Oh, wakin' up in the Warms,
> In the Arctic in the winter.
> It's a whole new kinda feeling,
> Wakin' up in the Warms.
> In the Arctic, in the winter, in the Warms!"

I sang out, to some long forgotten advertising jingle, ending with a little dance routine.

Phil laughed and dropped his book as I pulled him out of bed and together we leapt about the cabin singing made up songs to made up tunes. Chet danced with us, making little dashes at our ankles, while a fly resurrected from the moss bumbled about in confusion, thinking it was spring.

The cabin was piled high with possessions. When Phil asked for a treat, I searched for our two twenty-five-pound bags of flour. We had forsworn opening them until this day. After he soldered the holes in Chris Olsen's flour bin, we poured in the precious powder. The cloth bags were moldy and crusted from their long journey in the bottom of the canoe. I set them aside, planning to soak the flour from them to use another time.

Phil brought in fat bear flank, which I sliced thin and sprinkled with salt and sugar to make a sort of bacon. "How do pancakes, blueberry syrup, and bacon sound for starters?" I asked, although the menu had been planned for weeks. "Then we can go on to T-bone steaks with as much fat as you want and biscuits with gravy for lunch. And for dinner, I thought perhaps 'vegetable meef stoop,' that's dried vegetables-moose-meat-beef-bouillon-soup-stew."

"And apple sauce ice cream?" he hinted.

"And apple sauce ice cream. We can eat all day and never go outside if you want."

"Oh, this is the day we change clothes," he sang out. "From now on, I think we ought to change underwear every Sunday, whether we need to or not. Look how clean!" He held up a pair of panties, clothes we hadn't seen since that long ago Yukon day. I had forgotten clothes got that clean.

"I'm going to make a bookshelf so that we can look at all our books when-ever we want to," Phil declared, dancing over the floor in his bare feet and ragged T-shirt like some kind of dirty, bearded scarecrow. Aside from our rifles and sleeping bags, those books were our most prized possessions. Now that we were safe, we longed to look at them.

"Maybe you'd better wait until we finish chinking," I suggested. "They might get snowed on and warp." Phil looked so disappointed that I amended, "Well, it won't hurt to make the shelf anyway. Maybe I can fin-ish chinking that part today."

It wasn't a cold day but we kept a fire going constantly. Sky showing be-tween the upper logs made it seem a little less homey, as did the snow that still hid between some of the exposed joists. I lifted the door flap and stepped into a foot of silvery fluff. My bare toes sank through the stinging softness and I stood listening. What a different world waited out here! I had forgotten this place. Suddenly released from the cabin, my mind ex-panded. The Arctic was everywhere, as far as my thoughts could travel.

Inside I could hear Phil hammering away and humming an unrecogniz-able tune in some key of his own. About me the trees moaned softly, their tops rocking as they guarded the cabin from the wind that streaked down the exposed river. I watched great sheets of it sweeping our old camp at thirty miles per hour. It drifted like sand over the ice, building dunes, burying the tent.

How glad I am not to be down there, I thought. I wondered suddenly how the animals were faring. It wouldn't be a fun day to be a wolf. I breathed happily of the falling snow, standing contentedly in my bare feet and tattered pajamas. Let it snow.

Chapter 7

I STRETCHED and pushed back the covers. Phil was already up and the roar of the glowing stove filled the cabin. Two weeks had elapsed since we moved in, but there was much that needed doing to make it a home.

"It looks pretty hot," I said apprehensively. The stove was a cherry red and sparks flew from cracks in its worn old top. I reached out and flipped the draft shut, but it did little good. The stove was balanced on coffee cans, and the boards below it were smoking. Occasionally the whole stove had pitched forward, filling the room with cinders and smoke.

"I need to install a damper in the stovepipe," Phil said. "I'll get to it as soon as I finish the windows." He was pouring water between the floor boards as another rain of sparks descended.

"That layer of moss would make dandy tinder," I commented. "Not to mention all these wood shavings. It'd be terrible to burn the place down." The temperature had dropped to thirty below zero, giving us a taste of what life without shelter might be like.

"I should be able to start on the stove stand tomorrow," he told me. The stand would include a small table with a storage shelf beneath.

"You really think you can finish the windows today?" I asked in excitement.

"I think so," he grinned.

Real windows. I smiled to myself as I pulled on my daytime long underwear. "Where's Chet?"

"Playing Wild Dog of the North down on the river."

I threaded my way through the clutter and pulled aside the plastic flap that covered the window hole. On the river bank below me sat Net-Chet, attentively watching the far shore. On windy days she chased stray leaves that drifted past. Her gait was strong now, but she still had a few odd habits acquired while her leg was splinted.

I finished dressing and sat on a wooden crate to brush my hair. It was still coming out, though at a diminishing rate. It felt remarkably soft since being washed. My mother had told me that you never get any dirtier after the first few weeks. That may be, but I think my standards of cleanliness had changed. I discovered that daily bathing is very hard on skin when you live outdoors, especially the face and hands. Washing removes the protective oils.

"We need wood," I commented. "It's scary facing winter without a woodpile. We really don't know how dark or cold it will get."

Phil stepped outside for firewood. I looked around the room. The stove had slowed, and already a chill was returning. A damper in the stovepipe would help. So would windows. I glanced fondly at the new door, thinking what a difference it made closing the Arctic out. It took so long to build anything with an ax and plane. The cabin was piled with our belongings, and the sleeping bags, already filthy from the summer, were still underfoot on the floor. But the windows and stove came first.

He returned, stamping the fresh snow from his feet as he closed the door. It was small and covered with plastic to keep out the wind. A double plastic window filled the top, constructed to let in more light and conserve lumber.

"I want to try trapping this winter," Phil said, dumping the wood by the stove. He removed the pot of boiling meat and sat on a five gallon can. "It would be good survival knowledge and teach us about animals. Besides, the price of fur is sky high."

"I've been thinking about setting a couple of rabbit snares up on the hill," I told him. "I'd like to make fur caps for us. It would be fun to see if I can catch a rabbit." We hadn't seen one since they had turned white with the snowfall. "While I'm out, maybe I'll backtrack the caribou we saw yesterday and find out where they were coming from. If they follow the river or what."

The day before, Chet had proclaimed the arrival of the deer to our valley. While we scuttled for coats, mittens, camera, bullets, lenses, and rifles, they had trooped by our doorstep in their tireless migration. It was a little band of perhaps forty, all bulls, the fringe of a timeless tide of animals. Their trotting feet soon carried them behind the island and away.

"Do you want to shoot any?" Phil asked. He was blowing on a chunk of meat, skewered on his fork.

"We can always use the food," I answered. We didn't know how much meat we would need to see us through the winter, and we had already eaten most of a moose. "Caribou might make better mukluks," I said as an afterthought. We were still wearing our summer boots. "Moose hide is really too thick. I'll leave Chet and take my rifle just in case."

Phil chewed contentedly. I sat down near him and stabbed into the pot. The meat tasted very good. Everything did. The bland diet had sharpened my sense of taste. I could tell within a few inches of where a piece of meat had come off the animal. Although our consumption had dropped dramatically since moving inside, we were both putting on weight. It felt good to fatten up. It felt like success.

I chuckled and Phil glanced at me over his fork. "We'll be too fat to get out that little door soon," I commented. He grinned.

After breakfast I slowly ascended the hill. Shafts of noon sunlight streaked yellow between the trees, casting long blue shadows over the sparkling crystals. Each day the sun fell lower in its arc across the southern horizon. It was so weak now that only a few clouds on the skyline were enough to obscure it altogether.

I studied the tracks of the little invisible folk of the forest. Intricate paths marred the perfect snow, telling stories of the night. Hidden tunnels mined the snow and I stepped cautiously, my unseen feet punching into convoluted mansions buried beneath the surface of the snow.

Bunny "runs" were everywhere, I noticed. Young trees, bending under the weight of snow, were nibbled by the rabbits. Even spruce trees. A rabbit trail zagged under a fallen tree and I stooped to peer in. A foot of snow covered the trunk, raising the surrounding terrain and leaving a secret sunken place. With an exit. Rabbits never forget they are rabbits, fair game for every predator from owl to wolf.

It would be time to put on snowshoes soon, I thought, as I waded through the knee-high crystals onto a ridge that paralleled the river. I paused to check the wind direction. It was strange how erecting walls had separated me from the rest of life. I had never awakened in the tent without knowing the direction of the wind. How easy it is to lose track of the wilderness from inside a cabin. My life was now defined by a few logs. Somehow I had exchanged the Arctic for a safe and comfortable enclosure.

Ahead of me I spotted the caribou trail, a single deep set of tracks, wending through the stunted spruce. Their hooves were nearly as large as those of the moose and very round, snowshoes for an animal a fraction the size. Apparently they had all stepped in the same tracks to save energy breaking trail. I could see where they plunged for the river, and I followed the path through the thick aspens. It ran steep and straight, avoiding the worst thickets until it emptied over a ledge, sliding to the river below. I could not climb down the icy cliff, but sought out the trail with my eyes, tracing it downstream, out and around the island. I could see where they hit overflow and the single track split to forty, joining again on dry ice. I turned back to find where they had come from.

Their broken trail was easy walking, the prints placed at close to my natural stride. It carried me overland above Olsen Creek, choosing always the best ground. Before me a vast tundra opened, climbing westward. Caribou know how to walk, I thought. Down one mountain and up the next. They are designed for a country where food grows slowly. My mother once told me if you see a caribou and it's not moving, it isn't a caribou.

Turning my back to the bitter wind, I stopped to view my valley. How big it looked from up here. Away from the sheltering trees, the wind was strong, burning my cheeks. The private sound of my heart thudding inside its rib cage and my gasping breath brought a warm feeling of comfort. I stared south into the setting sun, seeing a sparkle of falling frost squeezed from the clear yellow sky by the dropping temperature. Downstream a faint mist clung to the river where water had seeped from under the restless ice. The sun slid sideways as I watched, rolling along the crest of the southern peaks, until it glimmered out.

I gazed over the expanse, home of the caribou. Again I faced the wind and continued up, up, hearing only the crunch of my feet breaking through the crusted snow, the wild song of my heart and breath and the fierce, cold wind. What was it like to roam baggageless through this land? Finding food everywhere and a shelter within one's own hide? How limitless the horizon! I was caught for an instant in the flow of my stride, feeling the muscles contract rhythmically as I placed each hoof, hearing the familiar rustle of the other caribou about me as we scaled the mountain. I lowered my head against the wind, steam ripping from my frosted muzzle as I climbed. Up one side and down the other, entranced by the simplicity of owning nothing even in this unforgiving land of extremes.

The sky was brilliant in flaming clouds scattered over a flawless distant gold, but the land was dissolving in purple and blue. I glanced about, shrinking into my own puny body wrapped in clothing. I remembered my cabin and fire. Shoving my hands deeper into the pockets of my down parka, I turned from the stinging blast. Tears of cold were frozen to my lashes, and ice sheeted the collar of my parka where the wind crept under to burn my ears. I wiped a mittened hand across my dripping nose as I looked about a last moment before starting for home. Back to the cheery little haven of warmth and food. Back to the small space that made my life possible. I was only pretending to be free. I left the winter tundra to the caribou.

Phil and Chet danced out to greet my return. This was the first time we had been separated in a while.

"You just sit right there," he said, pushing me onto a crate as he stripped away my mittens and cap. I had to laugh. It was our usual routine, but it had lost none of its charm.

"Oh, look at the windows!" I exclaimed, hopping up half shod. Despite having worn Phil's boots with extra socks, my feet were burning with cold. "Why, they're beautiful! Just look at the view!" Two 18- by 34-inch Plexiglas windows of ten panes each now graced the south wall of the cabin, allowing the mountains to pour in. They were set in whittled frames of willow, snug and tight, and combined with the window in the door to brighten the cabin considerably. With the peeled yellow log walls, the place looked very inviting.

Phil beamed as I examined the windows in delight. "Now sit down," he insisted.

"Oh, Phil, you shouldn't have," I protested, as he placed a cup of REAL hot chocolate into my numb hands and knelt to unlace the remaining boot. "Such a treat. You drink half." I tousled his silky hair. What a difference a bath makes.

I took a sliver of wood and lit a tallow candle from the stove. It had taken us awhile to work out a good system for making candles for tallow melts more rapidly than wax. This candle had been cast in a tin can, removed, and rolled in paper. The paper held the melting fat so the candle would last longer. After an hour, we usually extinguished the flame and lit another.

"What'd you see?" Phil asked as I sat again upon the box.

"They came down Olsen Creek, like we thought, cutting high and straight for the river. Phil, they just walk right over mountains. They take the shortest route."

I sipped the scalding cocoa while he removed the felt insoles from my boots and hung them up to dry. I stretched my cold, stiff toes toward the stove. There were only three pieces of wood inside, and I opened the stove door and pushed one through.

"Firewood gobbler," Phil teased.

"I'm going to be warm this winter," I declared defensively.

"We'll both keep warm, you burning wood and me chopping it."

"Okay, I'll get wood today. Well, tomorrow," I amended, glancing around the darkening cabin. This living from hand to stove worried me, especially with so little daylight. At least the windows were finished, and I had almost completed chinking under the eaves. We had made a mistake in not laying moss between the rafters and plate logs when we put the roof on. The cabin leaked air, but there was nothing to be done now.

"I'll spend the whole day tomorrow adding to our woodpile, such as it is," I assured him. But my thoughts were back on the darkening mountain with the caribou, caught in the ceaseless ebb and flow of an endless journey, hypnotized by the rustle of countless hooves.

The cabin glowed with rich tones in the dancing light. Exaggerated shadows bounced over the uneven logs, causing them to waver, bringing designs to life. Each log was unique, a product of life and growth and weather, furrowed by bark beetles, and stained by water, sunlight and ax.

"I used to deliver flowers when I was in high school," I said suddenly. "The beauty of flowers is their only value, and I figured that since I enjoyed them, I owned them as much as the person I delivered them to."

Phil was silent, accustomed to my monologues. He picked up the pot of boiled meat we had eaten for breakfast and put it on the stove. The floor was cold, despite the warmth of the room, and the meat had frozen. I sat looking into the candle. Tallow had melted around the wick, forming a dark pool inside the paper.

"That's the way I feel about land," I went on. "At best you get a lifetime tenure. And what's a lifetime to this earth?" Through my thoughts, like a whispered mantra, stirred the wandering hooves. I took scissors and trimmed the candle wick.

"Why is it," I asked, gazing out the windows, "that I stay inside so much? I should be out climbing mountains."

"Or chopping wood," he countered.

I glanced at him and returned to my mountains. I rested my elbows on the new windowsill, my breath fogging the panes. The peaks were light silver against the darker sky. A full moon sat fatly in the lavender east, lighting the world below. I felt Phil's arm slide around me. Together we watched. Color faded from the land and sky. Deep shadows striped the hillside as the cold moon climbed slowly over the peaks, luminous white against the royal blue.

"I could shoot two hundred yards by such moonlight," Phil said at length. It was true. The brilliant moon highlighted the snowy ridges, etching in every tree. The mountains gleamed like white satin beneath an inky sky. I could feel their call.

"All my life I've been seeking the 'essence' of experience," I said wistfully. "It's that elusive something that makes the world sparkle. Sometimes I can almost smell it. But I reach out and it dissolves. It can't be held." Down the silent valley wafted the voice of an owl.

"Sometimes I want to run out and embrace the Arctic," I went on after a minute. "I can see it over there, so clearly, way up where the mountain meets the sky. Calling . . ." I ran my fingers over the window panes, caressing the peaks. "Surely there! is the real Arctic." We were silent for a while, watching the faraway pass, so near in the moonlight. "But what would I find? More wilderness miles," I answered myself, "and the essence on the ridge somewhere beyond."

"You'd be cold," Phil said.

"It isn't real, is it?" I asked. "The essence? It's more like a memory of something. Like a memory of a smell."

"And that's not real?"

"Well, it's not something I can discover out there."

The owl continued his monotonous song. "Who? . . . who-who . . . who? . . . who?"

"You think too much."

I glanced back at him fondly, my friend Phil the spruce tree. He rested his chin on my shoulder and I pressed my back into his warmth. Moonlight filtered over the hushed valley. An element of sadness had stolen upon me, a strange nostalgia for this very moment as if I were remembering it from some distant future.

Taking him by the hand, I stepped to the door and opened it. Night suddenly flooded in, cold and vast and real. We closed the door behind us and entered that different world, shrinking to specks in the Cosmos. The owl had ceased, and I heard only the squeal of snow underfoot and the quiet hiss of my breath freezing and falling like snow in the sub-zero air.

"How silent it is," Phil whispered. I started to shiver. The smoke from our stovepipe cast crazy shadows on the moonlit snow. "Come, let's go back in," he said softly.

"Listen," I requested. The silence beat upon our empty ears. Not a sound. Nothing. My mind stretched into the wilderness night, listening. It was different from the muffled silence of falling snow which sucks up every noise. Neither was it the silence of plugged ears. This was the clear, cold music of thousands of miles of nothing to hear.

We lingered, breathing it in. "It's the silence of a million ears," I said at last. "Of life, waiting."

☙

A few days later, I set off up the hill to check my snares. In the cold clear dawn, the pink frosted mountains above Olsen's Creek stood out sharply against a pearl-gray sky. I had my wood-hauling slings and ax held loosely in one hand and smiled to myself, thinking of my mother's words, "Never return to camp without a load of wood." I suppose every daughter gets advice upon leaving home, but mine seemed more practical than most. "Don't shoot a moose in the water," she had told me. She also said to never pee on a fire, but like everyone else, I had to find things out for myself.

I felt a strange happiness as I entered the Cathedral of Trees. I left the packed trail, my snowshoes sending up billows of white as I climbed. I stopped, knee-deep in morning-blue snow, ax in hand, to view my world.

Overhead boiled the flaming clouds of dawn. The mountains floated like strawberry ice cream, protruding like islands from a sea of mist. How big it all looked! The sky stretched forever up and out, bordered in clear, sharp horizons and inked-in spruce. Nearby naked birch were silhouetted against a canary yellow sky. Somewhere below, a tiny cabin was nestled, folded into the hill, hidden even from any low-flying plane by the size of the Arctic.

Tired of waiting, Net-Chet floundered by, stepping onto my snowshoes as she plunged into the deep, soft snow ahead. She was trailing harness from the leather work collar given to her by Chris Olsen. She had business of her own, searching out secrets with her licorice-tipped nose. She told me a good deal, pointing out the doings of our neighbors.

Between the trees, I could see the river. I spotted a dozen caribou crossing the ice below the islands. We had shot one the day before, a poor animal, infested with parasites and devoid of fat. When I dressed him out I could find no bullet hole. Soon I uncovered the mystery. Phil had taken aim at one animal and hit another. The bullet entered near the anus, traveled through the body, and ruptured the liver. I smiled, shaking my head. Hey, Phil! Show us your famous liver shot!

"Okay, Chet. I'm coming," I told the impatient dog.

It was the last of October. What does that mean? I wondered. A moose, a sunrise, a storm. The leaves fall. The ice goes out when it's ready. We divide up life and call it time. With subtle currents, the wilderness was drawing me into its seasonal rhythms. The days spread out before me, almost as in childhood, an unstructured, undivided, now.

I climbed the ridge, and Net-Chet fell impatiently in behind me. The land was softened in smooth undulations where snow blanketed bushes or was lifted against the trunks of trees. Along the exposed muskeg, trees were stunted, and the wind had packed dunes which I alternately clumped over or plowed through.

I came to a group of trees and stood a moment, studying them. They were all probably the same age, though they varied greatly in size and conformation. Some had grown too close together. Others had been broken under snow or gnawed by animals or they grew on hidden rocks. That accounted for the differences. They were too old to benefit greatly from thinning, still it wouldn't hurt to remove the dead and dying. I enjoyed my role as tree friend.

I examined my tree. It had been killed the summer before, and a few yellow needles remained. Life was hard long before spruce beetles finished the job. I scraped my ax over the bark, peeling it easily away. Stepping back, I planted my snowshoes firmly and swung from the hips. The double-bit sank deeply with the solid "thunk!" of a green tree. I looked up in surprise in time to catch a face-full of snow. Yes, there was one green twig. I shrugged and swung again.

The next tree was truly dead, naked and practically limbless. The wood was twisted, and I could see the weathered grain spiraling upward. I was reluctant to clear away the brush for a good swing, but better to kill willows than feet. Besides, you can't kill willows, for they spring up stronger than ever from the roots the next summer. Cautiously, I knocked the snow free, butting the head of my ax against the trunk.

The familiar ring of dry wood echoed across the valley as I penetrated the years, scattering the snow with yellow chips. What had this old fellow witnessed through the endless swing of seasons? I tried to picture a green shoot, a sapling, a struggling pole. At one point, the snow had broken his crown, but gamely he had sent forth three more, crooked and spindly, yet a push for life. What could I learn from a tree? Was it conscious of me? I imagine we are too skittish to attract the attention of trees. I would need to sit for a month beneath one to be noticed. Life wasn't easy here. Maybe it never is. Hardship keeps a species strong. And individuals too, I suppose. Hardship is Life's ally.

I finished my main cut, then called Chet behind me while I sank a second notch on the opposite side. The sun was already disappearing sideways into the snow-covered peaks to the south. The clouds were brilliant red in its last rays, reflecting off the hills. The butt of the tree was rotten, making it tricky. After a few swings, I leaned on the tree and pushed. It heaved to and fro, then sheared forward in a loud twisting of splinters. There it hung in another tree while I flopped about, tripping over my snowshoes, trying to free it. This is life, I thought, as I grunted and strained. All the little failures and triumphs. No heroic leaps, no mighty lunges. Real heroism isn't heroic.

I limbed my trees, cutting the larger one in half. The top I fastened to Chet's harness and took the heavier portion for myself. My sling was a simple strip of nylon webbing sewed to form a large circle. By looping it under the end of a log and through itself, the sling tightened and formed a hand hold enabling me to drag logs weighing several hundred pounds. Together Chet and I hauled our loads back to the Cathedral, where I had my snares.

At first I thought the rabbit had gotten away, so complete was his camouflage. Then I saw the bloody, trampled snow and the frozen little white carcass. I could reconstruct the nighttime struggle of a frightened creature. This had happened while I ate or slept or read. And I had caused it. The rabbit had its head and both front feet through the snare and had taken quite awhile to die, tearing the skin from his slender legs. My cunning prey diminished to a terrified bit of life.

I picked up the body, retrieving my ax, and started homeward, dragging the firewood. I didn't reset the snare.

Twilight had deepened and the valley below was wrapped in soft blue-gray. I could see the frozen river through the treetops and the silver mountains beyond, light against a darker sky. The cold air was as quiet as only the Arctic can be. I stopped, feeling the vast wilderness miles. I knew that there was nothing but Arctic forever. Man had never been here. I was alone, alone perhaps on the planet.

But I was not alone. My mind became aware of another in the glade. I felt Chet stiffen behind me. Together we watched the white form of a wolf materialize from the snow, making itself known to us as if by choice. The wolf, parent of one I had eaten, studied us, human and dog. In the gathering gloom we three faced one another until the wolf, finished with the encounter, turned and melted like smoke into the dusk.

Coming down the skid trail was easy. Gently it ran, a firm white trough opening before me through the deep snow and ladened trees. I felt like a sled as swiftly I descended with my dragging wood, rounding one smooth turn after another. Quite suddenly the trees became taller and more dense. I rounded a corner and saw the meat racks. A hard turn around the toilet hole, and out of nowhere sprang a snug little cabin, cradled in the hillside. Smoke puffed from the stovepipe into the still evening air, and outside a man was splitting wood.

I was somehow surprised to see them there, the man and the cabin. The scene was so comfortable and homey, it seemed out of place in this wild spot. I greeted him and we went inside together and lit a candle, for already the darkness of a Halloween night was upon us.

Phil sat on a corner of the stove stand. On one side of the cabin, the birch skeleton of a high bed was beginning to take shape among knee-deep piles of shavings. Underneath would be Net-Chet's nest and the woodbin. The poles of the bed frame were mortise-and-tenoned together. It was pinned into the back wall of the cabin and into the joists below. The surface was of spruce logs planed on three sides and precisely fitted together.

We had decided to celebrate Halloween with "cranberry upside-down cake." One of the nicer gifts from old Chris was an oven. It was a rusted sheet metal barrel about a foot in diameter that fitted between the sections of the stovepipe. Inside was a smaller barrel, forming a flattened donut. Smoke traveled up the pipe, between the barrels and back into the pipe. It was an ingenuous device that baked and added heat to the room.

"I've been thinking we should take a trip when the sun comes back,"

Phil said unexpectedly.

I looked up quizzically from cooking.

"There are some old mines on the map, and we might find one in operation," he continued. "Most are at least forty miles away and far above timberline, but maybe we could mail out some letters. And get some treats."

"I know where your mind is," I laughed. "My poor, starved L'ammal." I reached over and pinched a roll. He squealed indignantly and lunged for mine.

"Not fair!" I shrieked, batting him off.

Soon a tempting aroma enveloped the cabin. As Phil lifted the hot cake pan with his pliers, it slipped, seeking its rightful position, upside-down on the floor. Undaunted, we plopped down beside it, spoons in hand. When the last wood shaving had been spit out, the maid was called in. With quick pink tongue, she polished the boards.

Phil tried to look bashful as he suggested one more little treat. "After all, it is Halloween," he argued.

While he read aloud by candlelight, I put the flour sacks to soak. Chet had finished the boards, happy with her unexpected good fortune, and was attempting to nose into the sleeping bags with Phil. He scratched her ears absently as he read. The greenish lumps of flour soon softened, and I worked them free with my fingers, kneading them into a thick paste. I added baking soda to sweeten the glop and it reacted with the cranberries. Soon the oven was filled with bloated cranberry sludge, bubbling and burning. We choked it down, smiling at one another and declaring how "not too bad" it was, eyes smarting from the ammonia reek that almost masked the taste of mold.

"We must be getting spoiled," I commented, an unwelcome burp rising in my throat.

Phil stretched and loosened his belt a notch.

Outside the long low howl of a single wolf echoed musically down the river. I trimmed the paper about the candle, and lit another. Quietly we sipped tea into the evening, playing chess on a miniature board as we waited for the trick-or-treaters who never came.

*

November days slipped by in gathering darkness, crystal days of pale skies and flamboyant clouds, back-lit by the vanishing sun, days as soft as goose down. November nights were long and sharp, as clean as glass beneath the dazzling moon or bathed in the silky blackness of stars and aurora borealis.

These nights were filled with talk of new adventures. From our very doorstep ran a great highway, a river now stilled in winter's sleep, that would carry us over the earth. In dream it stretched before us, connected south to the Yukon and then to the Bering Sea and on to the World. Our minds traced other arteries which, with years of toil, would lead at last to Hudson Bay and the mighty Atlantic: the inland Northwest Passage. We were tireless those long nights, hauling our austere outfit over passes and up nameless rapids through the years ahead, as snow drifted on our doorstep and the candle burned low.

"We could get by on much less than we had this time," one of us would say.

"We would have to," the other would agree, between bites.

And on we dreamed, making lists of equipment and plotting routes. Our biggest frustration was in not having access to information. Like food, it was something I had always taken for granted. The only references we had were stored in our heads or in the cherished few volumes of our library.

We spent much time together, one crafting candles or furniture or mukluks and the other reading aloud by candlelight. To our surprise, we found much pleasure in the dictionary and the almanac. Hardly a day went by that we did not settle a question with the "answer books." It was amazing how many topics arose in conversation, and like Pandora's box, once the books were opened, all sorts of things popped out. We finished the New Testament, but were finally lost somewhere in Israel with Moses and his Arc of many rituals. No, that was not what I was looking for, not a system, not a belief.

I had come seeking to the end of the earth and yet there was still that call. Well, seek and you will find, I thought. Don't and you won't. Some of us seem born to the quest.

Vaguely we knew that November is the month of national elections and wondered idly who had run and who had won. It didn't seem to make much difference in our world up here.

We talked of all these things as the sun dropped from sight and snow drifted in ever changing patterns over the river. Then one day the sun didn't come up and we entered the northern night, a time of white moons and northern lights and frost flowers on window panes. The day, unborn, became a dawn where the sun burned its fiery path forever out of sight, setting flame to the clouds for hours at a time while it slid from east to west below the southern horizon. Peace settled upon us, and like the tiny things we are, we walked under that great painted sky, gathering our firewood and dragging it home.

Beneath Phil's patient hands our bed grew, one hand-planed log at a time, until a high platform emerged. I read aloud while he worked. I sat among the mounds of wood shavings, speaking above the rhythmic swing of the plane. Net-Chet would lie with her head in my lap, honey eyes watching everything. She had become quite a beauty, her gold and white fur now tipped with black, the showy coat reaching a billowing length of up to ten inches in places. She was usually too hot inside, but endured it for our companionship.

As she entered adulthood, we had decided to feed her once a day. She responded by promptly exhuming a quarry of ancient bones, many left by an unfortunate cow moose some time before our arrival. These proved devoid of all but moss. She nevertheless greeted them as old friends. Even the wolf bones returned from their resting place on the Snackbar, proof that she sometimes strayed afield.

She had settled comfortably into our lives, deciding when we should awaken mornings. At night she became our shrew trap, thundering over our sleeping bodies in pursuit of her tiny prey. By day she watched for hours outside the door. As patient as a glacier, she waited for something to move. Her lonely vigil wasn't always in vain. While some animals sleep away the cold night, many must travel the land in search of food. Sometimes we would see a lean wolf slipping along the far shore. More often we would hear them talking across the distance. Who am I to say that wolves do not care about one another or that they do not say so? It was a wild and beautiful song to hear at midday dawn, cutting through our conversation in deep and haunting tones.

How did they make it, day by day, I wondered? Finding and catching food in the deep snow, traveling forever in the cold? And the tiny chickadees in the dark: what do they eat and how do they keep their match-stick legs from freezing at forty and fifty and sixty below? How do fish breathe under the thick ice? What do they do down there in the dark all winter?

There was a fox whose rounds took him along the distant bank. After alerting us with a low "Woof!" Chet would watch him, her tail twitching like a cat. The fox appeared almost to glide over the shoreline, cocky in his feather weight.

Rabbits are never cocky. Sometimes they would venture onto the exposed river, humble frightened creatures, but curious nonetheless. I never actually saw one out there, for they were scarce and invisible in their snowy garb, but I often saw tracks. Once I trailed the hippity-hop tracks of a brave rabbit onto the ice. It was followed closely by little leaping ermine paws. A fresh page of river snow told of the ermine's sudden veer and then nothing. Owl wing tips touched the snow where the hunter had become the hunted and the trail vanished.

Most of life went on quietly, hidden from us by darkness. In nocturnal

visits out-of-doors, I would stand gazing into the galaxy where stars like searchlights flashed colors from the velvet of space. Shivering in long underwear, I stood barefooted on the packed, sub-zero snow, the breeze on my behind reminding me of my mortality. We were timid nighttime creatures. Furtively I would glance into the shadows, feeling soft and fragile without clothing. Edible in my nakedness, I faced the Arctic with humility.

Like soundless music the northern lights would ripple above me. Awed by the vast stillness, I strained to hear. Great curtains of flame were flung across the night to stand trembling for another whiplash or fade, reappearing somewhere else. Giant castles of green and red would burst like flowers, sending stairways of light tripping across the stars. How could I hold it? I felt my body heavy upon me, the weight of gravity forcing me down. I would fly, soaring with the auroras this night, swirling joyously into the misty light, dancing over the earth, expanding into nothing and everything. I could almost remember . . . when was it? Like a sparrow I flitted inside my head, searching, searching until the cold ache of my bare feet reclaimed me. And I would scurry back to bed filled with happy wonder and a great sense of loss.

I recall standing one morning in the lee of Timber Island. It was snowing, the valley a misty gray about me. The only sound was the hiss of windblown snow. Before me a packed trail, drifted and marked with sticks, led into the falling snow to home. Then the faint, peculiar tone of Phil whistling "Summertime" came to my ears, so out of place. Far upstream a single wolf called, pulling me into kinship. I stood listening, reluctant to turn homeward with my load of firewood, but it did not come again.

As I neared the cabin twenty caribou caught my eye, sprinting downstream behind Timber Island. I dropped the wood and headed for the island with the hope they might afford me another look. It was difficult going in the deep snow, off the trail. Wind had packed the dunes just enough to necessitate lunging forward before punching through. How do the caribou manage, I wondered? Slowly I circled the island, seeing many tracks, but no deer. They had all come down Olsen Creek, heading east. Had our cabin been a mile upstream or down, we would have missed seeing them altogether.

I rounded the last island and faced homeward into the wind. But soon overflow forced me to retreat, my feet wet by the treacherous invisible water that sometimes seeps over the ice, hidden by snow. I cut between the two downstream islands, walking cautiously, my cap pulled down over my ears. I could see the tiny cabin ahead, so far away in the driving snow, so distant in all that space. When I arrived, my boots were full of slush, my socks frozen to them.

Our long-awaited Thanksgiving Day dawned warm and snowy. While Phil organized the cabin, I set about the last minute preparations for our royal dinner.

I had never had a real Thanksgiving before. Not that I hadn't eaten myself into a yearly stupor, but it didn't mean anything. Why should it? For weeks we had rationed our treats that this might truly be a day of celebration. We put on special shirts for the occasion. We set out plates and silverware. The cabin was tidy, belongings now stashed on new shelves or in bins.

The beans, bread, and blueberry pie were baked the day before. I worked happily preparing gravy, rice, dried vegetables, and cranberry sauce while the two stuffed grouse baked. I thickened the cranberries with flour, turning them an odd color, "like a lung-shot moose," as Phil poetically put it. Our treats would probably not have excited most refined palates. We often conserved sugar by substituting saccharin. Bear lard was our butter. The little oven didn't bake evenly. Our fresh foods were meat and berries, and we had little in the way of spices or variety. "Cranberry upside-down cake" was cranberries and saccharin topped with cornmeal, flour, lard, and baking powder; "chocolate moose" was candy made of tallow, sugar, powdered milk, and cocoa.

Last of all, I mixed up blueberry ice cream using berries, powdered milk, and a lot of fresh, fluffy snow. We set all the food on the bed and lit the lantern ceremoniously for a picture. Whenever I see that picture now, what I notice is that the ice cream is pushed to the front of the pan to make it look larger. We had wanted to impart to those who saw the picture later some of the thankfulness we felt.

We ate slowly by lantern light, reluctant to finish, recounting our blessings aloud to one another. A short while before we had no home, no winter food, no place to get warm, and a dog with a broken leg. Now we sat amidst abundance and were truly thankful. Of all the people sitting down to dinner this day, perhaps we were the most fortunate.

December came, cold and dark. As Christmas neared, we set out to cut a tree. We climbed the hill and entered the Cathedral Grove. The hill was cloaked in the exquisite serenity of new snow, the trees bending beneath it. Within a few days, a wind would free them, but now the woods seemed buried in mounds of white. I studied the frosted alder catkins in the cold blue twilight of December noon. They looked like tiny pine cones on bare sticks. Already the virgin blanket of snow was decorated in the minute train tracks of shrews, in one tunnel and out the next.

"I hate to cut one," I admitted, knocking a load of snow from a small spruce tree with my mittens.

"We don't have to," Phil answered.

"No," I insisted, resolutely. "We're going to have a Christmas tree. We can find a group that needs thinning." We hadn't figured out where we would put it, but we'd find a place. Phil had handcrafted the 32nd and final board of our bed, and we had moved to that warm and lofty sleeping place, leaving additional room on the floor.

"We've got a yard full clear to the horizon if you want, and we don't have to cut them."

"I want something I can decorate." I had been crocheting strings of colored yarn to put on the tree. After Christmas I planned to unravel them to knit mittens and socks, but now I wanted a tree.

Like children we were awaiting Christmas and, just as important to us, the winter solstice, when the sun would begin the journey back. We pretended not to notice as we sewed down booties as presents for one another. These would be our much-needed indoor footgear, protecting us from icy floors. When we wore boots in the cabin, the inevitable perspiration made for cold feet outside. I was knitting us each a new pair of socks and mittens for Christmas. Phil had almost completed mukluks for himself. I was to inherit his summer boots with plenty of room for extra insulation.

He was studying the grove. White ice masked his face, and only the eyes peered from under his hoary brows. Chet whined and I leaned sideways to let her scoot past. She burrowed by me along the waist-deep trough left by Phil's snowshoes. Abruptly she stopped and plunged her head deep into the side of the trail, leaving me her furry wagging behind for company. Satisfied with the news, she withdrew and wallowed up the hill after Phil, curly tail plume marking her progress.

I breathed happily of the cold air, rubbing the frost from my sticky eyelashes with my mittens. It was forty-five below zero. Christmas time. How are you, Dear Ones? Where are you today? I wish I could tell you what became of the two who set forth on the Yukon in an overloaded canoe that summer day so long ago. How I wish that I could share it all with you.

I trudged through the thickets of young trees, studying their tops. The best ones of course didn't need thinning. A trail of broken spruce tassels marked our progress up the hill, for trees are brittle at very cold temperatures. It's surprising how much colder minus forty is than minus twenty. You would think that "cold" would be "cold."

"How's it look to you?" Phil asked when I came up to him.

I smiled. "Better a scrawny tree," I agreed. "No reason to take the best." None of ours would have made the grade down south. Chet curled up and began chewing ice balls from between her toes as Phil cleared the deep snow away from the base of the little sleeping tree.

"Oh, what the heck, Phil," I said suddenly. "You're right. We've got a world of live ones. Let's enjoy them."

We grinned at each other, Phil over his ice beard, me with my flaming red cheeks. "We're old softies, both of us," he told me.

Hello out there! I thought joyfully. We linked arms and descended homeward together, clouds of new powder snow billowing about us as we cascaded down the slope. I hope you're as happy as we are this Christmas. From my window I will have the world with thousands of Christmas trees, no two alike, each one carefully decorated in purest white.

Chapter 8

JANUARY WAS the month of cold.

The early Norsemen are said to have had a calendar consisting of ten months with thirty days in each. The remainder of the year didn't count. Having neither fuel nor food to combat winter, families spent much time sleeping, not unlike some Arctic animals, until the sun returned.

It seemed like a reasonable system to us.

As the thermometer plummeted and darkness claimed the frozen land, layers of ice built upon our windows and white frost crusted the lower inside walls. Because of poor chinking under the eaves, we lost much heat into the vacuum-like cold outside. Wary of the hungry cold, we stayed close to home. It was an unknown, this temperature ranging perhaps 150 degrees below that of the human body. It was a cold that could suck the animal warmth from a creature in minutes, leaving a lifeless shell — a vast, waiting, all-devouring Cold.

Late dawn would steal upon us, sometimes soft and poignant as a solitary distant flute, sometimes with the grandeur of a full orchestra. Daily we made our little excursions for wood, always together. We would put on our down britches and parkas and set off hand in hand into the great pastel twilight.

At fifty-five below each breath comes like a drink of ice water. Snow squeals underfoot and axes are brittle. I was making trips from Timber Island with Chet, hauling small dead trees as Phil cut them. Net-Chet enjoyed the work, throwing herself gamely into the harness when I called out "Move!" She struggled along the packed trail, pulling her weight in wood, pausing now and then for me to catch up. A puff of wind, a breath too faint to stir a dried leaf, trailed from the north, and I stopped a moment to warm my cheeks in my wooly hands. I must knit more mittens soon, I thought. Logs are rough on yarn.

When I faced the breeze again I could hear the familiar hiss of my breath colliding with cold air, and see it falling in a fine snowstorm around me. I bowed into the breeze, pulling against the weight of wood, and resumed trudging. Chet turned without a word from me and pulled for home.

The cold made me uneasy. There's a deadly seriousness about fifty-five below. It was the ultimate test of our cabin and our wood pile. Still, we had passed the solstice, the darkest part of winter, and although I couldn't see it, we were on our way back into summer. I glanced back at the island, a frozen still life in pink and gray, remembering the sounds and bustle of summer. I shook my head, doubting if the sun would ever again penetrate this land.

At the base of our hill I unhitched Chet. She bounded before me heading back to the island, eager for another load. Ahead I could hear the steady, clear knock of an ax. The land lay soft about me and in the distance, the pearly peaks light against a deep violet sky. The moon, three-quarters full, hung low in the northeast. Net-Chet rolled happily in the snow, toboggan-ing along, propelled by her hind legs as she rubbed the frost from her snout, dry-cleaning her coat. Then she shook to fluff the fur. Her fur always smelled fresh, as did her breath, the clean land and meat diet keep-ing her in top health.

On the open river, snow was drifted in scalloped dunes, frozen waves built by the wind. A line of upright sticks marked the packed trail from home to the island. It was difficult to see the trail, for the drifting snow smoothed it over, but there was a raised ridge under the surface and you knew when you missed it. Chet leapt sideways and bucked forward a mo-ment in the deep snow. She galloped playfully around me, harness traces whipping out behind.

We found Phil back in the trees, cutting the limbs from an old dead spruce tree. He was swathed in an orange down parka, blue wool cap, and red down pants.

"My feet are cold," he told me, bisecting the log with a final swing of his double bit ax. "Let's head on in." He smiled at me through a glacial beard. Only the big green eyes gazing from beneath the white eyebrows were fa-miliar. His long dark lashes were frosted exotically. I could see mine too, white with the growing crystals. They felt gummy and glued together. I rubbed them a moment with a mittened hand and blinked to clear my vi-sion.

Already dawn was fading into winter dusk. A shifting land of purple snow lay before us on the trail home. Across the white desert, once a river, I could just make out a cabin tucked back in the dark trees. I found it by the sluggish puff of smoke. Chet whined impatiently, holding one foot and then another off the snow while I prepared her load.

"Move!" I called, and she threw herself forward. The log snagged in brush, and she glared angrily back at me. I kicked it free. "Move!" I sang out once more. And off she struggled.

I grabbed my sling and tugged a log out into the open, slowly crossing the ice homeward. Phil fell in behind, hauling the heavy butt end of the tree. His ax, stuck in the top of it, plowed into the snow as the log twisted. He stopped to reposition it.

"Good dog," I told Chet as we reached the cutbank before the cabin. I unhitched her and started back to help Phil. Together we pulled and the big log slid quickly after us. We arrived home panting. I curled my tongue over my front teeth and the frigid air whistled around it, warmed on the way to my lungs.

"You have a white spot on your cheek," Phil told me. Frostbite looks dead and waxy, a peculiar color of gray-white.

I held my hand over it a moment. He had given up wearing glasses and his belt buckle because of frostbite. Any metal next to the skin conducts the heat away. I had removed my little gold earrings and Phil had threaded a piece of fishing line with a couple of beads on it through my ears to keep the holes open.

Frost swirled about our legs as we entered the cabin, clouds of snow born in the assault of cold air on warm. Phil shut the door behind us just as Chet decided she wanted in.

"You moaned?" he asked with exaggerated politeness, opening the door. He had been training her to shake before entering. It is equivalent to teaching a person to sneeze. She would twist her head from side to side, trying to work up to it. Chet wagged in with another burst of frost and looked about for her dinner.

"Not yet," I said. "Go to your corner." She trudged sullenly to her stall under the bed, looking back to see if I was watching. With an elaborate sigh, she dropped into the shavings and sat licking the ice from between her toes while we shed our parkas and "hot pants." The windows were darkened with sheets of ice. When Phil lit a candle, the lower walls where we had used green logs sparkled white with frost crystals.

I built up the fire and put Chet's bowl on the stove to thaw. Anything left on the floor froze solid. Then I reached into Mightypot for a frozen slab of ribs and placed them in a pan in the frail old stove pipe oven. Phil was already perched on the bed removing his canvas and moose hide mukluks.

"I think we should bring in a moose hide and carpet the floor," I said, climbing onto the bed. We sat up high much of the day, reading and working on projects. Chet snaked her head out and whined irritably, wanting to be up with us. I glanced at her and she turned away meekly, folding one ear back. Then she shot me a petulant look and whined once more, very softly.

"Those skins are as hard as plywood," Phil answered, ignoring the dog. "We'll have a hard time fitting one in. But it's a good idea. I need some more rawhide too. I'm going to build a hand sled for our trip to the mine. I'll make a frame of birch and stretch the hide over the bottom."

To make rawhide, we cut a piece of skin and soaked it until it softened and began to rot. Then the thick hair was easier to scrape off. If we were making long strings of rawhide for lacing snowshoes or other such uses, we dried the naked skin and cut it in a diminishing circle, creating one continuous string. This was soaked again before use.

It was warm on the bed. The tea pot soon began to boil, spouting steam. I put on my down booties and hopped down to make tea.

"I have no idea how we'll soak that much hide," he continued.

"We could use the water bucket and hang it from the ridge pole so it wouldn't freeze," I suggested.

Phil took his mug and sat thinking. "We're going to need pemmican for the trip, too," he said after awhile. "And I want to design pack saddles for Chet."

I peeked into the oven, then shut the flimsy little door. Returning to the warmth of the bed, I crossed my legs under me. It was growing quite dark in the cabin. The only sounds were the crackling of the fire and the occasional pop of burning wood. I sighed, staring into the yellow candle flame.

Another low moan came from beneath the bed, and I looked down to see Chet staring impatiently up. "Her food is probably ready," I said to no one in particular, and slid from the bed, clicking my tongue for her.

I studied the cabin, wondering where we could dry meat for pemmican. Along the east wall was the bed and kitchen shelves. Phil's shop area took up the southwest. The stove was in the middle. And everywhere underfoot were piles of shavings. Phil generated them faster than we could burn them, making fire a constant danger. We had a close call once when the gas lantern had been knocked down, breaking the glass chimney and shooting a jet of flames into the shavings.

"We can string the meat between the purlin and ridge pole," I decided. Phil glanced up, obviously caught in other thoughts. "If we take a darning needle with heavy nylon twine, we can simply sew it through the meat so it won't fall down. Then we can hang the string from nails in the rafters."

★

The "way-belows," as we called temperatures of less than forty below zero, broke in mid-January with a snowstorm. It rarely stayed that cold for more than a fortnight. Within the warmth of the cabin we made plans by candlelight and talked of our coming journey to the mine. We sat inside, lulled by the singing trees and the gray thundering ocean of wind while snow drove over the river and a tireless blizzard raged on for days.

"I never thought a windy twenty below would seem balmy," Phil said, shutting the door behind him. I caught a glimpse of dove-gray before the cabin returned to the soft browns of kerosene lantern light. His arms were full of cut wood, which he dumped on the floor with a crash. He had been out splitting it in his shirt-sleeves. His beard was frozen, and he came towards me, a look of innocence on his face.

"Oh no you don't!" I warded off icy whiskers. "If you enjoy 'em, fine!"

I was leaning into Mightypot, scrubbing clothes. It was a hard job with little detergent and a scarcity of water. Because we had few clothes, we were loathe to part with them and they became very dirty. Unlike Chet's fur, the grease from our skins and the food we ate permeated the material even in the clean snows of winter.

"Holly's back," he said, indicating the window. It was now clear of ice. I left the clothes and went for a look. Phil started for the door to bring in more wood.

"Stay in awhile," I entreated, turning toward him. "Let them play. Ravens are shy of big people."

We crowded at the window, watching the daily spectacle. The large black bird sailed slowly upwind, beneath Chet's very nose, alighting heavily. Chet charged and the raven beat ponderously aloft, long midnight wings inching him upward a bound ahead of the dog. This would go on until Net-Chet tired of it. At first we had worried about Holly, for the act was very good. His moves were deliberately clumsy, his getaways painfully slow.

Net-Chet sat down, eyeing that elusive bird. Holly walked forward, short black legs stepping precisely over the packed snow. No response. He looked thoughtfully at some invisible tidbit, cocking his thick head to one side, and began to peck. That did it. Off they went again.

I know why a dog would play with a raven, but why would a wild raven come daily to play with a dog? I watched the big bird, sensing the rush of wind and snow. Above the storm I seemed to hear the whistle of air through his coarse pinions. Long had Net-Chet awaited a playmate, watching by the hour outside the cabin door. And the sky had sent a raven.

Phil was talking about our trip to the mine. ". . . and we can leave the meat outside for the two days we'll be gone on a trial run. But we should bring it all in when we leave for the mine to keep animals from getting it. This summer I want to build a meat-house so we won't have to worry next year."

We had been unable to figure out the use of a low structure at Chris's until we designed a meat-house. It was as big as the cabin and latched from the outside. I smiled at the thought of my anthropology teacher and his "ceremonial structures." Theories often discount the day to day existence of real people.

"I'd like to take our trial run as soon as the sun comes back," he added.

Outside Holly circled, gaining elevation. With a wild, musical call, he shifted, letting the wind catch him. Over the river he sailed, his form rapidly dwindling. For an instant he seemed to wink. I thought I saw him fall through the gray sky, flipping playfully in a roll. I stared, but could see only a raven disappearing into the falling snow.

Reluctantly I returned to doing laundry. Phil stepped out to retrieve a candle he had put on the wood pile to harden. He ducked back inside and ran into a face full of wet jerky, hanging from the rafters to dry.

"I'm ready to rinse," I said, wringing the last pair of long johns. They weren't exactly clean. Together we descended to the river carrying a pan full of clothes and the tea kettle. Phil had chopped a hole through four feet of ice and I stooped to skim out a bucket of water. With my fingers I brushed the floating chunks of ice over the edge, new ice forming even as I worked, and added a few cups of boiling water. This brought the pan up to ice cold. Quickly we rinsed and wrung the clothes. Then another pan and another. By the time we started back to the warm cabin, my fingers were stiff and blue.

The cabin was steamy with wet laundry. I set Mightypot on to heat and took a bath, washing my hair first and working down while squatting in the kettle. Then I heated a fresh bucket and ordered Phil in. His distaste for water had increased with cold weather.

Clean and dry, we turned out the kerosene lantern and lit a candle as the wilderness again settled into Arctic night. To the hypnotic bluster and howl of wind we ate a quiet dinner and curled up in bed together to read aloud by the flickering light.

After the candle was out, I lay for a long time, listening to the wind and thinking about our coming trip, wondering if we were making a mistake. Beside me was Phil's steady breathing, below me the hard wooden press of our narrow bed.

As my mind swirled down into sleep it was caught by the roar of wind. I drifted in a stream of voices, faint and rapid, yet distinct, as if I were eavesdropping on the Universe. They pattered through me, light and quick as rain, old and young in everyday mood, touching me here and there like feathers. I floated there awhile in a warm bath of Beings: tiny sparks within my mind. Then faint upon the wind I thought I heard a wolf call. I searched the ragged clouds for him, but the cry was not repeated.

A few days later the temperature dropped again, and through the melted space at the top of one window I could see the livid clouds of dawn streaming along the southern mountain crest. Any day now we will see the sun, I thought. It had been gone two months. I yearned for it. I fantasized about swimming pools and tanned skin and the taste of sweat upon my lip. Of green leaves and oranges and the dazzle of a summer afternoon.

"Well, we'd better go get wood," I sighed, reaching for my hanging boots. Chet flung her front paws onto the bed, smiling. She was always on the alert to unspoken commands and invisible signals. The slightest click, snap, whistle, or tap would suffice. Even an eye cast in her direction was invitation enough.

"You wanna go outside?" I asked, deliberately misunderstanding her.

She flashed me a meek "No," dropping one ear and turning her head to the side.

"Chet, you wanna go for a work?" Whenever we went out, she hauled or carried something to teach her to enjoy work. It seemed a good alternative to whips, the traditional method of training working dogs.

Oh, yes! Yes, yes! She sailed happily about the cabin, sweeping the furniture with her tail.

I pulled on several pairs of socks and Phil's big summer boots. Then I damped down the stove and ducked through the tiny doorway, fastening my parka. Maybe today we'll see the sun! I thought, exalted, as I sucked in the sub-zero air. Phil was already outside gathering snow in Mightypot to melt for water. The river had frozen clear to the bottom. He reentered the cabin and set the pot on the stove, then joined me.

Along the rim of the valley a curtain of clouds roiled, turning to molten flame. Suddenly a ray of sunlight leapt over the peak, licking past the corner of the world. Beyond the mighty Yukon it shot, northward over the frozen land. Pressing into the edges of the long Arctic night it raced, stretching its fingers out to us from the blackness of space. Up the Chandalar River, beyond the gold town, beyond the nameless rapids and bars, past Chris Olsen's place it flooded, filling our valley with sudden golden light. The long dark was over, leaving only a memory of sixty sunless days.

"The sun's back! The sun's back!" we shouted joyfully to one another as we danced and pointed and hugged.

Phil squatted on his slick-soled mukluks and slid down the steep hill. He sailed out over the bank and landed on the dog. They rolled happily together, legs and snow flying.

Phil was dusting himself off as the sun slipped sleepily away, dipping us back into familiar pastels. It had peeked up for only a couple of minutes. I joined him and together we headed for Timber Island. Chet's face split in a grin as she dashed around us. Phil smiled at me through his powdered beard and took my hand.

"Ow!" I complained, switching hands.

"I forgot your sore finger," he apologized.

I laughed. It seemed funny to bother about a cut. Last fall we had hardly noticed injuries, but now that we were safe and comfortable, each little scrape demanded attention.

The island was buried in snow, trees bent under it. Usually storms were ushered in and out by fierce winds, but this time the cold had returned in silence. Small trees sagged earthward, and I wondered how any survived to maturity. The majority appeared to be in various stages of tortured, twisted decline.

"Have fun," Phil called after me as I plodded slowly into the island, Chet following in the swath of my snowshoes. I was looking for dead trees and taking pictures while he bucked up the first log. I wanted a picture of Chet burrowing through the deep powder, but she was helpless off my broken trail and contented herself with plunging her icy beak into the tunnel wall, inhaling the secrets. I plowed through snow to my waist over a tangle of naked branches. Many sprang up as I shook them free, but others were snapped off or bent beyond repair. Birds had been among the alders, knocking the seeds from the catkins and picking them from the snow.

With my eyes only two feet above the snow, details of the little life were striking. Rabbit holes dove under submerged logs, hideaways created by the rising snow. Snow was swirled into dunes, false topography on the familiar island. I came upon a clearing, trees cut by people some long-ago winter. Their big caps of white were slanted out of the wind.

Such clearings are common on northern rivers. I have seen small valleys denuded of trees for mine timbers and firewood. Men burned the trees to thaw the ground for gold. Long after the gold is spent and forgotten, the holes remain. On tundra, where plant growth is slow and the bare ground absorbs sun, melting the permafrost, such pits may ooze almost forever. This is true any time the fragile sod is disturbed.

I stopped and listened. Out of the south came a low whistle of wind. To my right a burst of spray plotted the wind's course through the treetops. Another gust hit near me and I shielded the camera under my parka. The air was suddenly filled with flying crystals. As the trees about me flung off their burdens, I was deluged in snow. Fascinated, I watched this air-made-visible, as it touched the trees and shook them one by one. The sky had turned a delicate salmon color. I retraced my steps, shooting film between bursts of wind.

"What say we head for home," Phil called as I came into view, abominable snowwoman, my hair thick with snow. "I think we're in for a blow."

We labored along the familiar skid trail, dragging our logs. Looking back I could see a single blood-red cloud suspended in the liquid yellow southern sky. Out of the west came a vast shape of flying snow, whipped from the mountains and obscuring everything as it flew toward us. On it came, raging hundreds of feet high, a solid roiling wall of gray, devouring the valley. As it hit the nearby peaks it ripped the snow from their flanks and plumed it high aloft. Like rabbits we scurried for the shelter of our nest.

⋆

The day of our expedition dawned clear. We were off on a trial run of a few days with the dual purpose of breaking trail upstream and trying out our overland technique before setting off for the mine. We were up long before first light, tending to last minute details. By candlelight, we stuffed sleeping bags and balanced the dog's packs while she watched with anxiety, never letting us out of sight.

Sunrise found us a mile upstream. It was late February and the sun was rapidly returning. The day dawned crystal blue, sharp and bright beneath a pale sky. We left the wind-packed snow at the river bend and labored up the drifted cutbank into the dunes that covered the horseshoe swamp. All of us were packed heavy, prepared as for a week on Everest.

Near the top of the bank I stopped to catch my breath. Before us a quarter mile of muskeg cut across the loop of river. Deep snow, folded and dipped about scrawny trees, was crusted just enough to upset balance. I needed to raise my feet almost thigh-high, lunging onto the crust, only to break through with each step. Hidden sticks punched up through my snowshoes, tripping me. Net-Chet was impatient behind me, frequently stepping on my snowshoes. "Okay, smarty, you break trail," I told her, stepping aside to let her pass. She bounded ahead but was hopelessly bogged in deep snow and was soon forced to fall back. How do wolves do it? I wondered again.

The land looked softer under the snow, rounded and mellow. We hadn't been upstream since freeze-up. I made it to the far bend without falling down, wading through snow to my hips. Windblown, it had metamorphosed into coarse crystals that sang and crunched under foot like glass beads. When I came to the river again and started down the dunes that were packed against the bank, I floundered on my big feet and pitched face-down. My hands never hit ground, and it was some moments before I could shift my weight enough to lever myself upright.

151

Our shortcut across the bend had saved perhaps a mile, but taken time. Down on the wind-swept dunes the going would be easier. Across from us the blue-shadowed river wound like a desert, sterile and still. I tried to remember how it had looked, where the water ran. There was overflow down there, a turquoise streak of ice staining the center a hundred yards upstream. I sniffed uneasily, studying the silent snow.

I stood looking at the towering peaks, feeling small and bogged down in snow. There are so many levels to view things from, I thought. No matter where you stand, you can't see it all.

"Maybe going straight over the mountains would be best," Phil observed, catching my glance. That was the shortest way, and the driest. Before us the deceptive ice waited.

"Well, let's put in this upstream trail anyway and see how we fare sleeping out," I answered. Other people camp out in winter, I reminded myself as Phil led down the embankment.

Carefully we clumped along, sometimes backtracking from overflow. Where water had boldly gushed to the surface, cracking the ice under its weight, the exposed seep was often solid despite its malevolent appearance. But the innocent snow nearby could camouflage three feet of slush. The snow insulated these seeps even in the coldest weather, and often the only clue was the formation of ice feathers over the dunes or a faint uneasiness along the back of my neck.

I stopped and looked back questioningly at Phil. I was again in the lead as we switched off breaking trail.

"I think we should cut inland here," he answered, confirming my judgment. Another sweeping bend lay ahead where the river almost doubled back on itself. Cutting across the bend would be a hard trudge. I nodded, breathing into my mittens to warm my cheeks. Impatient at the delay, Chet was tromping a circle in the snow. She glared at me and whined.

"I'll break trail awhile," Phil offered.

I fell in behind him, scanning the landscape. It was difficult to pick out the lay of things under winter's disguise, but a muskeg must drain down through here. My elongated shadow stretched before me, undulating over the smooth frosting. Here and there bits of cotton grass poking through had drawn circles on the dunes where the wind had whipped them around. Stunted trees sprouted from the thick blanket, and many more snoozed out of sight, waiting to trip someone. Ptarmigan had been feeding in the willows near the bank, and their feather-footed tracks were scattered in the softer snow of thickets. About them the big prints of snowshoe rabbits touched lightly.

Phil thrashed on, cutting a trail inland. I fell into the steady swing of my stride and breathing, my ears muffled by my cap: the mantra of movement. There is a place of quiet between steps where the mind ceases to chatter and each rhythmic contraction is sufficient.

"Doesn't look good," I observed as once again we gazed upon the river. "I'll go first." The setting sun danced over the sleeping sprawl of islands, and we strained to pick out a course. The land lay still and blue before us, the sky a deeper blue above.

The snow was piled high, and it was a slow process descending to the river. Chet let me break trail to the packed dunes of the river bed and then jumped in front as I paused. She sprawled on the scalloped snow spread-eagle and wriggled backwards. Her feet had punched through to unseen water below.

"You stay there," I ordered Phil as I dropped my pack. Wearing his old boots with extra socks, I was less vulnerable than he in his canvas mukluks. "Wait'll I cut a path clear to the island."

I tried several spots along the shore as evening deepened. There were big trees on the island and we didn't want to camp in the open. Chet, now wary, stayed behind me. Softly I stole over the dunes, the unmarred white drifting beneath my scrutiny as I placed each foot. I was just congratulating myself on crossing when I noticed that Net-Chet had deserted me. Glancing back I saw my big snowshoe tracks filling with cold gray water. Only a bit further, I thought, and I'll reach shore. Suddenly I went in!

In panic I struggled to free my snowshoes, slush to my knees. They were caught under the thin crust and ladened with saturated snow. I lost my balance and pitched forward onto the snow. For the moment it held and did not drop me into the water. I fought free and crawled forward, dumping mounds of slush onto my down pants as the snowshoes flipped back on my heels. I scrambled to my feet, shaken but not seriously wet, in time to see Phil heading for me.

"No! Not here!" I waved at him.

When I reached the shore, I trudged downstream looking for good ice before starting back. My snowshoes were crusted with freezing slush that picked up snow, becoming heavier with every step. But the ice below me held. I cut over to my old trail, satisfied that it was basically dry. Chet might punch through in spots, but it would probably sustain Phil on snowshoes.

"I'm okay. Now give me my pack," I demanded. Phil was preparing to carry them both and looked doubtfully at my frozen pants and boots. "That ice won't take you with two packs," I countered reasonably. "I'm not badly wet."

We reached the island without further mishap. It was well timbered with large, somber spruce. We set about making camp in a sheltered hollow among their feet. Chet was disgusted with the idea of camping out. Relieved of her packs, she trampled a nest in the snow and glared at us as she chewed the ice from her paws and legs. Phil dropped a big dead tree, building a fire on layers of logs. Then he placed me before it and told me to change socks while he cleared a place for the tent. I put a pot of snow on the fire to start supper while my bootlaces melted free. It certainly was turning cold out. A deep blue silence flooded the land and a piercing chill that the blaze pushed back only a few feet.

Phil joined me by the fire, squatting in the snow, his arms resting on his knees. We had stamped down the deep crystals with snowshoes, but still his feet were buried. I offered him a scalding mug of tea. He cupped his mittened hands about it, sipping. In the fire warmth his frozen beard began to drip.

"It must be thirty-five, forty below," he observed, sniffing the calm air. The first star of evening glimmered low over the mountains to the north.

My bottom was getting cold despite down pants. I slipped a heavy down parka over the everyday one and shifted my weight on the log. Nearby, my thirty-pound showshoes leaned sadly against a tree. I thought for a moment of working with them, but decided on supper first.

"We didn't come very far," I said, lifting the lid from the boiling pot to stir. In fact we weren't far from where I killed the moose last fall. The big fire crackled merrily, sending clouds of steam into the darkening trees. There it clung in tiny crystals, frosting the needles in misty white. About us the old trees leaned like sleeping sentinels enclosing our camp.

"Too far for her," Phil smiled, indicating Net-Chet. She was curled in the snow, wrapped in her fur stole of a tail. Lengthy fur britches combined with her tail plume to cover her feet and nose so that little heat was lost. She withdrew her long face to register a sour complaint. I got up to dig out drymeat for her dinner.

Net-Chet was not a wolf and she knew it. She might play Wild Dog of the North, remembering perhaps some racial heritage as she stalked shrews, but her ancestors had relinquished their power to survive alone in trade for a relationship with mine.

Chet had finished her meal and sat grumpily by me a moment. I noticed that snow was melting into her fur. She wasn't designed for fires. The cold bit deeper as darkness thickened about the three of us, age-old companions in a wilderness.

"Why don't moose get frostbite?" I asked suddenly, breaking a long silence.

"Or do they?" Phil countered, raising his head from some reverie in the glowing coals.

154

I had to think about that one. The lives of wild animals are not easy. They probably never die of old age. "The ones I really admire are the mammals that live under ice," I said between chews. "Think of it. Seals live most of their lives in darkness, under ten feet of ice. But they are warm blooded and breathe air, just like us. They find their way between breathing holes and keep them open by gnawing. You wouldn't believe it possible."

"What about polar bears?" Phil added. "Living on seals that live under the ice. Emerging wet into sub-zero air. And why don't they get snow blindness? Why don't eyes built for hunting in winter darkness burn out in the glaring white of summer?"

I looked long into the fire, thinking. "There was a point," I began at length, "that I believed there were answers. Do you know what I mean?" I glanced at Phil. He didn't. "I studied biology because I thought it would give me the answers. I collected facts, hoping to piece them together into answers. But the deeper I looked into anything, the more there was to see."

Phil was shaking his head mutely. I began on a different tact. "Physics is that way. For years people thought they were rounding up the last few great facts that would add up to The Answers. Then along came quantum mechanics and the uncertainty principle, and we're back in the twilight zone. That doesn't refute everyday Newtonian physics, but the very nature of reality still eludes us. We are so permeated with our sensual data that we cannot even ask the questions.

"Once my Universe was a logical structure, a Little Yellow Box. There were shelves for each opinion. I could touch the walls and ceiling. Occasionally I heard noises outside, so one day I pulled up a floor board and discovered space beyond. I began to decorate my Box with new ideas, and they ripped it apart."

I glanced at Phil, but he was lost to me, a stranger that I loved. He was uncomfortable with my need to examine life. He took life at face value. What a paradox, I thought. We are each inseparably mingled in the life of a teeming Cosmos and each totally alone in our experience of it. Every organism belongs wholly to itself, even Phil. He was not mine, and never would be.

"What an adventure life is," I smiled, releasing him. "What a wonderful game. Strangely, I think the saving grace is that we all die in the end. That takes away the significance. We've already lost so we don't have to be careful."

I sat awhile, watching the fire and thinking. Then I continued, "Life isn't a book that starts and goes somewhere and ends. I keep waiting for it to all turn out. It's an experience, an adventure. If there are answers, they can't be taught, only discovered. Whether we find the meaning or invent it, life forms a complete whole because we are the end product of our choices. Things don't turn out. The sun comes up and goes down. I remain right here, right now, in my life, forever. It doesn't go anywhere. This is it."

Phil was silent. I gazed a long time into the fire until it filled all my world. There was a glowing cave, surmounted by a castle and flaming stair well among the embers. A log broke suddenly, collapsing the roof and sending up a shower of sparks into the keen blackness. The shadowy trees seemed to bend lower as if drawn down to the warmth.

"Did you lay out the bags?" I asked, breaking the spell.

"No. I meant to, but got sidetracked with food."

"You stay there," I waved him back. "I'll only be a moment." Actually it took me much longer, for the pad was curled into a rigid sausage and would relax only after I worked with it near the fire. Away from the warmth, the cold descended, penetrating my clothing. It was hard pulling out the stiff sleeping bags and zipping them together in the familiar little tent. I had an apprehension that the night would be most unpleasant.

And it was. Chet deserted the tent early in the evening for her own spot in the snow and seemed to have fared somewhat better. As for me, I was never so glad to see dawn in all my life.

In the bright, cold sunlight of morning, I hung the frozen sleeping bags over bushes. We had retreated to the bottom of the bags, and our breath had frozen within them as well as sheeting the surface with ice.

"Other people sleep out at thirty and forty below zero," I complained as I stooped over the morning fire warming my stiff hands. "There must be a way."

"You're still alive," Phil reminded me sweetly. He was running in place by the sluggish blaze, trying to thaw his feet. Chet glared out from her nest beneath a big spruce and moaned loudly.

"Barely. And to think our lonely little cabin waited all night for us and we slept over there!" I pointed to where the tent had been: a little hollow showed how our compressed, shaking bodies had melted into the packed snow.

"Next time we'll scrape down to the moss," he said.

"If there is a next time," I answered. My joints still ached from the miserable night.

"Maybe the only way to travel in Arctic winter is like the old-timers did. Fur parkas and bedrolls of caribou don't frost up. Canvas wall tent and stove to dry out. We'd need more dogs to carry the outfit . . ."

156

"And more moose to feed the dogs," I interrupted. We were at an old impasse. "And who said it was ever easy or comfortable?"

As the sun swam higher in the blank, blue sky, the temperature climbed to minus thirty.

"Shall we spend part of the day snooping upstream?" Phil asked from the bottom of his tea cup. We had voted to cut the excursion short. "With a broken trail, it shouldn't take us long to get home."

I agreed and we began the prolonged process of breaking camp, interspersed with many a fireside session. It seemed warm and still out now. With our bellies full of hot broth, we laughed gaily in the morning brightness, congratulating ourselves on surviving the night.

It was almost dark when we got home. The logs had lost their warmth, and now the cabin seemed a dim and frosty cave. Still we greeted it as an old friend, as tired and chilled we stepped from the purple evening dusk, hauling our packs in after us. Phil lit a fire at once, and I pulled out the bedding to dry and started supper. Chet whined until she was put on the bed. It wasn't warmth she wanted; she liked to be included.

We kept a hot blaze going until we went to sleep. Outside the temperature was back to forty-three below zero with a slight breeze trailing from the north, and the black sky was pricked with frozen points of light.

⋆

As the season advanced, we spent much time immersed in tedious projects preparing for our long journey. We could plan on making only four miles a day, and because we might not find people when we got there, we would start for the mine prepared to spend twenty days without resupplying.

"March ought to be a good month to travel," Phil said. "We have a lot of daylight now." It was warm in the cabin. Late February sunlight slanted mellow through the windows, and outside in the still air a squirrel churred.

I glanced up from pounding drymeat into a fibrous meal for pemmican. It is a good trail food that the Indians once used—dried meat, tallow, and berries (although we left out the berries). I grinned at him, saying, "'In August was the jackal born.'"

He looked at me, puzzled.

"Oh, it's something that my mother used to say. Kipling:

"In August was the jackal born;
    The rains fell in September
'Now such a fearful flood as this,'
    Said he, 'I can't remember!'"

Phil smiled broadly, but I persisted. "I don't trust this weather."

We were silent awhile, each with his task. "Do you know that I wanted to be a hermit when I was a kid," I said, changing the subject. "And now I am one!" I pushed meat crumbs into a cup and poured hot tallow over them. I had mashed the old horse jerky into the mixture for salt. We'll get rid of that stuff yet, I thought.

From the window I could see that the spruce across the river had taken on a faint greenish blush as if they too were beginning to awaken. Net-Chet was outside trying her paw at stalking squirrels. They were busy scattering the snow with spruce tassels, pruning trees for a cone crop they might never see. It takes two years for cones to come to fruition.

"Come on, Phil. Tell me about some of your daydreams. Everyone has them." He was making a spare set of mukluks, working the heavy moose-hide soles soft with bear lard. "Rhino leather" he called it.

He hung the sole on a peg and leaned back in his chair. We hadn't used the chair most of the winter, for it had been too cold to sit that low.

"Well, I always imagined that I would put a false culvert under a road someplace, entering and leaving only by night. I guess I never thought there could be a place where there were no people. My schemes were how to live among them without being seen."

"I built a bomb shelter when I was six," I broke in. "Well, first it was going to be an ocean. I had seen the ocean once and when I got home I started digging. I spent my savings (about half a dollar) on salt. I really intended to build an ocean. Later it changed to a swimming pool, then a bomb shelter."

"My brothers and I once built a neat fort in the middle of a great big bush," he told me. "It was a dandy fort, but the bush turned out to be poison ivy." He was scraping the hair from wet moose hide, rhythmically fleshing it with the back of the draw knife. The hide was for the bottom of the sled. Its birch frame was drying over the stove, steamed runners curling around a purlin.

I laughed. "I wanted to live in a forest. I would have secret tunnels under giant trees with stairways cut inside the trunks up to the branches. I didn't believe I would ever grow up. Growing up was a myth."

We were silent for a spell, each with his task. It was a comfortable, companionable silence. "My mother encouraged our dreams," I told him. "She was never what she called a 'cookie baking' mother. She didn't nurture as much as inspire us. I remember her bringing lunch up into the chinaberry trees. She used to let us build campfires in the front yard. One time a neighbor called the fire department. I suppose many people thought we were neglected or uncontrolled. I can hear her saying, 'Poor city kids.' She believed in freedom for children. For every living thing. Each man his own person."

I continued crumbling jerky, nibbling as I worked. "She grew up wild," I continued. "She was sickly, so her mother took her and my Aunt Janet to live on a remote lake in upstate New York. Her father, a brilliant and unstable doctor who didn't like her, stayed in town. When she was nine and ten years old, my mother used to slip out of the cottage and spend the night, sleeping in her canoe adrift on the lake. She had no fear of the woods or of being alone."

I was quiet, thinking about my mother as a lovely wild girl, roaming the woods alone, like a forest spirit or a fairy child. No wonder she used to say, "Poor city kids."

Phil interrupted my thoughts. "I miss apples," he told me sadly.

"Well, maybe we'll find some at the mine," I said. Then, as an afterthought, "I miss Chinese food and salads and sunbathing."

"Yeah, and apples . . ."

"I miss chocolate bars and music and talking with friends."

"And apples . . ."

"I miss swimming and pretty clothes and hot showers and coffee and movies . . ."

"And . . ."

"Yes, I know. Apples."

⋇

The omens were promising as the day of departure neared. Daily the sunshine grew in duration and power, and the warm, calm air seemed full of springtime. We now saw many signs of animals on the move. Moose tracks crisscrossed the river, restless for the new green shoots that would not appear for another two months. We saw no more caribou tracks, but the carnivores traveled long trails in search of the increasingly rare rabbit. This was the hungry season for them, when the snows are deep and last year's little folk have been well depleted. It is also the mating season for many, and they cover great distances to renew their species.

Bull moose who performed this vital function last fall had dropped their antlers, innocent of calves swelling in the warm dark bellies of their autumn loves. Safe from snow and cold, tender life waited its first spring in secret comfort. Heavy with the future, cows traveled with last year's calf, seeking out unbrowsed buds in the deep snow. Like the juvenile wolves, young moose had yet to survive their first winter. If they did, a sad surprise awaited them in late May, when their faithful mothers would drive them away in preparation for the new little life. They must then begin their solitary wanderings, heritage of moose.

Our troupe of traveling chickadees began adding musical twitters to their hushed wintertime calls, and birds that had been silent since autumn were speaking out once more, warming up for the spring concerts. A good deal of squabbling ensued as real estate took on some of its old value and new birds filtered into our area disturbing the established order. Oblivious of us they would come blowing into the yard like a swirl of dried leaves, bringing the exciting news of the coming spring.

On the first of March a snowstorm hit. We listened quietly as gray winds pounded into the cabin, rattling the stove pipe. Our thoughts turned to the journey before us. I remember that my own parents had almost died in a March snowstorm when they underestimated the Arctic. But they had been out of food and forced to travel in search of game. We were still well fed and could afford to sit home if we so decided. But you tend to get cocky when you're well fed.

We would remember March as the fickle month of winds.

Chapter 9

PERFECT SMOKE RINGS puffed from little holes in the stove, and a flickering light filled the dawn-gray cabin. A familiar rushing sound grew as the shavings caught. Shivering in my bare feet and dirty long johns, I blew upon the frosted window for a look at the outside thermometer. Rose-edged peaks appeared against a satin sky as the pane cleared.

"Eight below," I called cheerfully to Phil as he ducked outside in his long underwear and bare feet.

"And calm," he called back. "It looks like a good day." March days were already long, the sun returning in the spring as rapidly as it had left the year before.

We intended to hike up Olsen Creek and scale the mountains. From there we would drop into a large drainage that paralleled the Chandalar and follow it high into the Brooks Range to the mine. We had originally planned a circular route up the river and along a series of lakes before climbing to the mine, but after our experience with overflow, it seemed safer to go directly over the precipitous mountains. We hoped to find people and be able to mail the letters we had written on bits of notebook paper.

We were going well prepared. We had the tent and down clothing as well as pemmican for more than twenty days, an ax, rifle and camera equipment. I had even baked a treat of oatmeal cookies. We didn't plan to hunt, but the rifle was insurance. It all weighed a good deal.

Hurriedly we donned our clothing and set about the last minute packing. Phil loaded bulky items onto the little sled that Chet was to pull. It was a simple affair of hand-hewn birch planks. The runners curled up in front and the bottom was made of stretched rawhide. Over the load he lashed a gussetted tarp.

We finished breakfast as morning light filtered into the cabin. Phil lugged the heavy backpacks outside while I wrote a note and tacked it to the bed. It seemed unlikely that anyone would be here in our absence, but I outlined our plans, just in case. The darker side that neither of us mentioned was that if we failed to return, perhaps someday someone would piece together our story. I thought a moment and laid my journals beside the note.

Phil was lowering the frozen quarters from the snow-shrouded racks, complaining under the tumbling deluge when I appeared. We had already eaten two and a half moose, the caribou and half the bear. I wrapped a rope around my hand and dragged a side of ribs to the door. At last we had all the meat safely inside. I double checked the cabin and he wired the door bolt shut.

Getting all of us saddled up took time. While we adjusted our snowshoes, Chet danced gaily around and around, fouling her traces. Finally we heaved on the packs and set off for the cache. We planned to ascend Olsen Creek to its terminal amphitheater before confronting the peaks.

We didn't get far. It was soon apparent that Chet could not handle the sled alone. It caught on bushes and was too heavy for her. I stopped to adjust a snowshoe while Phil retraced his steps and stooped to untangle the dog. Delighted at this attention, she knocked him sideways and his heavy pack pulled him backwards into deep snow where he struggled feebly. Sensing his playful mood, Chet pounced happily upon the sprawled body, sled and all, while he beat at her helplessly.

We returned home to repack. When once again we set off up the trail, sunlight showered the high country, lighting the broad sky where clouds clung in a gauzy mist along the ridges. Chet now carried heavy packs while Phil wore his and trailed the ungainly sled. He hated to leave it behind after all the hours invested in it. I thought it a bad arrangement, but said nothing as he tied the traces to the back of his pack.

Net-Chet bounded happily ahead, delighted with a romp. She burrowed along the old packed trail, snow to her shoulders. The path was difficult to see, hidden under new snow, but led by some sense of her own, she never wavered.

When we reached Chris's cache we left the packed trail and my real work began. I searched out the old path, wading slowly through soft snow to my waist. We had not been up this way since autumn, when we had taken a day to explore the drainage. I remembered that the trail ran straight up Olsen Creek, sticking always to the best ground and maintaining a uniform grade. It had once been almost a road, four feet wide and dug evenly into the hillside.

The canyon bottom was brushy despite the trail, and we fought off laden alders as gradually we ascended into open alpine country. Small stands of spruce followed the creek bottom or clung in protected hollows. The little valley was far larger than it looked in the clear air, and at times major drainages merged with it, our trail taking one fork or the other.

Our progress was slow as I labored through the deep snows, Phil behind me hauling the sled, and it was late afternoon when, tired and hungry, we entered the great snowy bowl of the amphitheater. There at the last fringe of trees stood the remains of a small structure. It was a trap line cabin of Chris's and had his distinctive hinges and gable work. The roof had caved in long ago.

High above us loomed the towering walls of the giant amphitheater. I felt chilled and sweaty as I gazed at this grand scene of snowy desolation. An evening breeze spilled off the mountains where the feeble sun rested on the rim of the bowl. Even in summer there would be shadows here someplace. How big and wild it looked across the cold, clear distance. Remembering it in autumn garb with snowbanks splashed among the crags, I squinted into the last rays of the sun, choosing a route for our ascent tomorrow.

"We should camp where there are still trees," I said, indicating the barren slopes ahead. Already the sparkle was fading from the land, and a somber wilderness of vast silences hovered over us, blue with evening. There is a certain comfort in a world so bounded, I decided. It was awesome and grand, but we could see all of it. We turned aside from the lonely cabin, leaving it to guard the memories of another era.

The fringe of trees ended abruptly a few hundred yards ahead. I studied them, choosing a place to camp. Phil looked very tired. By the time he had chopped firewood, I had the tent pitched, bags laid out, and supper started. Chet circled about us, disgruntled at the prospect of sleeping out. I felt strangely at home. Tired and contented, we sat before the hot blaze, encircled by scrawny black spruce standing twisted under winter's harsh embrace. Above us the silver cliffs contrasted sharply with the darker smoky-blue of the sky. High thin clouds had settled in, and occasional big flakes floated down as we shared dinner.

Phil's mukluks were becoming rimed with ice as he sat before the fire. When he got stiffly up and went to his pack to dig out dry footgear, I noticed that he was limping.

"What's wrong with your leg?" I asked as he settled again on the log beside me. Reaching for the boiling tea pot, I singed the fuzz on my mittens. Carefully I poured steaming water into two cups balanced on a strip of dead bark.

"I twisted my knee awhile back, and it's getting stiff sitting here." He untied one mukluk and pulled it off, hanging it over a nearby twig.

"Phil, I know how much time you put into that sled, but it isn't working out."

He took a sip of the tea and spit out a spruce needle. "What do you suggest?" We had dreamed of hauling home a few goodies, perhaps donated by some kindly person.

"We've been on a trail so far, and on fairly level ground. Tomorrow we go over the mountains." I gazed up at the overshadowing pass. It was only slightly lower than the brooding peaks. "I think we should tie the excess baggage onto our packs and leave the sled here."

To my surprise, he agreed.

Chet started uneasily from her snow nest as a deep wolf voice came trailing through the twilight. We were in new country now, and she stayed close, sniffing with apprehension. This was probably one of our wolves, I thought, but that will change when we cross the range tomorrow.

Most animals are territorial. It insures adequate hunting grounds for some and a detailed knowledge of exits for others. We were no different, and the familiar contours of our valley had come to mean security.

Chet dropped back into the snow, ears still twitching. She had experienced her first estrus at Christmas, and we had worried that she might stray. But she was in no danger of motherhood unless a very sporting rabbit or shrew gave it a try. Chet had a healthy respect for wolves.

She flicked her ears half listening to us, searching the silence.

"Well, let's turn in," Phil said and stretched. "We've got a long day tomorrow."

Early the next morning, I led off through the deep, crusted snow. It wasn't easy, and I was soon panting from the exertion. Where summer walking was a matter of finding a way from place to place, winter was a tedious process of breaking trail. Above me I could see that the ridges were swept nearly bare in spots, but snow was piled deep in the bowl. I wallowed slowly out of the ravine and began to switchback up the steep slope onto a ridge.

Phil's knee was quite stiff, and he allowed me to break trail, content to be carrying the heavier pack. He could normally handle perhaps thirty pounds more than I, his top limit around one hundred pounds and mine closer to seventy. He insisted that he was okay, but I stole a few items from his pack anyway.

I was sweating profusely as we mounted the knees of the mountain and stopped to remove our snowshoes. I could see why caribou traveled the high country, avoiding the deep drifts. The ridge was packed hard and as smooth as glass. I stomped steps for Phil into the mountain as slowly we wended our way ever higher, mounting onto a steep ridge. The slick moose-hide soles of his mukluks turned the granular snow to ball bearings, and he had a difficult time keeping his footing.

Away to the east the sun was wreathed in a beige glow. As we rested a moment, looking down on the headwaters of the newborn Olsen Creek, the first gust of wind struck. We shouldered our packs and, shoving mittened hands deep into our trouser pockets, angled on up the endless ridge. Distances are deceptive above timberline, and we climbed slowly into a shifting dream of cold blowing snow and thickening mist.

Despite the exertion, the constant wind sucked body heat away, and I stopped to dig out my parka with shaking hands. Below me Phil appeared as a blurred dark figure, struggling over the slippery sharp rocks or plunging into hidden, snow-swept holes. The ridge was a jumble of jagged slabs turned edgeways. Phil was falling repeatedly, unable to manage the footing and favor his knee.

"Come on, let's get out your parka!" I yelled at him over the rush of the wind. We could no longer see the canyon below. I helped him drag off his pack and slid the fastening toggle with nerveless fingers. Misery welled up within me. The precipice rose endlessly above us with sheer drops into gray nothing on either side.

"Are you okay?" I shouted. He nodded wretchedly. "You just watch your feet and I'll choose a course." The stinging blast tore the words from me and flung them into space. Granular snow streamed by, making the ground dance. It was hard to see my feet. Net-Chet scurried uneasily ahead and snow drifted about the twinkle of her legs. She would stop and tramp a nest into the snow as she waited impatiently for us to catch up.

Soon we were forced to use our hands, clinging to the sharp, bare rocks as we mounted always higher along the knife-edge of the ridge. We should have reached the pass by now, I thought, anxiously peering into the tawny, drifting haze. Looking up I could make out the sky, pallid and distant. I suddenly realized how huge the land up here was and that we could become easily disoriented.

At last the ridge began to flatten and finally stretched into the no-man's-land of a broad pass.

"Where are we? Can you reach the map?" Phil yelled at me above the wind. His beard was matted with snow.

"Oh, let's just get down from here!" I shouted back. I had never seen a more godforsaken spot. Only hard exercise was keeping me from freezing to death.

Chet moaned loudly.

"We have to study the map!" he insisted.

With numb hands we drew it out, sheltering the precious paper with our bodies. For a moment the clouds pulled back, displaying the land beyond. It was unbearably dismal, not a tree in sight. Across from us lay our chosen route, a deep valley between great, frosted crags that marched awesomely into still higher mountains until they were lost in the blowing snow. It was the kind of scenery, vast and grand, that belongs on calendars, and my heart withered at the sight of it. I had known that the mine was way above tree line, but was unprepared for this fierce desolation.

Phil tucked the map into his shirt and then extracted a small cloth bag. He began working the strings free with his teeth. "I figured we could use a little cheering up," he told me. He grubbed out cookie crumbs with his mouth, for his hands were dead cold, and offered them to me in his bare palm.

We scrambled and slid over the broken ground, falling often in our steep descent, following another exposed ridge that cut above a series of cliffs that continued on out of sight into the blowing snow. I was afraid that we might become trapped, unable to get down. There was no place to stop or even pitch a tent. No way to build a fire. Perhaps we had overextended ourselves. What would I do if Phil's leg gave out? I couldn't carry him. And we would both soon die on this high exposed place.

The ridge continued to drop sharply until it dumped us into a narrow, twisting ravine. There we donned snowshoes and floundered slowly down towards the valley through thickets of little willows. Here at least was a bit of shelter and something to burn should we be forced to camp. The air was now thick with falling snow. Walls of stone closed about us, funneling us down the tortuous gully.

Phil was slower now, obviously pained by his knee. I looked about, wondering what I would do if he were to badly injure himself in one of his frequent tumbles. I was acutely aware of our complete isolation. No one would even find the bones. Let's face it, I thought grimly, no one would even look for them. I glanced at the frowning peaks that overhung us with a feeling akin to loathing.

"Hey!" I yelled, startling Phil and the dog out of their respective suffering. I shook my fist at the towering icy cliffs. "I'm glad you're up there and I'm not!" My thin voice puffed into the wind and disappeared unnoticed. I felt smaller than ever.

Phil looked up, frosted face gray in the filtered light.

"I refuse to kill myself for the chance to tell people I'm doing fine. The mail can wait until spring," I told him. I waved at the canyon below us and the rocks beyond. "All I want is to get out of this wind. Where will we even camp?"

"We can go downstream if you want to call it off."

"Yes. This is senseless."

"There will be trees down around that bend," he said, pointing south.

We had rounded a corner and could now see the valley floor dimly below. It looked grim.

I stared doubtfully. "Maybe by the time it hits the Chandalar River, twenty miles downstream."

Chet was moaning loudly at the delay. I was shivering.

"No, there are old cabins on the map. Where there are cabins, there'll be trees."

I shrugged. What did we have to lose? Our planned course lay upstream, but that was just too depressing.

The steep gully emptied us into a valley formed by a large creek, now frozen in winter sleep. This too seemed endless as we wandered slowly downstream in the gray of a snowy evening. The valley was bigger than I thought, perhaps three hundred yards across with mountains rising sheer from the floor on both sides. Hummocks obscured the route ahead as wearily I broke trail, plodding numbly through dips and over hillocks.

Ahead rose a gentle hill, the jutting toe of a mountain mass where two streams joined. It was suddenly fringed with spruce, dark and pointed against the drifting white. We labored forward, drawing gradually near. Already dusk was pressing into the margins of the day, blanketing the light. As the canyon swung southward, we found ourselves at last in the merry company of great old trees, larger than any we had seen. A narrow ribbon of spruce wound along the frozen white stream bed, cut off suddenly by the mountains. It was like coming home, this natural haven, this gift of the wilderness to the cold and weary.

Soon old cabins sprang up here and there, a little community of days gone by. We felt revived at the sudden change.

"How did they pack in all this stuff?" I wondered aloud, dropping my burden inside a stoutly built cabin with an intact roof. The floor had been carefully removed by someone, exposing the joists. I lowered my body onto an old straw-filled bed frame where a porcupine had spent a previous winter. Chet curled up on the ice between the joists. It was cold and dark inside, and my sweaty skin contracted uncomfortably over sore muscles.

Phil shook his head. He was busy examining the woodwork, chuckling inanely to himself whenever he discovered something of interest.

I felt annoyed. "Do you want to stay here?" It was getting late and we hadn't seen the sun since before the pass, or stopped walking since breakfast, ten or twelve hours ago.

"We can do better I think," he said. "Whoever removed the floor probably built a new cabin nearby. Anyway we can't have a fire in here because the stove pipe is missing."

"At least it's out of the wind," I answered, beginning to shiver. Damn him for his patient interest in antiques.

Chet looked doleful as I buckled her packs back on, my fingers stiff and gray. Back into the twilight we went, pushing our tired bodies along to restore circulation. Soon we lost the trail. The promised better cabin began to fade from my vision, and pain descended once again. What was wrong with the other one? I thought irritably, upset with Phil for his pickiness.

We struggled on through alternate forest, muskeg and stands of large, tough willows in the gathering darkness. I wanted to go back. I felt like crying in my exhaustion, forcing one aching step after another. My shoulders hurt, my feet were numb with cold.

I looked back at Phil, stumbling and limping along. This is stupid, I thought suddenly. Have we lost all sense in our weariness? We were in the midst of a beautiful grove of ancient trees, a secluded dell encircled by living wood. From high above came the gray rumble of wind, but very little penetrated their vigilance. Why had I forgotten? We needed no dank old cabins.

"This is home," I declared, taking charge with my remaining strength. I let my pack fall against a spreading patriarch and unsaddled Net-Chet.

It was reassuring to build our nest and make a home in this great wild land. Soon a fire drove back the darkness, and golden shadows danced over the snow and the friendly tree trunks enclosing us. I extended my fingers to the warmth, as wood released the sunlight gathered in long seasons past. We found ourselves laughing together over boiled pemmican, enjoying the hot cheerful blaze and the big trees. Here to the limit of its existence, this sliver of forest had crept, hardy giants sheltering one another, and now us, from the storm.

"Who would destroy so thoughtlessly this hard won gift of Nature?" I wondered aloud. It was safety and protection for the men who had dwelt here. Yet they had cut down living trees to thaw the ground, often chopping into old giants only to abandon them. Many of these lived still and will perhaps when I am forgotten, bearing the scars of selfishness and stupidity.

I leaned back against the wide trunk of an old tree and sipped my scalding tea. Phil forked a rabbit pellet out of his cup, one of the hazards of snow-melt.

"I'm glad we're turning around," I said, passing him the spoon and cooking pot. "You could make it with a broken arm or rib, but if a leg gives out, you've had it. A person who can't walk is helpless. What would we do? I doubt if I could carry you far."

Phil ate in silence, staring into the coals.

"We could have died up there today," I continued. "It wouldn't have taken much, a small accident or finding those cliffs at the wrong place. Any of a dozen things. We can't afford to go so far out on a limb with no backup. Lord, I dread going back over that pass. Do you realize that by walking downstream, we have backtracked in a circle? A fork of Olsen Creek ought to be right over the mountains to our east."

"I was thinking of that," he answered. "The shortest route home is that way." He pointed across the canyon. We were hidden in the strip of forest, but somewhere off in the night would be another bleak pass dropping into Olsen Creek. "What do you think?"

I was thinking that I'd rather travel ten extra miles than break a new trail. But then there was Phil's knee. "May as well have a look at the new country. We're about ten miles from home, I'd guess. If we push, we could make it tomorrow."

"No reason to push," he replied. He was stuffing more snow into the charred little tea pot. Carefully he balanced it over the fire. "In fact, we should take a noon break when we can. We didn't eat all day. It's not smart to get so overextended."

I agreed, thinking how stupefied we had been this evening, somehow unable to choose. "Accidents happen when you're least prepared. We really have no reason to rush, as you say. Except on the pass."

"This wind makes me uneasy," Phil said. We both listened. "It feels like a big storm blowing in."

Although our trees protected us from most of it, we could hear the steady throb of black air seething through the darkness above. Enfolding us in big, strong arms, the spruce whispered nameless tunes of comfort, eternal in the wisdom of their ancient kind. I listened contentedly, filled with affection for these, my fellow life forms. I was lifted on their night-time song of wind and living branches. We arrogant mobile creatures must never forget that it is the gentle silent plants that nurture us and give us life.

"What about your sled?" I asked suddenly.

"Well, it's not really litter, being only moose hide and birch. The skin will be gone before long. The frame in a few years."

"All your work, my L'ammal!"

"It wasn't wasted," he said slowly. "The next one I build will be better. The only regret I have is not sending the mail. And apples."

I woke sometime in the night, feeling rather than hearing the sound of snow ticking soft and thick onto the tent, blanketing the black and seething canyon. How beautiful life is, I thought, tears coming to my eyes. How miraculous each breath of my body, never to come again. I hung there, cradled in the lullaby of that wild spot, rocked in the arms of the night, joyful of my living breath, in love with the sound of my heart.

We were late breaking camp, reluctant to desert the sheltering forest. The wind seemed stronger than ever, but realizing that it might well last for weeks, we trudged slowly out of our hidden hollow into another small drainage. We were pleasantly surprised to find the deep gully sparsely timbered. It rose steadily before us, twisting into the mountain mass.

When at length the ragged spruce gave out, dissolving into the sheer white sides of the mountain, we traveled up a narrow stream choked with stunted willows, finding still some shelter from the stinging wind and snow. Finally our canyon abutted into the peak. Above us loomed the last bare ridge to the pass. It began abruptly and we packed away our snowshoes for the final ascent.

Again we entered a dream land of mist and snow as we crept up the wind-swept ridge. It was very steep and we could look down on either side and behind as our little battle carried us upward. How inadequate legs appear with a mountain under them! One step at a time we toiled on.

This pass seemed somehow friendlier to me as we lumbered up the final broad curve of skyline, white mountain against white clouds. Perhaps that was because it was my land that I now looked down upon, Olsen Creek and far away the familiar loops of the Chandalar River. Still, we did not tarry.

Descending another steep crest we found ourselves in a large tributary of Olsen Creek. Like the opposite side, this was a gentle canyon, cutting far into the mountains, and a better route than the final amphitheater. When we hit good stands of timber we stopped for tea, and because it was growing late and cold, we decided to camp. Within a mile or two we would find our broken trail and be safely home by noon the following day.

We broke camp early the next morning, anxious to be home. Phil fell steadily behind as the day progressed. After we rejoined the broken trail, I waddled slowly before him, singing little songs and telling him stories to shorten the trip. Net-Chet scurried ahead, satisfied to be going home. Gamely she helped out, carrying packs that were too heavy for her. For practical, humane packing, one third of an animal's weight is a healthy load.

We arrived home stiff and tired in the late afternoon, but the meat needed to be rehung before we could move back into the cabin. The sky was clearing off although the wind still blasted, drifting snow down the exposed river. From the peaks I could see plumes sprayed aloft, trailing rooster-tails of snow, and I shuddered to think what the high passes were like. I was glad to be home.

Suddenly a little plane shot into view a few hundred feet over the river, the first one we had seen all year. Almost before we heard it, it was gone, flashing red and white through the trees. Still excited by this brush with another world, we went back to dragging quarters from the cabin, piling them outside the doorway.

And then he was back! He circled once, eyeing the river, then dropped from the sky and settled noisily upon the dunes. With short, splayed legs extended, the skis slammed over the packed dunes at a remarkable speed and the plane came to rest before our very door.

We looked at one another in wonder. I scrambled off the hill and was plunging awkwardly through the crusted snow even before the magic little bird drifted to a stop. A door swung open and I grinned stupidly up at a giant pink-faced man in sunglasses and a clean blue uniform. He looked so well scrubbed that I didn't know if it were proper to offer my own chapped and grubby paw.

"You're the first person we've seen in most of a year!" I blurted inanely.

He peered over his sunglasses and hauled a black leather note pad from within the white fleece of his jacket and asked, "Are you the folks who have a mother in Canada?"

I stared at him in confusion. "Why no," I answered weakly. "You must be looking for someone else." To my great disappointment, he turned back toward the plane and I resisted an impulse to grab him. He was going to hop in and fly away!

But instead, two other men climbed from the little Cessna, a large man in a pressed khaki uniform and a strangely familiar little Indian figure dressed in dark, friendly-looking clothing and a wool cap.

"Now let's see," said the one in blue, starting over from his notes. "Your mother's name is Helm . . . ?"

"Yes, yes!" I replied, delighted to have something we could agree upon. He would stay a moment! "Do come up to the cabin and get out of this wind." He seemed to agree to that also, for we migrated toward the cabin, the big men plodding solemnly through the drifting snow, Chet and I wildly herding them on. Phil was still limping out to greet us.

"I got a letter here from your mother in Vancouver," he began again as he stalked up our familiar hill.

I nodded vigorously this time, for I did indeed have a mother.

Reassured, he went on. "She was worried about you and asked if we might try to locate you. She sent a money order to a . . ." here he stopped and consulted the mysterious black notebook . . . "Bertha Fred in Venetie and asked her to buy groceries for you. Mrs. Fred is also keeping your mail. Quite a lot, I understand."

The khaki man didn't look very friendly, and I addressed myself to the smiling blue one. The little dark Indian kept grinning and I grinned back, too overwhelmed to think.

We stepped over the frozen carcasses adorning our yard and I flung open the door. Phil was skipping about on his stiff knee, shaking hands with anyone who would shake back, oblivious to his long icy beard and hair ladened with twigs and snow. His hoary eyebrows looked more formidable than ever, the big bright eyes gleaming unnaturally in a dirty face. Self-consciously, I ran my grimy fingers over my own tangled locks and flicked a bit of breakfast from my stained parka.

I darted inside and turned in time to see Blue crack his skull on the doorframe. Khaki stooped awkwardly and fared better, rising into a face full of frozen meat. Our door had always seemed adequate to me before.

The cabin was cold and unlovely. Meat and snow were scattered over the floor. And for the first time, seeing our home through the eyes of these laundered men from the sky, it seemed dark and dingy.

"How's it going, Bobby?" Phil boomed, vigorously pumping the Indian's hand. At last I recognized Bobby Mark, the man who had hauled us upstream so long ago. They fell into conversation about trapping and game and weather.

"We just got back from trying to hike over to the mine on the other side of the mountains," I said to Blue, offering our only chair. "We wanted to mail some letters. Could you do it for us?" Our little cabin seemed bursting with loud people.

"Be glad to. You're lucky you turned back. There's no one up there," he told me, deep voice jolly after hours of searching. Alaskan State Troopers try to keep an eye on people in the bush, but it is a vast country.

Carefully I extracted the wrinkled scraps of notebook paper from my pack and handed them to the Trooper. "We don't have any envelopes or stamps," I apologized.

"Don't worry about it," he answered. "I'll send Hanson in with your mail and the groceries next time he's up this way. I stopped in Venetie on the way up and the entire village came down for news of you."

On the other side of the cabin Bobby was saying to Phil, "You got mighty fine trap-line cabin here. Maybe you let me trap up here next winter?"

I frowned. I didn't want to open this area up for exploitation. Normally the Indians didn't come up this far, for their boats couldn't make it. But with a cabin here, it might be worth flying in for. I felt dizzy with so much happening at once.

"Oh, I think we're planning to stay awhile," Phil answered him. It was true that we really hadn't decided.

172

"I bet you got lotta furs," Bobby grinned back. "What kinda furs you got this winter?"

Phil told him that we hadn't trapped and Bobby laughed and looked like he didn't believe it. A whole winter out and no furs?

"Well, gotta go," Blue said, cautiously ducking through the door. "Glad to see that you folks are okay."

Before we knew it, they were gone. Net-Chet chased wildly down the river bed, as the little bird, trailing a spume of white crystals, regained the sky. We watched them circle overhead, gaining elevation, and then slip southward, quickly dwindling into nothing. All that remained were penciled tracks on our familiar river. Somehow everything had changed, and yet we were as alone as ever. We could still starve or freeze to death. We still had only ourselves to depend upon.

Their visit jolted me back into an awareness of the Twentieth Century. Looking after the vanished plane, I realized that they would never know how big the country is or what it was like to live as we did. No matter how they studied the land beneath them, they were only an hour or two from hot rolls, coffee, and the morning paper.

It seemed more than coincidental that they should have arrived at this very moment, and I was inclined to laugh at the vagrancies of fate. God has a sense of humor, I thought. I turned to catch Phil staring at the strange tracks. "They were really here?" he asked in a dazed tone.

"Sure," I replied grinning. "Come on, let's unpack. Hey, Phil! Who do you suppose is President?"

❀

Suddenly aware of appearances, I started cleaning. I swept the cabin with a little patch of caribou fur, carefully combing the moose-hide carpet free of shavings. I washed clothes, cut our hair and trimmed Phil's beard. With a bit of our remaining flour, I even baked cookies, saving them for our expected guest. Phil had never put much stock in tidiness and my two companions tiptoed nervously about the cabin.

One snowy evening, the ghostly form of a small plane roared suddenly from the clouds. Lumbering low between the islands, he circled upstream trailing snow, skis outstretched for impact. We rushed down to greet the laughing young man that crawled forth. It was David Hanson, flying a tiny two-seater red and orange Super-Cub. Born and raised in my home-town of Tucson, he had come to Alaska with his wife to live in the bush, but never got closer than Fairbanks.

"This must be the right address," he grinned, swinging on to the hydraulic wheel-skis. Snowshoes were strapped to the struts. "You folks expecting some mail?" Out of the cramped plane he began dragging boxes of groceries and parcels.

He seemed very much at home in our little place, sitting comfortably in the chair while I fed him cookies and Phil looked hungrily on.

"I brought you some books of my own," he told us. "Figured you would probably enjoy some new literature. And there's a stack of back news magazines. I hardly ever get the time to read them."

"We were just starting *Hawaii* for the third time," I burbled, pushing more cookies at him. "Would you like it? By the way, who's President?" I pulled out a list of questions.

"Old Tricky Dick is in for another term, so you may as well stay here. Oh, you probably haven't even heard of Watergate. Well, you ought to enjoy the magazines."

I laughed and clapped my hands with glee and then timidly withdrew. I wasn't used to talking with strangers. My voice seemed too loud and fast. I watched Phil and David conversing happily, and wondered if Phil had the same sense of confusion and awkwardness. I thought so, for he seemed overly hearty.

David's eyes were light Nordic blue. They were eyes that missed nothing: cop's eyes. He wore a khaki shirt of remarkable cleanliness with soft cream-colored long johns showing at the wrist and throat. Over his uniform was a heavy fleece jacket which he refused to remove. I caught the momentary flash of a shoulder holster. Like the other men, his hair was shorn in a military crew cut. I studied him furtively, wondering if his head got cold.

"I have three little ones now," he was saying, "so I doubt if we'll ever do it. But I do envy you folks the experience."

Net-Chet had been her least-mannered in the excitement. After getting up the courage to sniff David over, she had forced herself into his tailored lap and, despite frequent removals, was rubbing a bit of the valley off on his immaculate trousers. We evicted her and she wailed her lament to the hills, willing to be anything but excluded.

"She's normally very well behaved," I found myself repeating to our skeptical guest.

All too soon the visit was over. David glanced at his big gold watch, exposing clean, even fingernails, and said, "I've got to be off before dark. I don't have radio contact until I climb above the peaks." He set his full cup of tea and half-finished cookie down and rose.

We followed him to the plane, still jabbering in our excitement. Chet remained locked in the cabin because of her wild desire to chase planes. Her sharp voice trailed after us and I could see her teetering in the window, balanced on a five-gallon can, face plastered to the pane.

With a rush of wind, David was gone. At the last possible moment, the little plane shook itself free of the snow, and raking the treetops, popped into the featureless sky. He circled once as he rose and then slid south to vanish in the falling snow. I stood a moment, sending my thoughts after him. Every second carried him days from us and I watched hoping he wouldn't crash. People are small up there too, I thought. The plane serves them well. But if it fails, they are as much in the country as we are. I hoped David was prepared.

"Hey!" Phil laughed, swinging me in a circle. "It's Christmas!"

Chet was silent as we ascended the hill, arousing my suspicions. We opened the door to see her beady brown eyes staring truculently from their hairy sockets. The cookies were gone.

Bertha had used the money order well despite Venetie prices, and twilight found us sorting happily through our bounty by candlelight. There were staples like oatmeal, flour, powdered milk, and sugar as well as special treats such as hard pilot biscuits, canned butter, and jam.

"No apples," Phil said sadly when the last bundle had been opened.

"They wouldn't keep well in these temperatures," I reminded him. "I think she did a very good job of shopping."

He had to agree. "Do you know that we have 8160 matches here?" Phil asked, looking up from his figures. "At our present rate, that should last another twenty-three years." He was sipping David's rewarmed tea and mopping up the crumbs Chet had missed.

The cabin was a shambles of containers and paper. Phil patiently folded away every scrap as we transferred supplies to permanent containers. I was reading letters aloud. One large cardboard box was crammed with mail, letters, and packages sent from our families and friends with love.

Phil's parents had sent a shoe box full of prepared spices. My sister Anny sent a box stuffed with chocolate chips, coconut, and nuts. My mother was our most faithful correspondent, sending a dozen thick letters telling in hilarious detail of her adventures in Vancouver. For she really did live in Canada now, having remained after a raft trip down the Fraser River.

"Your brother is getting married!" I said, scanning a letter from his folks.

"Just read it," he intoned.

"Okay . . . 'We're going out to their wedding in June. Jeanie, your sister made a beautiful bride . . .' Beautiful bride!" I zipped down the lines. "It doesn't say who she married!"

Phil laughed, slapping his thighs. "Go on! Go on!"

"'. . . we are now in the new apartment and your Dad is doing very well after the heart surgery. We had a hard time with selling the house. You know your Dad. After all the years he put into it, no one could keep the place like he did. We finally took old Junior to the vet and had her put to sleep . . . She was so old and crippled up, it seemed the only kind thing to do. Your Dad, with all his gruff talk, you can guess who had to take her . . .'"

"L'ammal, I'm sorry . . ."

Phil said nothing, indicating that I should finish reading. But his eyes were swimming, and at last I put aside the letter. Silently I slipped my arms around him, remembering the gray-muzzled female dog named Junior, his childhood friend.

⋆

While our past reclaimed us, the Arctic was coming awake. Without our help, and for the most part without our knowledge, every twig and crystal followed its own path in its own time. Each bud, perfect to its kind, awaited the signal; each snowflake, blown hither and yon by the restless air, mirrored the advancing days.

The winds of change thundered endlessly down the river, exposing at last the ice below. As March progressed, more and more pale-blue ice stood naked under the glaring sun. Our raven, Holly, had deserted us, but Net-Chet spent much time playing Wild Dog of the North, chasing the dried leaves that were wrenched free and tumbled for her delight. Phil, active as always with new projects, was building a full-length counter under the windows, planing logs while I read aloud to him through the storms of March. From my perch upon the bed I could see snow streaking down the river and hear the constant bluster of the wind. I was glad we were home and not on our way to the mine.

One evening the wind stopped. For three weeks it had blasted, carrying tons of snow southward. We stood in the eerie stillness of dusk and listened. A pink glow suffused the land, blushing the motionless dunes and frozen peaks. Every few seconds a CRACK! ZZZzzinnnnngggg! rocketed over the silent river, zipping swiftly past the cabin and into the distance. Not since the uneasy rumbles of autumn had we heard such ice-talk. I studied the river, half expecting to see a rift appear. But it remained impassive.

With the onset of still days we went outside to play. Under the spring glare, our hill had started to thaw. The snow became like sugar, coarse and granular. Down on the dazzling river we spent three days building an igloo, for the fun and experience of it. We intended to camp out there some night, but never did. We cut blocks of snow from the hard-packed dunes with a hand saw and built a structure we could almost stand in.

Net-Chet lay panting in the nearby shade as we worked, her thick pelt beginning to shed. The sun was warm on my bare shoulders, and about us the happy birds flitted to the feeder we had erected in the front yard. It was made of moose antlers, fitting enough, for moose cracklings was the dish served. From the hill came the intermittent racket of squirrels, and on the bank a troupe of chickadees whooped it up as they refilled their crops with sand from a patch of brown earth, compliments of Chet's overgrown nails.

Before the end of March we began to dry our remaining meat. In many ways, summer is the off-season in the Arctic. It is a time when travel in the low lands is difficult, when game is thin and meat spoils. It is a time of bugs. We soon found ourselves with more bones than Net-Chet could handle. This bounty we carted to the Snackbar to share with the wolves. These bones were our only garbage. We had nothing to spare. Any can or piece of paper was carefully saved and reused. Wishing to disrupt the wilderness as little as possible, we even burned toilet paper.

We kept the camera ready, but with the sun's return, our neighbors had become shy, hunting mostly during the dwindling twilight that partitioned one day from the next.

One morning Phil burst into the cabin and grabbed the twenty-two. "There's something peculiar up on the hill!" he told me. "A sick wolf, I think. Keep Chet here."

He had been gathering firewood behind the cabin. I restrained Net-Chet while he hurried back up the hill. I slipped a rope leash onto her collar, finding it with difficulty beneath the heavy fur. Proceeding cautiously, I finally spotted Phil through the trees. He was bending over something, and as I came closer, it materialized into a large, gray wolf.

"He's dead," Phil told me, looking up from where he squatted over the animal.

I glanced around. No snow covered the carcass. "He must have died recently," I said. The body was curled against the bole of a large spruce tree, and the ground about was littered with half-digested bones and his final tracks—the bitter end of a trail. The animal had survived its last weeks here, eating the barren moose bones that Chet had scattered. White droppings contained pulverized bones and nothing more.

I lifted a paw, raising the stiff body from the snow. The frozen, sunken eyes stared lifelessly back. "He hardly weighs a thing, poor beast," I said. "She," I corrected. I gazed down over our friendly hill, seeing it through the hunger of a wolf. It wouldn't look quite so homey to a starving animal.

"Looks like one of last year's pups," Phil suggested. "Probably a sister of the one we ate. Doesn't make our little murder seem so awful, does it? . . . Better get Chet away," he said suddenly. She was intrigued by this spectacle, drinking it in with eager nose. "She may have died of starvation alone or been helped along by disease."

I pulled Chet off, and started back down the hill.

"I'll drag the body over to the Snackbar," he called. "Otherwise Chet'll just sneak back as soon as we're busy."

⋏

April. Even the name sounds magical. An end and a beginning. I had been born one Easter Sunday, twenty-three years before, so I always think of April as my month.

The sun made daily headway and darkness departed for another season, stealing off with the full moons, the stars, and the aurora borealis. Snow crystallized into coarse, wet grains and our paths became muddy. On the river, twigs and leaves sank into the ice, forming delicate patterns. Furry willow buds, looking like hungry caterpillars, climbed suddenly up the awakening shoots. I brought in a bunch and soon had a living bouquet sending forth leaves and roots. Still our white front yard, which ran to the far horizon, seemed changeless under an arching dome of baby blue. It takes a long time to thaw the North.

We spent much of each day outside now, happy to be alive and alone in the vast yawning wilderness. There was an almost perceptible stretching in the ground, an impatience to throw off winter. Here and there riverside boulders began to sun themselves on bright days. We could sense the tide turning as spring warmth flooded up the south sides of hills by day to be beat back with the sinking sun. We were caught up in the pressure of a land awakening as it swelled against the grip of winter. How gentle it seemed, yet here was a restless power nothing could withstand. Already the ice groaned and cracked, blisters piling in uneasy mounds as waves of tension swept the river. Although the ice was no thinner, I could feel the mounting strength of the water beneath. Drip by drip, the sun was winning.

We wore snow goggles now and became sunburned as we snowshoed shirtless in the still, crisp air. One day I looked up and saw that the ridges were no longer white. Up where the wind had ruled all winter, the sun now shown without relief. Great slabs of brown greeted my eyes.

Travel became steadily more difficult in the wet grainy snow. I spent a good deal of time on photography. The drip and scallop of frozen water formed a moving canvas of intricate ice-art for my lens. I devoted whole days to tracking down bird calls, in particular one that sounded like a sheet

178

of metal being wobbled. I came up with owls, jays, shrikes, squirrels, and a dozen assorted tweeters, but never a wobble bird. At last I found this most elusive bird, only to discover my old friend the hawk owl. The great gray owls sang too now, filling the blue dusk with their deep booming "whoooooos."

One day a turquoise stain appeared, spreading over the ice. We walked up river to take a look. It was good to hear the laugh of running water again, and we stood beside the expanding color watching the insatiable snow turn milky blue as the water gushed forward. It would be even with the cabin by nightfall, cutting us off from the islands. A resonant gurgling came from deep within the ice and great belches of air escaped as pressure ridges sagged under the added weight. Three-inch fissures opened into the bowels of black ice.

As we plodded homeward we could see our little cabin gleaming golden in the low sunlight, so small and friendly against the beautiful wild mountains. I felt a sudden pang in my chest at the thought of leaving it. Had a year almost passed? So soon? We still hadn't decided where the next year would find us.

By sunset the overflow was merrily babbling by on its way to the Olsen Creek junction, eating the snow before it and buckling the old, scarred ice. But a few cold nights later found me creeping hesitantly over the new ice. It was beautiful, layers of green and gray and brown in a mosaic. A dark runoff from our hill had joined the seep and lay stratified beneath me as I stole over the slippery surface, following Net-Chet. With her bare feet and keen ears, she had an excellent sense of the ice and seemed to know where it was weakest even when I had no visual clues.

This new ice was by no means solid. In many places open water rippled the surface. Where I walked an inch of glass covered the saturated snow, which extended a foot or more to a solid floor of old ice. Here and there delicate feathers of frost decorated the slick surface and a collage of leaves or bubbles were fixed stark and clear below.

I had long desired to see the source of overflow, and suddenly ahead loomed a black depression, frozen in mid-gush. I tiptoed close, drawn by the spooky dark hole. Fractured blocks angled away from the collapsed pressure ridge in a still life of violence. I crept as close as I dared. There were rocks down there, I noticed, fascinated by the inky danger. It really was a hole in the ice, a place one might fall into and disappear. The fact that the water was scarcely four feet deep didn't lessen the thrill.

It was almost May when winter rallied one last time. One day summer had been upon us; the next, it was twenty below zero. Our open seep froze in nameless blues that reflected the cold crescent moon. Frost flowers curled once more on the window panes, and the honey-combed igloo stiffened in its decay.

The snow that followed retouched the landscape, dangerously hiding the painted, pockmarked ice and freshening the woods in purest white.

On this virgin snow, Chet and I set out for the island the next morning to cut firewood. I crept over the blank surface, so different from the day before, stopping to look back at the cabin through the falling snow. A stampede of big flakes blurred the outline of the hill, but upstream I could detect the dark stain of creeping water. A cold wet nose thrust deep into the bare palm of my hand and I knelt and put my arms around Chet's soft neck, and we stood together, two dots in eternity.

I was remembering the haunting news that David had brought us with the mail. Another pair of kids had spent this winter in the bush, and he had been sent to search for them. A boy and girl they were, like us, out adventuring in the Arctic. A pilot dropped them in the wilderness last fall with backpacks, two dogs, a bag of beans and, no doubt, a how-to- live-off-Arctic-roots-and-herbs handbook. They were vegetarians.

They hiked until winter caught them and then built a tiny shelter in what David described as a "god-awful place." Their beans ran out in December, the dark month. They had but one light-weight mummy bag, and into this they crawled, head to toe, cradling one another's feet to keep from freezing and pulling their dogs over them.

In the icy dark of December he went to bed, saying that if he must die, let it be there. But she refused to surrender and continued cutting wood for their fire and dragging it home on frostbitten feet. She laid branches on the roof spelling out S.O.S. in the snow, and no doubt learned to pray. But the Arctic is big and the chance of an unmarked shelter being noticed from the air is very small indeed.

January, the month of Cold came, and February, the month when the sun returns. Through March, month of deep snows and strong winds, she kept the little fire going beyond all hope.

And one day a plane spotted them. She ran joyfully out, throwing herself face-down in the snow, arms outstretched in supplication as he circled. But the pilot, seeing smoke from the cabin, disregarded the signals and flew away convinced that all was in order. He had only circled so that his passenger, a tourist, could photograph the scene.

How heartbreaking! How bitterly disappointing it must have been to see that straw of safety snatched away! What frozen tears of anguish she must have cried, lying there in the snow as her life vanished with that plane, leaving a greater desolation.

But the pilot couldn't forget that strange little shelter and the figure cast upon the snow, and some days later mentioned it to a friend who spoke to a State Trooper. A short while later, their Arctic winter was over and they were tucked into hospital sheets.

They had come foolishly unprepared, poor city kids. And they suffered for their lack of judgment with months of misery and starvation. They had wanted to live in Nature and now may never wish to see a tree again. People can laugh at their stupidity, but it takes courage to commit yourself to your dreams. Even being prepared is no guarantee. An old-timer froze to death this same winter when his cabin burned down. Another couple almost died of tularemia, a disease normally caught from uncooked rabbit, that was in their water. Again a chance plane made the difference. Even David almost died once of appendicitis. One must approach this country with humility. Knowledge does not replace respect.

But then life isn't safe, no matter how carefully you plan it, I thought as my ax bit deeply into an old dead tree. You may as well enjoy the ride.

I finished cutting the tree. Gathering up my load, I started slowly for home, dragging the wood. The land swirled about me, fuzzy and gray in the driving snow.

The sky was beginning to clear and the snow had almost stopped by the time I reached the cabin. The peaks stood in fresh relief, clean against the falling twilight. Soon the overflow bubbled darkly past us on its way downstream.

Late that night we were awakened as if by a distant memory. Soft and steady a drenching spring rain beat upon the cabin, bringing with it the smells of long ago.

Winter was over.

Chapter 10

THE SNOW had melted considerably by morning. Large patches of bare ground splotched the hill as I slowly picked my way up the familiar trail. Sniffing deeply of the rich smell of dead leaves and cold rain, I penetrated the Cathedral of Trees and stood looking back over the valley. Low gray clouds obscured the mountain tops and wisps of fog trailed over the ice below, swirling oddly in the sluggish air. From the earth, a mist began to grow. Swelling silently into the dawn, the ragged vapors crept up draws, snagged in dark dripping trees and caught in the crevices of hills. The call of a single bird echoed through the space, clear and sweetly monotonous. I watched the wilderness disappear until only a few ghostly spruce remained and that lilting solitary trill that seemed to come from everywhere at once.

The next day the flies arrived. Up from the snow they came, thawed by the gentle rains of spring. I opened the door to a sunny morning and was swept up in the happy drone of big, green-backed buzzers warming themselves in front of the cabin. Squatting comfortably by the woodpile, I watched their resurrection. They had lain frozen, unresisting and dead these long months, awaiting the call. Now they were everywhere, mating in the dappled light, redistributing their genes for the new season. They swarmed happily about me trying various couplings until arriving at the correct combination. Their iridescence seemed as much a part of spring as the few stiff butterflies who were also about. Here were the garbage collectors come to remove the accidents of winter. They would clean the earth and with their millions feed the new birds and fish.

I shook myself, reminded of the souring meat I had come out to fetch. Barefooted, I stepped towards the meat rack and the tedious job of drying the last of our provisions. Net-Chet lay panting beside the path in a mud hole of her own design. Tufts of her faded winter fur were scattered about her. She raised her head in greeting at my approach.

On the island below, six ravens screamed at one another over our scrap pile, and a cry from above drew my attention to a gull drifting dazzling white against the blue. Eyeing the bone pile, he slipped upwind into a soft landing a few feet from the ravens.

The river ice had a blue granular quality, darkly saturated in places where water seeped up through its rotted structure. Tea-colored streams trickled off the land, flooding the ice and eating the surface into a living sculpture of white and blue and brown. Water and twigs percolated through the layers, forming a vertical crystal lattice that permeated the ice from top to bottom. One could feel it now, four feet of ice giving slightly underfoot, weak and dangerous. Currents undercut it further, gnawing up from below or sucked down into cracks from above, molding and carving it.

For months the Arctic had waited as the sun gathered strength. Now all at once, spring swept over us, routing winter and pursuing it northward in a babbling flood. A score of new bird calls erupted overnight as the migrants began arriving in droves, carrying the future through trackless miles within their small bodies. Soon the twilight of summer night echoed with their ceaseless songs.

There was a humming in the air, and my ears long accustomed to silence, tingled with the merry voices of water. In countless places, drop by drop, it chuckled with new liberty as the rigid crystals dissolved. Boughs sprang up and leaves unfurled. Moss stretched as the blankets of snow became fluid and trickled down its stems, slithering between root hairs to arouse the plants from slumber. Water gushed off the hills, its impatient roar sounding even from under our floor. At first these rivulets rested with the sinking sun, but before long a constant drone joined the birds in proclaiming an endless day.

One day six caribou trotted over the rotting ice along the far shore. Soft crunching sounds came to us clearly, and the afternoon sun slanted through their twinkling legs, casting long shadows before them. They were traveling north along the river. Whenever open water blocked their progress they would drop into it in single file, scarcely slowing their pace. They seemed to sense our presence for they stopped a moment, listening towards us, before continuing their journey. As they rounded the upstream island, we grabbed the camera and raced along the bank.

The beach was naked in many places, and a broad stream gurgled over the ice near shore. Every rock and bush stirred memories for me. Even our old footprints were as we had left them, souvenirs of fall. Now thawed and free of snow, they were oddly familiar, like dinosaur tracks in sandstone, footprints of another world long ago.

The caribou trotted into view. They spotted us and with a clatter of small stones, bolted up the embankment and into the trees before we could photograph them. Phil eyed me dolefully and recapped the camera.

"Look there!" I said, drawing his attention to a gray shadow tracing the far shore. A big, lean wolf was traveling the route of the haggard deer, only slower. Where water glinted blue, he changed course, edging along the crack until he could leap it. He looked tired and footsore.

Wolves keep the caribou strong. I thought again of the old Eskimo saying. I can dissect an animal down to the last molecule and still be no closer to the great mystery of his being. Perhaps the Universe is holographic rather than additive: the smallest bit, a microcosm, the tiniest part containing all of the secrets. I looked down at my familiar hands, wishing I could comprehend the mystery of a single cell of my own skin.

"I'm going on up to the bend," I told Phil. He handed me the camera and lenses as he turned for home.

I picked my way over boulders and through the soggy yellow sedges where runoff flowed in a hundred little rills. Already, green shoots were climbing from the sand, forcing through last year's faded garments. Scales were popping from willow buds, and a bright flurry of leaves pushed against my bare legs. "Behold, I make all things new," I quoted to myself.

With staff in hand, I dawdled up the bank, shepherding blocks of ice out of the shallows and into the current. Many were as clear as glass and cut with complex holes and furrows. On my elbows and knees I chased them with my camera, trying to capture spring and make it be still. Again I squatted to turn over a rock and watch the ants hurry their lumpy charges underground. They had brought the larva up to warm.

At the river bend I cut inland, hopping over the muskeg where snow still obscured the deep potholes. A moose had been there, coming around twice in a loop, as they often do, walking, walking. His big, heart-shaped prints bit into the moss and saturated snowbanks, heedless of water or bushes. Each animal leaves an endless stream of history, a dotted line that trails him until death overtakes, sometimes by following those tracks.

I returned to the beach and scrambled up the game trail that skirted the cliffs. Cautiously, I moved onto an outcropping and settled above the river to observe the restless ice below. The sun was warm despite a breeze, and I planted myself in the damp fragrant earth, nestling my spine into the overhanging rock. Lulled by sun and river-song, I was soon enveloped in a miniature world of waxy, cream-colored flowers that sprouted from the bare granite a few inches from my head. Down, down into the satin petals I looked. There, in a marble hall, sat a tiny cream-colored spider, staring back from the lip of a bud.

My attention was drawn abruptly to the rumble and grate of ice. Upstream a ponderous block broke loose and careened into the shore-fast ice below me, sending spray far up the cliff. Momentarily, the balance was lost and water piled wildly up, driving into the barricade and flooding the downstream ice with new frozen jewels.

Ground squirrels were out. Their sassy voices carried clearly above the grumble of ice and current, shrieking an alert. From my perch, I scanned the beaches for the intruder. Then I spotted him on the beach up river. A grizzly!

I hurried for the river, wallowing slowly through deep slush, sinking clear to the ground with each step. I worked my way into the willows that fringed the exposed bar, knowing that I could not retreat with any speed through the drifts, yet drawn by this rare opportunity.

A few yards away the bear was intently turning over stones. He was far larger than the one we had eaten, and for a moment I considered a quiet exit. Grizzlies are meat eaters and have been known to successfully hunt bull moose. Photography takes more skill than killing, for you must get close enough to make it interesting and be in a position to see well. Still, the wind was in my favor, wafting power noises off the ice, and I continued to advance.

I froze to steady my telephoto lens against a spindly spruce tree. The bear filled the frame. I clicked off a shot and his head jerked up. I was standing in the open, fringed by stunted trees. The grizzly was perhaps twenty-five yards away, but I didn't think he could see me. Bears have very poor vision, although their hearing and sense of smell are remarkable. They are intelligent animals and are, as my mother had drummed into me, dangerously unpredictable.

At my next picture, the grizzly came up on his hind legs, a towering intensity, swaying slightly as he searched the wind for me. Slowly he rolled forward, smooth as a cat despite his size, big head scanning from side to side as he tasted the air and focused his small furry ears. The sun glinted like polished bronze from his frosted coat as he rose again, blunt brown nose questing for me. Scarcely breathing, I readjusted my focus and continued to shoot, the rough bark beneath my fingers adding little reassurance.

On he came, head searching from side to side. The muscles rippled under his fine coat as he swayed towards me with that peculiar waltzing gait of a bear. I could clearly see his power with every movement. Twenty yards, fifteen, ten. I thought my heart was thumping hard enough for him to hear, but I kept taking pictures. I had decided to charge and yell at the last moment, a move that had once saved my life while photographing wild buffalo. Running from a hunting animal did not seem wise, and bears have been clocked at thirty miles an hour for short sprints.

Suddenly he caught my scent. A few molecules of me had drifted to him, eddied back on the blustering breeze. With a speed hard to follow, he turned and ran. Splashing through the slough he vanished uphill, leaving tracks as big as dinner plates slowly filling with muddied water.

As I squatted over the tracks, my heart still racing with the fear and excitement of my encounter with this fabulous animal, I heard the distant bark of geese. A strange warm thrill crept over me and I looked up to see a wild V printed across the sky. Suddenly the geese spotted me, wise old honkers peeling from formation, shunning me in a fear well earned.

All wild life runs from man. I felt a sadness that this should be so. Natural predators like wolves travel almost unnoticed with the herds of caribou, each knowing the restrictions of the other. But man has learned to kill like no other creature, and even animals who have never seen a human run in panic at our approach.

↟

Two days after I photographed the bear the ice went out.

Phil had just stepped outside when I heard him yell, "Come quick! It's moving!" By the time I reached him, the solid ice of our front yard was still again. The river waited and we stood watching it.

"Right there," he said, pointing excitedly to a fifty-foot crack that marred the scarred old terrain.

The minutes ticked slowly by while far upstream a terrible tension was building. An unseen wall of ice was piling up at the bend, damming the river.

And then it started to go! I remember only frames of it, like the pictures I was taking, and of shouting with Phil above the din. Great seams rippled as cakes the size of houses split free. Then, slowly gathering momentum, it all began to move. For nearly eight months the yard had remained a dependable and solid highway, carved with our trails. And now it was under way! I saw the old igloo sail slowly past, a sight somehow as odd as if the land were moving.

The ponderous slabs hit our reef and slivered into blocks, hundreds of tons in weight. With massive force they piled skyward until the mounting pressure behind pushed them over the barricade. Like oversized toys, the great blocks bobbed and tossed, gathering speed. Soon they spun past at a dizzying rate, irresistible, flushed in a mad stampede. The river couldn't handle it fast enough. The packed flood shot up banks, mowing down the trees. They rammed together, fifteen feet high, in a grinding, jostling roar. How useless was the faint struggle of lower spruce as they whipped a moment and then were plowed under.

I glanced down to see the water climbing towards me. The choked river rose eight feet in the first three minutes, and we scrambled higher, fleeing the boiling current. Although a small outcropping deflected the major assault away from us, our yard was invaded by playful bergs. For the first time I was truly grateful for Phil's patient cabin site selection.

The big rush was over in about half an hour. When the water began to drop, tons of ice were stranded at our doorstep. These were blocks between four and five feet thick, their bellies heavy with stones that had frozen in from the river bottom. Within an hour, the flow had thinned, leaving the islands buried under blocks of ice. Only the forested areas remained inviolate, guarded by dying trees.

⋏

Winter departed rapidly. The enormous blocks of rotten ice fell apart in long tinkling crystals and within a week there was not a trace of them. Snow disappeared from the low country and the land turned green overnight.

With the change of season, our wandering spirit returned. We chose to postpone the decision on whether or not to remain at the cabin. We would spend part of this summer exploring the country north of us. We planned to hike into the mountains, perhaps as far as the Arctic Continental Divide, and return home by log raft, floating down the Chandalar River, a six-week journey of about two hundred miles.

It didn't take long to pack. Our main food was dried moose and tallow. The distance we could travel on foot was limited by what we could carry. A person consumes perhaps fifty pounds of dried food in a month. In addition, we took the little tent, sleeping bags, cook kit, our camera, an ax and two rifles: the .22 for small game and a 30.06 for insurance against starvation.

We started out in the same direction as our previous trip, deciding that it would be easier walking if we didn't attempt to follow the wide loops of the river. The day was blue and hot, hung with fleets of thunderheads, the clouds of summer. Olsen Creek raged in a torrent of amber water encased in a sluice of ice. It was hard to recognize the friendly little stream as it cut under ledges and pounded through thickets with incredible power.

Along the creek bed grew stands of birch, their tender leaves opening before our eyes. As we climbed, the valley stretched below, turning greener by the moment. Tiny red flowers speckled the blueberry bushes where already summer's work was underway. Black storms licked the ridges ahead, washing the vivid colors as banks of clouds crept northward.

I stopped thrashing through the tough willows and looked about. The

188

roar of mosquitoes could be heard even above the creek. They had arrived the day before, June 9th. There had been a few abroad since early spring, parents of this sudden population. When we woke there seemed more, and by evening, the air was choked with tiny flying bodies.

Shifting the heavy pack on my shoulders, I studied the bushes, lost in thought. On the nearby hill, slender willows stretched their few buds to the open sky while many lay crushed by winter snows. But here in the stream bottom where the moose had been browsing, a forest of sturdy shrubs was bursting with vigorous life.

Absently I fingered the buds. "Why, it's turn about!" I said aloud. Just as caribou need wolves, so too do plants depend upon those that eat them. The healthy hedge about me showed years of pruning by moose, who need forty to sixty pounds of buds each day. The neglected hillside plants were over-grown and had been broken by the weather. Somehow I had always imagined plants as the silent, martyred base of life. The relationship is far deeper and more beautiful.

In my excitement, I lumbered through those steel willows, looking for Phil. I found him examining a half-eaten moose antler.

"Probably porcupine," he said, pointing out the tooth marks.

I disclosed my new discovery to the back of his retreating head as we picked our way through the high bushes. Between one breath and the next, the gardeners bolted by us. It was a cow moose and her yearling calf, still far from grown. They were thin, their long winter coats faded and tacky. Ballet dancers, they melted through the thickets and vanished like smoke. There is grace in even the largest of wild creatures, a poetry of movement that is lost with domestication. Perhaps it is danger that keeps them so.

We reached the amphitheater and plodded across the broken mossy ground that separated us from the rock ribs of the mountain. A wide fan of sloping boulders was pitted with deep, wet holes and overgrown in a tangle of bushes. The final obstacle was a ring of "slide alders," guarding the ridge beyond. They are named this because the branches grow down-hill so that they will not be broken in avalanches. They are often almost impenetrable.

Net-Chet gamboled by me, red packs bobbing, as I paused to enjoy the cool touch of wind on my sweaty face. The center of her own hairy little world, she stopped to grin up at me, jaws gaping. Directly ahead Phil waited in the bushes, sitting by his backpack, rifle, and ax. I swung my pack onto one knee and dropped it to the ground. Propping the packs to-gether, we drew a tarp over them and crouched beneath while a brief storm chased over. The three of us huddled there (with a host of mosquitoes) reading aloud while hail pounded into the barren thicket.

As the storm passed on, we could look down upon the river. The muddy water looked blue-green, reflecting the sky and trees in the late sunlight. We could see ducks dropping like petals from the deep blue sky to ponds below. The sweet smell of growth seeped from the ground beneath us, and birds called, flute-like in the stillness.

Although it was late, we decided to climb further. There was no level place to camp, and probably would not be one until we reached the valley on the other side of the mountain.

The brush ended abruptly leaving a soggy carpet of moss and rock trailing into the clouds above. Clear pools of melt-water remained among the stones, adding to the fairyland of miniature plants. Lichens of white, red, brown, and yellow grew like coral, curling daintily in the green and orange moss. Dwarf berry bushes pushed up through this sponge adding to the under-sea appearance of a magic world. God is very good at detail.

The ground fell away sharply below us as we climbed and evening filtered over the land. Many had trodden these heights, and we found traces of porcupine, caribou, moose, ptarmigan, bear, and wolf. Distant mountains rose slowly into view, their naked sides protruding from snow.

Near midnight we topped a small peak that straddled the ridge only to see the mountains stretching ever up beyond. In the shelter of rocks we rested, eating drymeat and discussing our course. Little birds glided shrilly over the rocks, flinging themselves recklessly into the abyss below us.

The steep canyon walls looked barren and brown. "Look at the difference in the north and south slopes," I said, staring across the vast amphitheater. Plants that flourished on the sunnier south side were absent from the north. Each change in terrain was distinctively marked in vegetation.

Phil squatted beside me, his back pressed into a rock overhang out of the cool wind. Net-Chet levered his arm up, drawing herself under it, and sat down between us. She watched me intently as I gnawed drymeat and passed the fibers to her.

A low moan of wind whistled through the crags. I listened to the wind and gazed out over the mountains. A little white flower caught my attention, poking bravely between the gray rocks at my feet. It consisted of a single stem, perhaps an inch long, with one wrap-around leaf. This was crowned by a tiny white star. It grew alone among the stones, a whisper of defiance to the harsh winds.

What could you build that would last the millennia? Where would you put such a legacy? Mountains dissolve and are lifted again; deserts become oceans. Yet the genetic code, that intricate blueprint of life, has been passed on in an unbroken chain for more than two billion years. The fragile individual is the link between yesterday and tomorrow.

"I suppose we are just putting off leaving," I said suddenly.

Phil glanced at me and shrugged.

"But then things turn out as they should. We leave when we leave." Not very profound perhaps, but true. The ice goes out when it's ready.

Another squall swept the lonely ridge, and we shrank into the outcropping as hail danced on the stones. Mist rolled down the mountain, disintegrating before it reached us, but advancing. Swirling tendrils spilled into the canyons on either side. Stiffly we roused ourselves and climbed through trailing clouds onto the gentle swell of the pass. It was a meadow adrift in a sea of big yellow flowers. The pass dwindled into the distance or faded in banks of clinging fog. Here, on the hilltop of the world, the song of nesting birds surrounded us and patches of old snow glinted from among the scattered pools in the growing morning light.

By the time we reached timberline on the far side, a snowy day had dawned. The ground was slippery with big new flakes. Wearily we dropped into the valley and trudged south to make our camp in the friendly old trees. I was practically asleep on my feet, having walked for twenty-two hours, and Phil entertained the slow miles away with descriptions of foods he had known.

$\star$

Row upon row of mountains marched before us, becoming steadily more serious. They did not seem to be arranged in any order, but splattered randomly across our path. Sometimes we would follow up a clear brook, fishing for grayling in swirling deep pools and cooking them over the stunted little willows that sprouted from the gray slate beaches. At other times we would slog overland, pitching through the chaotic jumble of muskeg and thicket caused by melting subsurface ice. There were high mountain lakes, hung like jewels between stark cliffs where streams cascaded white from the snowfields above. And sometimes we fought through black peat bogs guarded by screaming mosquitoes. The larger rivers we forded, preferring the higher ground to their overgrown sweeping bends.

Occasionally, we needed to cross a precipitous pass where the old snows plastered the gullies like mashed potatoes or hung in thirty-foot blue cornices, carved by the wind. Bleak crags jutting into an unforgiving sky. Summer never conquered these forbidding heights. From their dismal slopes we could look down over the grand desolation of shimmering gray shale, tinted in a blush of green and gold, and see the sparkle of countless rivulets and ponds snaking through the upland tundra. Sunlight and cloud patterns would chase themselves over the land below, spilling colors from a leaden sky and dusting the peaks with lacy new snow.

The play never repeated itself. We think of seasons as repetitive, but this is because our attention span is short, I decided. Could it be that cycles are only an illusion of our limited perspective? True, the snows come yearly, followed by mosquitoes and then snow once more. But every year is different, every hour. The driving force of Nature is creative abundance. It is another name for God. The river flows by me, different water every moment. Is it the same river or not? Always different, forever the same.

I felt small and frightened by the peaks and their casual drapes of ice.

Yet even here, wild flowers hugged the rocks and nesting birds called out in alarm at our approach.

It was in such a place that we found the mine. A bleak and inhospitable ramble of trailers and sheds clung to the canyon walls, all but lost in the landscape. Here a twisted airstrip angled dangerously into the mountain, the remnants of a plane attesting to the perils of landing. Erosion is very fast at this raw edge of the world. Creation is unfinished up here, and the mountains were crumbling out from under the shabby dwellings. Tons of rock were embedded in the twenty-foot snowdrifts that covered some of the buildings. These had been peeled from the overhanging peaks during winter storms and flung down the slopes at the dreary, deserted settlement.

High above, a mine shaft tunneled into the ridge, its frozen walls entering between glacial deposits of snow. Shored up with timbers dragged from friendlier lands, it had been worked by a determined few men off and on for half a century.

As we entered the shaft, the walls and ceiling glittered in fragile designs. Shimmering in the light of a match were forests of ice-feathers, butterflies, flowing icicles, and crystal palaces. Gently I brushed them away, revealing the gray, frozen mud for which men suffered so much. Somewhere within would be elemental gold. You can't transport ice-butterflies into the sunlight. They grow only here where no one will ever buy them. You can't set one on your dresser or wear it about your finger. They are free. Here unnoticed lies a transitory elegance as priceless as wild flowers. Melting, growing, dripping, changing. Exquisite. Delicate things of untold power: water, ice, life, the seedling that splits and devours rock, love.

We made camp one night on top of the world, snow capped peaks rising about us. The tent was pitched in a patch of waist-high willows in a narrow, rocky gulch. Three weeks had passed since we left home. For several days we had traveled above tree line, climbing beside a milky-blue alpine stream through a green and rolling upland. On either side had marched the vast slate peaks, gleaming silver in the sunlight or black and forbidding in storm. The slate beaches were made of flakes the size of dimes, that crunched like crackers underfoot, their silver-blackness offset with pink and yellow flowers.

When once again the dark heights had blocked our way, we spent a hazardous day traversing a pass and were still uncomfortably exposed high on the other side. Tomorrow we would descend to a large creek and follow it up the final ascent to the Arctic Continental Divide.

"I don't think the fire is hot enough," Phil said, poking a biscuit for the tenth time. "Maybe we'd better just eat it?" This was a special treat, the dough spread on a flat rock and balanced over the fire to bake.

I grinned at him across the small, smoky blaze.

"They're warm," he told me, extending a tentative finger once more. I could see he didn't want to wait.

"We could start with the fish," I told him. "They really will be better if they cook."

A fine drizzle settled from a steel-gray sky, whipped up the stark canyon by a gusty wind. I sat cross-legged on the bare wet rocks, holding my chapped hands over the fire. A fist-sized blaze was tucked between two stones, and into it I fed a continuous selection of tiny twigs, our only wood this high in the mountains.

Willows are wonderful plants, the unsung heroes of high latitudes and elevations. The roots send out new vigorous stems to replace dead tops. In some places, a visual gray zone separated the winter-killed tops from this year's growth. Even in defeat, willows are victorious. When a raging stream gouges out a plant, tumbling it downstream in a matted wreck, it will lodge upon some rock and soon take root. I have seen bleached driftwood putting out new leaves. Would that I could be as the willow.

I finished my boiled fish and dumped the bones, feeling unsatisfied. Turning the dough again, I sat back on the cold stones. Above the crackle of fire came the thunder of water cascading into a chasm a few feet below camp, a torrent squeezed from the snowfields above. Here towering limestone cliffs closed abruptly, forming a cataract jammed with enormous blocks of blue ice. Down this twisted slot bounded the young creek, gray as dove feathers.

"So much for naming it 'Slick Crick,'" I said, looking toward the canyon that had stopped us. "Friendly Crick" and "Graystone" had also been proposed earlier that day, in a custom we had of identifying our nameless course through this nameless land. "More like the Grand Canyon. What now?"

Phil was studying the map, shielding it with his wool shirt. Like me he was cold. When it rained, we got wet, and there was not much use in fighting it. His face was dirty and weathered, blistered by the constant sun and wind. His soggy moose-hide boots were coming apart in the continual wet. Even in the rain, clouds of mosquitoes hovered about us. I glanced at my hands. The great outdoors isn't very romantic.

"Well, it looks pretty grim," he admitted at length. In this giant landscape, a wrong choice could cause us days of backtracking. He leaned forward to show me the map and traced a possible route with a dirty finger.

The map had become a maze of lines. Contour lines squeezed together

194

and curled back on themselves, taking up the extra paper in a most ingenious fashion. It was difficult to determine which way was up, and I would have shrugged it off, had not the terrain been similarly arranged, each little squiggle representing a two hundred foot drop in real life. I studied it awhile.

"Looks like we're going to have to cut high here and go around the gorge," I said at last. "I wouldn't trust it, even if we could get through this first part. It looks like a real trap to me."

Phil nodded agreement.

"This creek over here should be no problem," I continued, running my own finger along the stained and tattered map. "It's that final ascent to the Divide that will make or break us."

We both bent low, following the intricacies.

"I think they're done enough, don't you?" Phil asked, poking at a biscuit again. The drizzle was almost stopped and a somber evening had set in.

I nodded. "Go ahead. Dig in."

He lifted a slab of warm dough from the rock and crouched there, chewing contentedly. I reached down and ran my fingers over Net-Chet's damp coat. Her pads were worn, and I examined them carefully.

"You know, I've been thinking . . ." I began.

"As usual." He licked his fingers and reached for more, offering some to me.

"I know I'm different from you." I took the offered bread.

"I'm sorry. I didn't mean to make fun of you. It's just that you're always so full of deep thoughts. Don't you think about anything else?"

"What else is there?"

We sat together in silence. The ominous roar of the canyon filled my thoughts. I could almost hear the tempo of my mind slow, feel the breeze off the glaciers above. The fingers of my consciousness pressed into the icy rock, exploring the textured surface, knowing it intimately. Physical reality.

"Danger is our animal heritage," I said finally.

"And death?"

I shrugged. "It's the other side of life. One could not exist without the other. Creativity is all we have. Creativity is motion. There are no endings, only beginnings."

"You suppose."

"I suppose. But it doesn't matter anyway. Death is death, and I shall know when I get there. Or I won't. In the meanwhile, I may as well live life to the fullest."

Phil nodded slowly and then shrugged. "You're right. It doesn't matter."

"Phil, the power in life comes from not holding on," I said suddenly. He retreated a bit and lowered his head into the biscuits. "Security is a myth anyway. We are not containers to collect things. Think instead of being a tube, a glass pipe perhaps." I stretched out my cold arms, extending my fingers. "Our power lies in the ability to direct the flow in our lives and to let go of it. The minute you grab life, you flip into a vessel and become finite."

Phil did not care for the direction of my thoughts. I sat there feeling very sad and alone.

"It doesn't mean anything," he said at last.

"Of course not. It's only the truth. The truth never MEANS anything," I snapped. I was immediately sorry for my impatience. "What I'm struggling with is letting go. To love and live and let things be as they are."

I stopped and gazed about. Somewhere unseen the sun was sliding below the peaks, and the clouds about us had turned a luminous tangerine, their margins woolly red. Below us the canyon fell away into darkness; above, the silver glint of black peaks were striped with snow. I gestured out over the fading land. "How beautiful it all is. Is life."

I sat there a long time, feeding the tiny fire, thinking. Our camp was littered with mossy bones. Generations of wolves had run caribou down this very draw. Here the frightened deer had seen the gorge and known their ambush. The ebb and flow of life giving to life.

That night I wandered through dreams searching for Phil. From room to room I traveled throughout the bowels of some cavernous, deserted building, finding only traces of him, a mitten or pocket knife. Then I saw him in a tunnel a few paces away. I hurried to catch up, but he seemed always a turn ahead and he could not hear me. I rounded a corner in time to see him step through a kind of window. Through the glass, I could see him gradually vanish into the falling snow outside.

I woke sobbing, "Don't leave me! Please don't leave me, Phil!"

He shushed and held me until finally I drifted off to sleep again.

꙳

Four days later we began the final ascent to the Divide. Because of the sudden and dangerous weather at these heights, we decided to push on through the night until we were again low enough to camp. We were five thousand feet above tree line. We would not drop down to the North Slope, but angle right, entering the headwaters of the Chandelar.

As we left even the little willows behind, the going became steadily worse. Raw alluvial fans and naked moraines were dumped into our twisted canyon. The ground was broken and jumbled with new rock.

Above us brooded the pass, massively blocking the colorless sky and dwarfing our feeble progress. Not wanting to be caught on those treacherous glacial slopes, we climbed on into the cloudy evening. No bit of green relieved the tortuous gully as we wound ever higher over the snowfields and sheer slopes of red shale. Here and there, trails of mountain sheep transected our way, and I wondered what they ate. A constant frigid wind spilled from the glacier above, funneled over the saddle, as slowly we clambered upward, reaching at last the knife-edge of reality.

Standing on that lip of the world, we looked down on the birth of the Chandalar River. To our left, the route lay open to the Arctic Ocean. Below us, red and gray, the stark peaks pushed edgeways into the sky, their bare bones rising in wall after wall of lifeless rock and snow. Deep-cut ravines zig-zagged downward in a steep maze of canyons. Far below, the glinting ribbon of the young river was stained with a touch of green, and towards this haven we descended, sliding perilously downward in the dawn.

We were caught up in the evolution of a mountain range, ants traversing a stretching monster. The slanting snowfields were littered with rock, often several feet thick, that had been blasted from the peaks during the gales of winter. A torrent of meltwater plunged for the valley, tearing away its bed as it rushed dangerously under the ice, a hollow rumble beneath us. Where the snow was gone, a thick fluffy layer of stones littered the frozen slope. We moved to a constant tinkle and rustle of shale, and I thought it the music of sheep hooves. Chet enjoyed the snowfields, often tobogganing down the steep slopes on her belly.

I was dizzy from the fatigue of twenty straight hours of hard work when we finally reached the small meadow where our flood joined another. There we set up camp among the brief bouquet of summer: Iceland poppies, tiny pink and black orchids, daisies smaller than snowflakes, miniature dandelions, and hairy, gray-green herbs that smelled of mint.

For a week we dallied down the growing river. It wound easily west and then south, gaining strength. We found ourselves in a broad, U-shaped drainage, a glacial remnant where the stream branched into dozens of clean, clear channels. Walking often in the creek to avoid brush, we talked and laughed while showers and rainbows chased up and down the valley. Caught in a rush of nesting birds and clouds of knee-high flowers and clear Arctic air, we smiled at the grim peaks that hung above us still but no longer threatened our homeward journey.

Often we sat upon a sandbar at noon, fishing the tumbling bright pools and enjoying the sun. Our clothes were worn and filthy, frayed to ribbons by the bushes. Our boots were coming apart. Despite the fish, which seemed of little substance, and an occasional ground squirrel, we were running seriously low on food and were looking forward to a fast trip home. We were beginning to feel overextended in this land. There was no one to come to our aid, but unlike the summer before, our world now had a center: home.

When at last spruce trees began to appear along the southern slopes of the shore, the river had pulled together, drawing itself from the wandering channels and bars into a single purpose. For two days we gathered dry logs and constructed a raft. It would have taken us weeks to walk home, and we were almost out of food, but we hoped to float down in a few days.

Lashing our packs aboard, we set out. At first all went well. For half a day we sailed downstream at a healthy clip, working hard together with long poles to keep our craft straight in the swift current and set it around the numerous rocks. Chet cowered on top of the packs, very displeased with this turn of events. When the river rallied and shot into a gorge, I began to have second thoughts. By then, of course, it was too late, for the three-hundred foot cliffs dropped straight into the water.

The raft was a ponderous affair, and our only means of steering it were the poles. As the river snaked through cliffs, piling up at each abrupt turn, we were frequently rammed against the walls, out of control. Still we managed a wild ride, shooting through in a sort of dynamic disaster and recovering from each near-catastrophe. Down over the frothing rapids we flew, zipping between boulders while the river raged about us and our yelled commands bounced off the overhanging cliffs.

I saw it coming, but there was nothing I could do. We had just swept over a seething mass of bedrock and the raft swung about, putting me in front. Ahead a great, gray wall of jagged shale leaned far out over the water. I caught a glimpse of tangled trees where the current sucked away into blackness beneath it. Frantically, I shoved for the bottom with my pole, but the water was too deep. At the last instant, I rammed the stick into the cliff, hoping to deflect our course, but there was not a chance in hell.

The impact of the raft drove us under the ledge, the entire river thundering relentlessly down upon us. I was smashed against the black rock and forced to my knees beneath an overhang, the pounding water to my chest. Phil was thrown from the raft and swept under. I screamed and grabbed for him, catching his hair with my fingers as he vanished. His hand clutched my wrist as the current dragged him under the raft, pulling him towards that black oblivion beneath the mountain.

Sobbing hysterically, I pulled with all my strength against the torrent. Another feeble hand caught my arm, almost unfelt under the weight of water. Madly, I groped downward into the blackness.

The raft was disintegrating under the force of the current, twisting into a wad of sticks. Any moment the frail parachute-rope lashing would rupture, dropping us all into the churning abyss.

"Phil! Phil!" I kept screaming, my voice drowned in the roar of water. My free hand found his shirt somehow, and bracing my body into the crush of the wall, I strained with all my might.

His face broke the surface a moment, wild and frightened, and one hand caught hold of the raft. Again I pulled with every bit of my remaining strength, inching him onto the submerged pile of twisted logs.

"We can't stop!" I yelled. The river belted down on us, mercilessly smashing us further under the ledge. A precious two feet of air separated the water from the rock.

Phil was shaking with exhaustion, his eyes bulging. My body had turned to jelly against the tireless flood. "Brace your back against the wall and push!" I shouted above the roar.

My legs felt like water. My head swam as I strained.

"Shove!"

Suddenly something gave. The raft contorted with the force and then swung out from the wall. It collided with the torrent and was rammed back.

"Chet!" I screamed. Phil turned and lunged for her. He snatched her aboard just as the raft drove into the rock, nearly crushing her.

Again we pushed, drowned rats, plastered under a ledge. Again the raft surfaced.

"Keep it out! Keep it out!"

We fought off the cliff, throwing everything we had into that one effort, that one chance at life.

"Keep going! Keep going!" We nosed into an eddy and swung around the horrible trap.

And still we could not stop. There was no place to get out of the river. Down through more rapids we were dragged, exhausted almost beyond endurance, clinging like kittens to this bit of safety. My knees were shaking so badly I could scarcely stand. I had lost my pole, my only means of steering, in the fight.

At last we hit an open stretch, where the current was brisk but the water was only a few feet deep. Falling overboard, we towed our sodden outfit to the bank, tying it securely in a rocky shoal with numb fingers.

As I pulled myself ashore, I started to cry. Shaking and sobbing, I fell into Phil's arms.

"I almost lost you!" I said, over and over, clutching his chilled body to me. "What would I have done? I never would have even found the body! How could I have looked in this gorge? What would I have done?!"

The horror of it hit me in waves. If I had escaped alone into this wilderness! To walk the weeks home without him! Never even knowing! Again and again I saw Phil's beloved head slide under the water, saw his terrified, outstretched hand.

Like wet and frightened children we stood together trembling and crying on the rocky shore of that uncaring river.

It was evening by the time we had camp set up, and our belongings strung like some collection of junk from every bush and tree. Luckily we always carried matches in water-proof containers, for little, except the camera, had escaped the general soaking. The only thing we had lost was the map which Phil carried inside his shirt to plot our course. Considering the circumstances, it was no small loss. As incredible as it sounds, we were to find it, still in its plastic bag, lodged on a rock in mid-river two days later.

We sat beside the fire, drying clothing and wondering if it was worth going to bed in soaked sleeping bags. We also asked ourselves if we dared return to the river or had best tighten our belts for a long walk.

The mosquitoes weren't bad by the fire, and here at least was real firewood again. I shifted on my sitting log, turning a pair of socks on my knee. Phil handed me the cook pot and spoon. I smiled tenderly across at him, acutely aware once more of how precious each moment is, how totally irreplaceable. I reached through the rangy, drifting haze of smoke and stroked his cheek, feeling again the fear.

About us scraggly spruce were lit in the low evening sun, yellow light streaking gently through the still air. A few feet away, the emerald river sailed steadily past, strangely quiet and benign. Here and there a grayling popped the surface, disturbing the ragged reflection of the far shore.

Looking up I suddenly saw a moose. Phil's jaw stopped chewing and he turned slowly to follow my gaze.

Like a painting she poised, knee-deep in the orange gliding water. It was a moment before I made out the tiny creature at her flank. The mama peered anxiously ahead, big ears working silently, long hooked nose probing. No larger than Net-Chet, the calf nuzzled her belly, unsure in a world so new. The cow dropped her head to sniff him.

In long easy strides she flowed into the water, the little calf pumping doggedly at her side. Together they crossed to an upstream bar, drifting silently before us like shadows. At one point, I thought the cow uttered a low call of encouragement. Chet awoke from some dog dream with a start, and the cow's head shot up. She could not smell us, but her ears twitched uneasily and the new moose froze at her side.

They stood for perhaps a minute thus before melting into the wilderness, the great dark cow and her newborn calf.

Life giving to life.

Epilogue

THE LOG RAFT served us well, and we arrived at our cabin three days later. On the way down we finally decided to leave the wilderness, at least for a while. A week after getting home we loaded the canoe with our few belongings and drifted downstream to the Yukon River, erasing in a week what had taken us all of the previous summer to accomplish. It was difficult for our little motor to push us up that mighty river to Fort Yukon, but with a light canoe, we made slow headway.

One evening, while camped on a sandbar below the town, we saw a river boat approaching, beating its way up the swift current. We were happy to see people, and put on the tea pot. As they drew near, we could see that they were white people. They pulled slowly abreast of us within a few yards of shore. Then to our astonishment they snapped our picture and continued upriver without so much as a wave. We were back in civilization.

We spent the rest of the summer in Fort Yukon, earning money to go back to Tucson. A generous Indian family took us in, not waiting to discover if we were riffraff. Phil and I were married in a little log cabin church in Fort Yukon with our Indian friends in attendance.

As it turned out, we spent only five months "outside" as the Alaskans refer to the lower states, working on a ranch to earn another "grub stake." In March we flew back to our cabin. Net-Chet was pregnant with our two other dogs. We ended up spending a total of nearly four years at the cabin. I built the meat-house while Phil added on to the cabin. We grew a marginal garden and corned meat and explored the country as far as our feet would take us. We became experts at building log rafts to come home on.

It was a time of great change for Alaska. The famous pipeline was being put in a couple of hundred miles to the west and outsiders flooded the North. For the first time in history, a road linked Alaska's Arctic with civilization. It was also a time of political turmoil. As a Territory, all the northern land had belonged to the federal government. Now the state was in the process of partitioning up this last great untouched wilderness.

Large tracts became state lands, and millions of acres were given to the Natives. Where our cabin stood became state land.

All of this went on without changing the cycle of the seasons for us, but within the space of those years, we started to see people. They were often helicopter crews of girls and boys, working for mining companies as a huge land grab ensued, with billions of dollars at stake. They flew into places like Caro and hauled away the artifacts for their living rooms back home. It was the end of an era.

With the growing comfort of our cabin, I began to feel the urge to move on. When I was starving and cold, there was nothing more wonderful than our cabin. Now that I was comfortable, I felt the need to face new challenges. I didn't want to leave the Arctic, but something inside pushed me. It is the process of life that holds my attention, not the end result. Phil was content and probably could have remained living there forever.

When we left the cabin for the last time, we talked of burning it to avoid opening the country for fall hunting or other exploitation. But there was too much of us there to destroy it with our own hands. So we wired the door shut and left a note telling our story. When I wrote the first drafts of this book, I changed the name of the Chandalar River, for I didn't want to call attention to any particular piece of wilderness. But in the end, I wrote it just as it was and I leave it to you, the reader, to treat this land with the consideration it deserves.

We returned to Tucson, where I planned to finish my degree in biology and apply for medical school. Phil and I were divorced shortly afterward. My marriage, like my mother's, was built on the Arctic and did not survive civilization. Phil remarried and moved to Alaska, but never got back to the bush. He lives near Fairbanks with his wife and three sons and works as a mechanic.

Net-Chet and her two daughters returned to Alaska with Phil. Net-Chet, true to form, preferred town living. As far as I know she is still alive, an old lady dog of sixteen. When I last saw her, it was hard to tell if she remembered me.

The cabin is still standing. Alaska is considering a law that would allow people in "trespass cabins" to own them, and I have encouraged Phil to claim it. In the meantime, I am sure that the roof is beginning to rot. I know that vandals flew in and stripped it of tools and supplies, littering the area with those items they didn't want.

I never did get into medical school. I became an artist, a profession at which I still work. I have come to believe that art is not just something I do, but a way of living.

I met my husband Tom Irons, also a seeker, in 1981. He was a glass artist in the process of building a home-studio in the Tucson mountains. We slept on our roof in the silence of desert. Now houses have grown up around us, altering the face of the land. Perhaps it is true that we kill the thing we love. But I still hold we can learn to share the planet with other living creatures.

My mother died of breast cancer last spring. The biggest disappointment of her later life was that she lacked the money and stamina to keep on exploring. Like the story of the grasshopper and the ant, she sang away her youth in adventure and her own wild worship of God, while the more prudent of her contemporaries were "slaving away" (as she used to call it) for security. When the autumn came, she had only herself and her glorious life behind her. But who is the wiser, the prudent ones or she who drank the whole cup?

Looking into the mirror, I strangely find myself more like her with each passing day. I didn't always enjoy her and swore never to be like her. But somehow the similarity feels oddly comfortable and familiar. Recently my sister Anny, a single mother in her mid-thirties, told me that she realized it was time to take her two pre-teen children on an expedition. I knew what she meant, though I don't suppose many people would. It was our mother's gift.

Sixteen years have passed since Phil and I set out on the Yukon. Last summer Tom and I took our young son Luke to Alaska and spent five weeks in the Brooks Range. As I picked the ripening blueberries with my baby, I could almost remember my own mother picking them with me. He followed me through the low bushes on his unsteady legs, as happy as a young bear cub. I realized then that when Luke is older we will return to the Arctic: to complete the cycle for me, and pass on the dream to him.

✤